SO-AGF-716

The
1700s

HEADLINES IN HISTORY

Books in the Headlines in History series:

The
1700s

HEADLINES IN HISTORY

Stuart A. Kallen, *Book Editor*

Bonnie Szumski, Editorial Director
Scott Barbour, Managing Editor

Greenhaven Press, Inc., San Diego, California

Every effort has been made to trace the owners of copyrighted material. The articles in this volume may have been edited for content, length, and/or reading level. The titles have been changed to enhance the editorial purpose.

No part of this book may be reproduced or used in any form or by any means, electrical, mechanical, or otherwise, including, but not limited to, photocopy, recording, or any information storage and retrieval system, without prior permission from the publisher.

Library of Congress Cataloging-in-Publication Data

The 1700s / Stuart A. Kallen, book editor.
    p. cm. — (Headlines in history)
  Includes bibliographical references and index.
  ISBN 0-7377-0541-8 (pbk. : alk. paper)—
ISBN 0-7377-0542-6 (lib. bdg. : alk. paper)
  1. Eighteenth century. 2. Civilization, Modern—18th century.
3. Enlightenment. 4. Europe—Civilization—18th century.
5. America—History—To 1810. I. Kallen, Stuart A., 1955–
II. Headlines in history (San Diego, Calif.)

CB411 .A16 2001
940.2'53—dc21

                                                        00-052799

Cover photos: (top, left to right) "The Bloody Massacre perpetrated in King Street Boston on March 5th 1770" by Paul Revere, AKG Photo; "Catherine the Great as legislator" by Dimitri Grigoryevich Levitsky, AKG London: (bottom, left to right) The storming of the Bastille, July 14, 1789, AKG Photo; "Peter the Great at the Battle of Poltava, July 8, 1709" by Gottfried Tannauer, © Scala/Art Resource, NY
Library of Congress, 27, 96, 128, 182, 192, 209, 220
North Wind, 74, 110, 118

Copyright © 2001 by Greenhaven Press, Inc.
P.O. Box 289009, San Diego, CA 92198-9009

Printed in the USA

CONTENTS

Chapter 1: 1700–1720

1. The Absolutist Rulers of Europe
The eighteenth century is known as an era during which
great power was concentrated in the hands of a few very
powerful European monarchs who managed to wrest
power from the church and nobility. Little concern was
shown for the average citizen, who lived in dire poverty.

2. The War of the Spanish Succession
The War of the Spanish Succession was essentially a world
war, fought by hundreds of thousands of soldiers from almost
every kingdom in Europe. At issue was who would become
king of Spain after Spanish king Charles II died leaving no
heir to the throne.

3. The French Rout in Flanders
Things had already been going badly for the French in
the War of the Spanish Succession when they were
met in battle by the British in present-day Belgium. As
described by the Duke of Saint-Simon, a member of
the royal court, the French commander refused to
move from his comfortable quarters to command his
troops and the conflict turned into a rout against the
French.

4. A Day in the Life of Louis XIV
Louis XIV gained absolute power by persuading the
nobility to surrender their power in exchange for land
and wealth. Memoirs of the royal courtiers tell the
story of the lavish daily life of the French Sun King.

Chapter 3: 1751–1763

FOREWORD

Chronological time lines of history are mysteriously fascinating. To learn that within a single century Christopher Columbus sailed to the New World, the Aztec, Maya, and Inca cultures were flourishing, Joan of Arc was burned to death, and the invention of the printing press was radically changing access to written materials allows a reader a different type of view of history: a bird's-eye view of the entire globe and its events. Such a global picture allows for cross-cultural comparisons as well as a valuable overview of chronological history that studying one particular area simply cannot provide.

Taking an expansive look at world history in each century, therefore, can be surprisingly informative. In Headlines in History, Greenhaven Press attempts to imitate this time-line approach using primary and secondary sources that span each century. Each volume gives readers the opportunity to view history as though they were reading the headlines of a global newspaper: Editors of each volume have attempted to glean and include the most important and influential events of the century, as well as quirky trends and cultural oddities. Headlines in History, then, attempts to give readers a glimpse of both the mundane and the earth-shattering. Articles on the French Revolution, for example, are juxtaposed with the then-current fashion concerns of the French nobility. This creates a higher interest level by allowing students a glimpse of people's everyday lives throughout history.

By using both primary and secondary sources, students also have the opportunity to view the historical events both as eyewitnesses have experienced them and as historians have interpreted them. Thus, students can place such historical events in a larger context as well as receive background information on important world events.

Headlines in History allows readers the unique opportunity to learn more about events that may only be mentioned in their history textbooks, or may be ignored entirely. The series presents students with a variety of interesting topics that span cultural, historical, and political arenas. Such a broad span of material will allow students to wander wherever their curiosity will take them.

INTRODUCTION

During the eighteenth century when the great empires of Europe battled for dominance at home and across the globe. From India to Africa and from the North American wilderness to the kingdoms of Europe, France, England, and Spain carved up the world according to who possessed the greatest armies and navies.

The unfortunate peoples caught in the middle mattered little to the leaders of the great empires. The kingdoms of Africa were decimated by the slave trade. The ancient homeland of the Native Americans was fought over, divided, and conquered first by the British and French, and then by the people of the new nation of the United States.

Like almost every other century, war dominated the lives, politics, and budgets of most nations. But the eighteenth century was also a time of great expansion in the arts, music, architecture, and philosophy known as the Age of Enlightenment. Great composers such as Johann Sebastian Bach and Wolfgang Amadeus Mozart wrote intricate and beautiful music that stirs the emotions. Philosophers such as Voltaire, Jean-Jacques Rousseau, and Immanuel Kant explored issues of religion, government, liberty, and freedom of thought that inspired the founders of the United States to form a republic based on democracy. Since that time, this model of constitutional government has been admired and imitated throughout the world.

While the influences of earlier centuries may seem lost to modern people, the repercussions of eighteenth-century events still color the present time. The horrors of the slave trade have remained a frame of reference on which some people continue to judge race relations today. The bright neon lights of modern Native American casinos stand as a testament to the strength and perseverance of people who once lost all they had to an invasion of European settlers. And the fledgling democracy founded by George Washington, Benjamin Franklin, Thomas Jefferson, and others has grown into the richest and most powerful country in the world.

The eighteenth century was a time when wars in Europe and other factors pushed millions of people out of the Old World and into the New World, while close to 7 million were brought here against their will from Africa to inhabit a land once ruled by Native Americans. Yet somehow all of these people were united as Americans, espousing the ideals expressed in the Declaration of Independence, the Constitution, and the Bill of Rights. Those words still unite Americans in spite of the incredible changes brought by modern technology. Although the founding fathers could not have envisioned airplanes, automobiles, televisions, and computers, their words and ideals echo through time from the 1700s to the twenty-first century.

Enlightenment and Revolution

The eighteenth century is often referred to by two contradictory terms: the Age of Absolutism and the Age of Enlightenment. The term *absolutism* refers to the unconditional rule of despotic kings such as Louis XIV of France (1643–1715), Frederick II of Prussia (1740–1786), and Peter the Great of Russia (1682–1725). These men created nation-states by extracting power from aristocrats and the church and governed with absolute dictatorial power, which they believed was granted to them by divine right. Louis XIV, also known as the Sun King, wrote that "God appoints kings as the sole guardians of the public weal."[1]

In part a reaction to the oppression and injustice inherent in such a system, the Age of Enlightenment was born in the era of absolutism. A large group of philosophers and writers such as Voltaire, Jean-Jacques Rousseau, Denis Diderot, and others became famous for their criticism of society's rulers.

Rousseau is considered one of the greatest thinkers of the eighteenth century. He believed that social manners and politeness hid humanity's basic brutal and egotistical nature. In *The Social Contract,* Rousseau stressed that the will of the majority might not necessarily be for the common good. These beliefs inspired the leaders of the American and French revolutions.

George R. Havens explains in *The Age of Ideas:*

> The eighteenth century in France was above all notable for its literature of ideas. The abuses of [power, especially political power] were many and blatant. In angry protest against the crying evils of injustice, oppression, and torture, there arose a brilliant corps of writers wielding their pens with a vigor and an originality rarely equalled. The leaders of thought at this crucial time were masters of a style which compelled the attention even of their enemies. Seldom has literature been forged into a more potent weapon in the slow battle for progress. These were authors who never forgot that the war in behalf of the unknown future must be won or lost first of all in men's minds.

In an age of repression and censorship, the ablest writers of the day learned to beat the government's game with wit, allegory, clever fiction, or surreptitious publication. The general public, in turn, eagerly patronized the contraband peddlers of forbidden books or manuscripts. As the century wore on, the French authorities themselves, half-conniving, often looked discreetly the other way, tacitly permitting the circulation of whatever seemed not to threaten too loud an uproar.[2]

Enlightened Philosophers

The philosophers of the Enlightenment were deeply influenced by scientific theories and strongly rejected the unbending religious dogma of the day. They believed in human reason as opposed to religious miracles. They believed in human self-expression, free from censorship by church or state. They opposed religious intolerance and the repression of the people by absolutist monarchs.

This sort of thinking had its root in the Reformation of the sixteenth century, when the Protestant Christians split from the Catholic Church. By the time of the Enlightenment, Calvinist, Lutheran, and Huguenot religious scholars were examining the history of the church with increasing criticism and detachment.

In the wake of this revolution, a new school of thought, known as deism, came into fashion. Deists maintained a belief in God but believed that God revealed himself through scientific laws, not through miracles or divine intervention. Rousseau and Voltaire were deists, as were many of America's founding fathers such as Benjamin Franklin, Thomas Jefferson, George Washington, and Thomas Paine.

In *Age of Enlightenment*, author Peter Gay summarizes deist belief:

> The deists did not deny the existence of a God: the whole universe with its beauty, its vastness, its intricate design, testified to His presence and His superb skill. But the deist God was like a great Watchmaker, or—as some of the deists liked to say—a great Mathematician; He had created the world, given it laws to run by, and then had withdrawn. Thereafter, the world, following His immutable laws, ran itself.[3]

The philosophers of the Enlightenment dreamed of a society in which truth would triumph over ignorance, reason over superstition, and where liberty and freedom would topple repressive despotism.

Monarch and Wars

While the philosophers and deists debated their lofty ideas, the monarchs of Europe continued to divide up the world as they had for centuries. England, France, Spain, and other powers clashed not only over their possessions in North and South America but also over who would sit on the thrones of Europe. This jostling for power resulted in long, bloody wars that raged across the European continent.

Major wars occupied European armies from 1702 to 1714, from 1715 to 1721, from 1733 to 1748, from 1756 to 1763, and from 1775 to 1792. Minor wars filled the years between. Indeed, war occurred somewhere on the European continent for two out of every three years, or two-thirds of the eighteenth century.

Two wars involved almost every country in Europe. The war over who would succeed the king of Spain when he died, known as the War of the Spanish Succession (known by the English as Queen Anne's War) involved almost every country west of Poland and lasted from 1701 to 1714. The Seven Years' War, fought from 1756 to 1763, was ostensibly a battle over who would control a small region of present-day Poland but an offshoot of that war was fought in North America as the French and Indian War.

In modern times, people assume that whoever rules a country such as Spain will be chosen more or less predictably by the Spanish people. In the eighteenth century, however, no mechanism existed, such as democratic elections, to name leaders. Instead, when kings and queens became ill or died, dozens of factions maneuvered, fought, and killed in order to elevate the next person to the throne. Oftentimes this involved wars with tens of thousands of military and civilian casualties.

These battles were further complicated by the fact that many eighteenth-century European monarchs were directly related to one another. The parties who fought the War of the Spanish Succession were a case in point, as Nancy Mitford explains in *The Sun King:*

> The War of the Spanish Succession, in which Austria, nearly the whole of Germany, Denmark, Holland and England leagued against France and Spain to dethrone [Louis XIV's grandson] Philip V in favour of the [Austrian] Archduke Charles broke out in 1702. [English king] William III, the great animator of the Protestant world, was dead; but his policy was carried on for a while by England under Queen Anne. Like all European wars of those days, it was fought with close relations in the opposing camps—Anne against her half-brother, the Pretender [James Francis Edward Stuart], her other half-brother [James Fitzjames, duke of] Berwick and her first cousin once removed Louis XIV; Berwick against his uncle [John Churchill] the Duke of Marlborough; the Holy Roman Emperor Charles VI against his brother-in-law and first cousin Louis XIV; Prince Eugène [of Savoy] against his first cousin, the [French general Louis Joseph,] Duc de Vendôme; the Duke of Savoy, once he had changed sides, against both his sons-in-law, Bourgogne and the King of Spain.[4]

Wars of Succession

This cast of characters is large in the War of the Spanish Succession and their motivations were as intricate as chess strategy. The war began because the king of Spain, Charles II, died in 1700 leaving no heirs to the throne. The childless Charles was the last Hapsburg king of Spain, meaning he was descended from the Hapsburg dynasty, the ruling house of Austria, one of the oldest and most distinguished royal dynasties of Europe. The Hapsburgs had inherited the Spanish throne through marriage in the sixteenth century and so ruled the Spanish holdings in America, the Spanish-held cities in Italy (Naples, Sicily, and Sardinia), the Netherlands, and also the Hapsburg German and Austrian possessions.

When Charles II, a weak-minded leader prone to convulsions and bouts of insanity, died in 1700, he left his Spanish kingdom to French king Louis XIV's grandson Philip V, from the ruling Bourbon dynasty. If Philip turned down the offer, the throne would go to the Austrian Hapsburg archduke Charles, second son of Holy Roman emperor Leopold I.

At the urging of Louis XIV (who himself was half Spanish), Philip took the throne and also retained the right to take the French throne when Louis died. This consolidation of Spanish and French military power alarmed other European nations. According to Will and Ariel Durant in *The Age of Louis XIV:*

> If [the Catholic king] Louis won, he would dominate Europe and imperil Protestantism [in England]; if [Prussian field marshal] Leopold won, the [Holy Roman] Emperor, holding the Spanish Netherlands, would threaten the Dutch Republic, and would soon reduce the autonomy of the German states. Commercial as well as dynastic interests were involved: English and Dutch exporters supplied most of the market for industrial goods in Spain and her colonies, and received considerable gold and silver in exchange; they were loathe to let that trade become a French monopoly.[5]

This complicated situation left the Grand Alliance of Britain, Austria, several small German kingdoms, Denmark, Prussia, the United Provinces (present-day Netherlands), Portugal, and Savoy (southeastern France) to square off against France and Spain. The Grand Alliance raised an army of 250,000 soldiers. The French and Spanish raised a huge army of 450,000 men. No war of this scale had ever been fought in Europe. Early battles routinely saw the death of up to 20,000 soldiers.

The fighting and dying changed little, and the war was finally ended by diplomatic means. The treaty known as the Peace of Utrecht in 1713 and 1714 prevented the French and the Austrian Hapsburgs from taking the Spanish Hapsburg throne. Philip V became king of Spain, as originally intended, but renounced claims to the French throne. Austria took Milan, Naples, Sardinia, and the Spanish Netherlands from the Spanish crown. The British benefited the most, with Britain receiving Gibraltar from Spain and Nova

Scotia, Hudson's Bay, Newfoundland, and Saint Kitts from France. England also was granted a thirty-year monopoly over the Spanish-American slave trade.

Like the War of the Spanish Succession, the War of the Austrian Succession was fought when another King Charles, this time Charles VI of Austria, died without a male heir. This war, fought from 1740 to 1748, pitted Prussia, Bavaria, Spain, and France against England, Holland, and Austria. As in the previous war of succession little changed at the war's end, except that Prussia gained the populated and wealthy Silesia region in present-day Poland, which elevated Prussia to a great European power.

Tensions over Prussia's control of Silesia exploded into the Seven Years' War from 1756 to 1763. This time Britain and Prussian king Frederick the Great fought against Austria, France, Russia, Saxony, Sweden, and, after 1762, Spain. In this war, Prussia and Austria fought over Silesia while England and France continued to battle over control over the North American wilderness in Canada, Ohio, and western Pennsylvania.

Fortunately, the enlightened age of the eighteenth century was an era of relatively limited warfare, when warring states believed in gentlemanly conduct that often spared civilians from unrestrained violence. In limited-warfare battles, finely uniformed soldiers lined up facing each other and fired their muskets at close range. Though this type of war was as vicious and bloody as any other, it inflicted less destruction on towns and villages. Peter Gay explains in *Age of Enlightenment:*

> Although the two great empires of England and France fought each other intermittently all through the century, their encounters were contained military actions, fought much like chess games over fixed terrains, for the purposes of imperial expansion. Compared with the wars of the preceding century, which had devastated much of central Europe, they seemed relatively mild. In fact, to men of the 18th Century, their age seemed one of peace.[6]

Even with great wars raging, citizens of large European cities were free to live their lives largely untroubled by warring factions.

Baroque and Rococo Culture

Spared widespread destruction, the people of Europe made great cultural gains during the 1700s. The era was known for its baroque and rococo architecture, a style fancied by kings and queens that was marked by luxuriant ornamentation bordering on the gaudy. Will and Ariel Durant explain the style in *The Age of Voltaire:*

> A revolution in art mirrored the change in politics and morals. After the . . . War of the Spanish Succession . . . the spirit of France turned from

the gore of glory [in war] to the pleasures of peace. . . . [Dwellings] and rooms became smaller now, but their decoration was more delicate and refined. Baroque [style] began to pass into rococo, the style of irregular forms and abundant ornament took a turn toward an almost brittle elegance, running to playful and incalculable fantasy. The delight in exquisite finish, bright colors, and surprising evolutions of design became a mark of the [regal style]. The classical orders disappeared under a frolic of dainty curves, corners were concealed, moldings were lavishly carved. Sculpture abandoned the Olympian grandeur of [palace of] Versailles for smaller forms of graceful movement and emotional appeal. Furniture shunned right angles and straight lines, and aimed at comfort rather than dignity. . . . Charles Cressent, chief cabinetmaker to the [French king], established the Regency style with chairs, tables, desks, and bureaus brilliant with mother-of-pearl [decoration] and . . . conscious loveliness.[7]

As the century progressed, great beauty was seen as desirable in all living spaces. Artisans and craftworkers constructed intricate and artistic furniture, wall panels, tableware, and other household items. The homes of the well-to-do were decorated with wall panels made from porcelain, furniture sculpted with intricate figures, lushly adorned tapestries, boxes and cups of silver and gold, and ornaments of Venetian glass.

Everyday People

For most European citizens, styles in art and architecture did little to mitigate the hardships of life. As they had been for thousands of years, in the early part of the century most people were farmers who spent up to sixteen hours a day attempting to scratch a living from the soil. Most small villages were self-contained; inhabitants grew their own food, cut trees for lumber and fuel, hunted small animals in nearby forests, and bartered for any small extras. Housewives baked bread, brewed beer and wine, sewed the family's clothing, healed the sick with herbs, and performed most other domestic chores with the help of their children.

In large cities, such as London, as Will and Ariel Durant write,

The streets were noisy with carts, pack horses, hackney coaches, and private carriages, all drawn by horses with hoofs clattering against the paving stones; there were also peddlers—many of them women hawking a hundred kinds of food or clothing; traveling artisans offering repairs, drivers disputing, dogs barking, beggars soliciting, street singers bawling ballads, organs bouncing their melodies from wall to wall. The people complained of but loved these noises, which were the vital medium of their lives. Only the pickpockets and the prostitutes worked silently. . . .

A considerable part of the population was packed into slums filthy with garbage and offal, breeding a hundred diseases. In the Wapping and Limehouse sections of London nearly every second inhabitant lived from hand to mouth, depending on charity, theft, or prostitution to secure lodging and food. Children ran barefoot, unwashed, and unkempt in the streets, clothed in rags and schooled only in crime. In these slums men and women seldom bothered to marry; sexual relations were a passing incident, a commodity marketable without ceremony or law. There were hardly any churches there, but beer shops and taverns abounded. Here too were the lairs of thieves, pickpockets, highwaymen, and professional murderers. Many of the criminals were organized in gangs. Watchmen who interfered with them had their noses slit. One group, the "Mohocks," was wont to sally drunk into the streets, prick passers-by with swords, make women stand on their heads, and gouge out the eyes of unaccommodating victims.[8]

As the century progressed, many of these problems were exacerbated by a population explosion that affected all of Europe. The European population rose from around 100 million in 1700 to 120 million in 1750, then jumped to around 190 million by 1800. The population of England alone rose from 6 million in 1700 to 9 million by 1800. In 1740, with 725,000 inhabitants, London was the most populous city in the world. Paris was next with 625,000 people, followed by Amsterdam, Vienna, Naples, and Rome. (By comparison, in the year 2000, London housed almost 7 million people, Paris 2.5 million.)

Population Explosion in the Thirteen Colonies

As the populations of Europe grew, millions of people decided to leave the oppressive kings, wars, and rigid social structures of the Continent and begin life anew in America, which experienced a proportionally greater population explosion than Europe. The population of the British colonies alone grew from 250,000 in 1700 to 5.3 million in 1800. (The thirteen colonies were New Hampshire, Massachusetts, Rhode Island, Connecticut, New York, New Jersey, Pennsylvania, Delaware, Maryland, Virginia, North and South Carolina, and Georgia. For most of the century, Florida was held by Spain and Canada was a French possession.)

As the population increased, the towering hardwood forests of the East Coast fell to the axes of settlers as cities, towns, villages, and farms began to dot the landscape. This population explosion had a deep impact on Native Americans who lived in the forests west of the original settlements along the Atlantic coast. By the 1760s, the growing population was pushing deep into the wilderness beyond the Appalachian Mountains. Western New York, Pennsylvania, present-day Ohio, Indiana, Kentucky, and Tennessee were invaded by wave after wave of settlers from Scotland, Ireland, Germany,

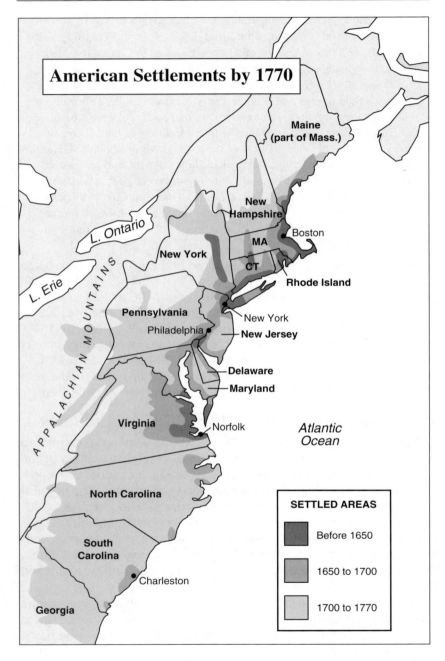

American Settlements by 1770

Maine
(part of Mass.)

New
Hampshire

L. Ontario

New York

Boston

MA

CT

L. Erie

Rhode Island

Pennsylvania

New York

Philadelphia

New Jersey

Delaware

Maryland

Virginia

Norfolk

Atlantic
Ocean

North Carolina

South
Carolina

Charleston

Georgia

APPALACHIAN MOUNTAINS

SETTLED AREAS

Before 1650

1650 to 1700

1700 to 1770

France, the Netherlands, and elsewhere. While most of the East
Coast tribes had been driven from the colonies by the end of the seventeenth century, in central New York tribes of the Six Nations of
the Iroquois, including the Mohawk, Seneca, Oneida, Onondaga,
and Cayuga, were doing all they could to resist white settlement.

The Native Americans were greatly outnumbered and had no resistance to several European imports—diseases such as smallpox and
scarlet fever, and alcohol, which killed nearly as many people as disease. In *The Shaping of America,* D.W. Meinig writes about the clash
between Native American and European cultures:

> Atlantic America was the scene of a vast unplanned, uncontrolled, unsta-
> ble, and unending encounter between European and Indian societies. . . .
> It could hardly have been otherwise. Europeans were intruders. . . . Their
> leaders arrived as military adventurers with charters from their govern-
> ments granting them authority over foreign lands and peoples. . . . And thus
> inevitably the disparate nature of the two cultures with reference to such
> fundamental concepts as authority, property, territoriality, contract, moral-
> ity, justice, and social prestige meant that what might have begun as a more
> or less balanced political negotiation soon foundered on the myriad prob-
> lems of coexistence. Grievances and misunderstandings begat quarrels,
> quarrels begat violence, local violence begat more systematic coercion,
> and successful coercion in one locality was aggressively extended to other
> localities. Much of the violence was gratuitous, powered by a brutal op-
> portunism that in turn engendered hatreds and retaliations.
>
> Overall this encounter can be seen as a vast collision of cultures that pro-
> duced chaos: a long period of harassment, expulsions, wanton killings, war-
> fare, destruction, punishments, executions, enslavements, and subjugation
> that sooner or later engulfed every seaboard region and radiated ever more
> deeply into the continent. It was chaotic because no power could control it,
> because there was no authority on either side capable of halting it even
> though many individuals, officials, and leaders tried to do so.[9]

The Growth of Slavery

Native Americans were not the only people to suffer as America
grew. The first African slaves were brought to the North American
colony in Virginia in 1619. As the country grew and the climate
proved beneficial for raising tobacco, rice, cotton, indigo, and other
crops, greater numbers of slaves were imported to work the fields.
By 1700 over 27,000 black slaves lived in the colonies, with over
16,000 in Virginia alone. That number grew, and by 1775, on the eve
of the American Revolution, more than 187,000 slaves lived in the
colonies—almost half the population, but most living in southern
states.

The use of free slave labor enabled white plantation owners in the
South to become incredibly wealthy. As huge plantation replaced
forests and fields, a white aristocracy grew up in the wilderness of
Virginia, Georgia, and the Carolinas. Fearful of slave rebellions, and
with no formal laws to restrict their behavior, the whites in these regions savagely penalized slaves who attempted escape or insubordi-

nation. In *African Americans in the Colonial Era,* Donald R. Wright lists the punishments incurred by slaves for even minor infractions:

> [When] the proportion of slaves to free persons began to rise, or even portended to do so, white anxiety mounted. The result in South Carolina and Georgia was the steady erosion of rights for blacks until they faced the strictest laws with the most harsh punishments of anywhere in the English mainland colonies. . . . "Suspicious gatherings" of blacks in the streets of Charleston set whites on edge, prompting the organization, in 1721, of a "Negro Watch" to stop slaves on sight (with instructions to shoot any black not stopping on order) and to confine blacks found on the street after 9:00 P.M. In the same year the colonial militia took over previously irregular patrols in rural areas. Powers of patrolmen were arbitrary and almost without limits. They could administer twenty lashes to a slave found off the plantation without authorization, search slave dwellings indiscriminately, and kill suspected runaways who resisted or fled. . . . Punishments for those judged guilty were swift, severe, and frequently inhumane. They included castration; nose-splitting; chopping off of ears, hands, or toes; branding; or burning at the stake. Overseers and masters administered their own justice and punishment on the plantation, and those acts varied from reasonable to arbitrary and depraved.[10]

The French and Indian War

While individual colonies were dealing in their own manner with African and Native Americans, European empires were engaged in battles over who would control the vast wealth of the Americas. By 1749, with the population of the English colonies pushing beyond the Appalachians, the French, fearing a disruption of their fur trade in the region, began building a string of forts in the Ohio River Valley. The French and English had been fighting in Europe for eight years previously in the War of the Austrian Succession (1740–1748). With hostilities between the countries barely settled, the new forts in this disputed territory soon touched off another war.

In May 1754, Virginia governor Robert Dinwiddie sent Lieutenant Colonel George Washington to the French Fort Duquesne, near present-day Pittsburgh, to warn the French that they were to leave or be forcibly removed. The French and their Indian allies easily defeated Washington's forces.

Washington wrote Dinwiddie about his stunning defeat: "I luckily escaped [without] a wound, tho I had four Bullets through my Coat and two Horses shot under me: It is supposed that we left 300 or more dead in the Field; [about] that number we brought off wounded."[11]

Most non-Iroquois tribes, including the Delaware, Shawnee, Abnaki, Ojibwa, Ottawa, and Potawatomi, were trading partners with the French and so became their allies. The Iroquois remained neutral.

Despite several sporadic battles, the war did not escalate until 1756. That year, the French began a long string of victories with the defeat of the British at Fort Oswego. In 1757, they destroyed Fort William Henry.

The next year saw a reversal of fortunes for the French when the British took forts at Niagara, Ticonderoga, and Frontenac. When the French city of Quebec was conquered in 1759, and Montreal in 1760, the war was over in North America. Battles continued in Europe until 1763, but France had been defeated by the British.

The war with the Native Americans, however, was just beginning. In the west, Ottawa chief Pontiac organized thousands of warriors to fight British subjects who were now moving onto lands formerly held by the French. In the spring and summer of 1763, Pontiac and his Chippewa, Sauk, Delaware, and Mingo allies attacked dozens of British forts in Ohio, Michigan, Pennsylvania, and elsewhere. In one of the first cases of biological warfare, General Jeffrey Amherst decided to infect the natives with disease. Amherst wrote to his field commander: "Could it not be contrived to send the *Small Pox* among these disaffected tribes of Indians?" [12] The field commander responded by sending smallpox-infected blankets to the Native Americans. Within a month, an epidemic had swept through the Native American forces, and Pontiac's rebellion was soon quelled.

By 1763, France and England signed the Treaty of Paris that ceded all of North America east of the Mississippi River, including Canada and Florida, to the British.

The American Revolution

Victory over the French and Native Americans provided security for the people in the British colonies to expand into the new frontier. Americans no longer felt dependent on Great Britain for protection. They lived in a land of full employment, good wages, cheap land, and basic liberties denied to most citizens in Europe. They controlled their political affairs through elected state assemblies in which men such as John Adams, Thomas Jefferson, Benjamin Franklin, and George Washington oversaw their affairs.

The war, however, had cost the British treasury a fortune. As such, King George III and his representatives in the British Parliament felt justified in taxing the colonists to pay for the war from which they had gained so much. In 1764, the British Parliament passed the Sugar Act, which placed a duty on imported molasses. In 1765, Parliament passed the Stamp Act, which place a tax on all legal documents, newspapers, playing cards, liquor licenses, college diplomas, and other paper items. This was the first direct internal tax to be forced on the colonies. Next came the Quartering Act, which demanded that Americans provide free room and board to British soldiers stationed in the colonies.

These provisions raised the cry of "taxation without representation" because the American colonies had no representatives in Parliament. The legislative houses of Virginia and Massachusetts quickly voiced their disapproval. Within weeks, rioting mobs in Boston had burned down the houses of several men appointed to collect the stamp tax. Meanwhile, merchants in New York, Philadelphia, and Boston had agreed to boycott British goods until the Stamp Act was repealed.

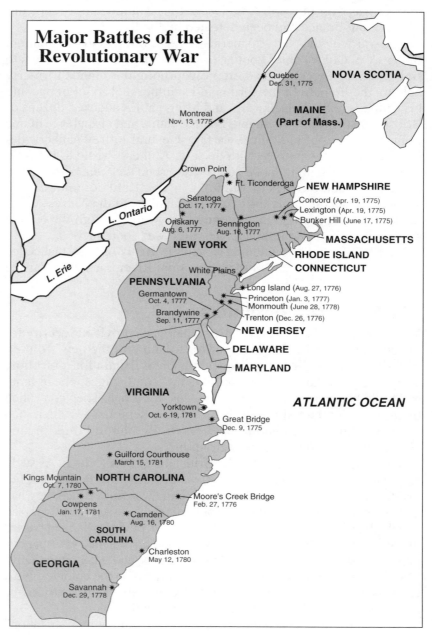

Major Battles of the Revolutionary War

Quebec
Dec. 31, 1775

NOVA SCOTIA

Montreal
Nov. 13, 1775

MAINE
(Part of Mass.)

Crown Point

Ft. Ticonderoga

NEW HAMPSHIRE

Saratoga
Oct. 17, 1777

Concord (Apr. 19, 1775)
Lexington (Apr. 19, 1775)
Bunker Hill (June 17, 1775)

Oriskany
Aug. 6, 1777

Bennington
Aug. 16, 1777

L. Ontario

NEW YORK

MASSACHUSETTS

RHODE ISLAND

CONNECTICUT

White Plains

L. Erie

PENNSYLVANIA

Long Island (Aug. 27, 1776)

Germantown
Oct. 4, 1777

Princeton (Jan. 3, 1777)
Monmouth (June 28, 1778)

Brandywine
Sep. 11, 1777

Trenton (Dec. 26, 1776)

NEW JERSEY

DELAWARE

MARYLAND

VIRGINIA

Yorktown
Oct. 6-19, 1781

Great Bridge
Dec. 9, 1775

ATLANTIC OCEAN

Guilford Courthouse
March 15, 1781

Kings Mountain
Oct. 7, 1780

NORTH CAROLINA

Cowpens
Jan. 17, 1781

Moore's Creek Bridge
Feb. 27, 1776

Camden
Aug. 16, 1780

SOUTH
CAROLINA

Charleston
May 12, 1780

GEORGIA

Savannah
Dec. 29, 1778

Volunteer soldiers called Minutemen were trained and organized into military companies ready to fight "at a minute's notice" against the British in the Revolutionary War.

The Stamp Act was repealed in 1766, but while the colonists rejoiced, Parliament forged another scheme for collecting taxes in the colonies. In 1767, the Townshend Acts were passed, placing taxes on imported lead, paper, tea, paint, and glass, to be collected at the ports. Another round of protests and boycotts forced the British to remove all the taxes save the one on tea. Meanwhile, Britain ordered more troops to Boston in case the growing unrest led to rebellion. The troops, known as "redcoats" for their bright red wool uniforms, were a constant source of tension for the colonists. On March 5, 1770, after an unruly mob gathered at a Boston customs house, British troops fired into the crowd, killing five.

War of Independence

The "Boston Massacre" aggravated an already tense situation. In 1773, Britain passed the Tea Act to give the British East India Company a monopoly over tea sales in the colonies. Most Americans resented this monopoly on their favorite nonalcoholic drink. In protest, a group of colonists sneaked into Boston Harbor on December 16, 1773, ill-disguised as Native Americans. They boarded three ships and dumped into the water 342 chests of tea valued at £9,000.

British authorities were incensed at this piracy and passed the Boston Port Act on March 31, 1774, which closed Boston Harbor to all commerce until the British East India Company was compensated for the destroyed tea. In May the British banned all town meetings not authorized by the legislature, and in June it passed the Quartering Act allowing British troops to requisition houses and empty buildings to house soldiers. Known collectively by the colonists as the Intolerable Acts, these laws soon mobilized the people of the colonies to fight for their freedom. In September 1774, the First Continental Congress met in Philadelphia and formally condemned the British actions. When Britain sent three thousand combat-ready troops to Boston in 1775, war seemed inevitable.

On April 19, a column of seven hundred redcoats began a ten-mile march from Boston to Lexington to find and destroy a munitions dump. When they arrived, a ragtag army of seventy villagers calling themselves Minutemen barred their way. Someone fired a musket and a battle ensued. When it was over, eight colonists lay dead. The redcoats then marched to Concord, where another firefight broke out. Two Americans and three British were killed, and when the troops tried to march back to Boston they were sniped at the entire way. Seventy redcoats were killed that day, and the Revolution had begun.

On March 10, George Washington was appointed general and commander in chief by the Second Continental Congress. Washington assembled a small colonial army that was aided by state regiments and American patriots. On July 4, 1776, the Continental Congress, meeting in Philadelphia, unanimously adopted the Declaration of Independence, written by Thomas Jefferson, which declared American sovereignty over British rule. By April 1778, France had joined with the Americans to fight the British.

The war dragged on for several years; most fighting was concentrated in New York, New Jersey, Pennsylvania, and Canada. In May 1780, the British began terrorizing the South as they took over Charleston, South Carolina. In 1781 an army of well-trained and well-equipped French soldiers arrived in New York.

Meanwhile, Washington learned that a large fleet of British ships was sailing to Yorktown, Virginia, with 17,000 troops led by Lord Charles Cornwallis. On September 28, 1781, Washington's 9,000 troops joined with 7,800 French soldiers on the outskirts of Yorktown. On October 9, the American and French forces began bombarding Yorktown. French ships blocked the British from escaping to the sea. Cornwallis realized his situation was hopeless. On October 17, 8,000 British troops surrendered. Two days later, Cornwallis's soldiers marched out of Yorktown while church bells rang and victorious Americans held parties in the streets.

In Paris, John Jay and Benjamin Franklin negotiated a peace treaty with the British that recognized American independence and ceded all land from the Appalachians to the Mississippi River to the new United States. The final Treaty of Paris was signed on September 3, 1783.

Adopting the Constitution

After the war the new nation faced some old problems. Taxes needed to be raised to pay soldiers. There were land disputes between the states over new territories. And Native Americans were resisting American settlements in the west. The country needed an entirely new system of government to address these problems.

On May 25, 1787, fifty-two of America's most prominent political thinkers gathered in Philadelphia at the Constitutional Convention. They met in the same room where the Declaration of Independence had been signed in 1776. George Washington was elected to lead the convention.

The new government they were charged with establishing would have to levy taxes, organize an army and a navy, regulate trade, and make laws. It would also have to issue money, sign treaties, and wage war. Reporters and visitors were barred from the meetings so delegates could debate in private.

That debate was famously contentious. The delegates at the Constitutional Convention were divided: Some, known as Federalists, wanted a strong central government. Those who wanted to give more power to the states were called anti-Federalists. Federalist Alexander Hamilton proposed that the states should have no power at all. He believed that their interests were too provincial, and that they would ignore federal laws.

Hamilton wanted a House of Representatives to be elected by popular vote, and a Senate whose members would serve for life. Hamilton called for a court that would review laws and strike them down if they violated the Constitution. The next day the delegates voted to form a government with three branches based on Hamilton's ideas. The new government would have a legislative body (Congress), an executive branch (the president and his cabinet), and a judicial system (the federal courts).

In September, Hamilton worked to rewrite the various committee motions into an official, complete document. With careful wording and elegant phrasing, Hamilton produced the U.S. Constitution, which was approved by the convention on September 17, 1787.

Many states refused to approve the Constitution unless amendments were added to protect the individual from government intrusion. After the ten amendments of the Bill of Rights were added, the Constitution was finally ratified by all the states in 1790. Even before the last state approved the document, George Washington was elected president in 1789.

The French Revolution

The same year that George Washington became president of one of the first democratic republics in history, America's former allies, the French, were beginning their own long, bloody march toward democracy.

The money and arms supplied to the Continental Army by the French had nearly bankrupted their treasury. France was the most populous nation in Europe—and the most powerful—but centuries of absolutist royal rule had left its economy in a shambles. At the beginning of the century, royal power had been purchased by Louis XIV by allowing the nobility—traditional rivals to the king—to exact tolls, levies, and taxes on the peasantry. These tolls were assessed with a ruthless efficiency that caused growing resentment among the French middle class.

In addition, France had been involved in a series of expensive wars throughout the century. And social fallout from France's role in the American Revolution fueled unrest: French citizens could not help but notice that the colonists were rebelling against a government much less repressive than their own.

Desperate for new moneys to keep his country solvent, Louis called together the Estates General, a national assembly made up of three tiers—the clergy, the nobility, and the commons. The governing body had not assembled since 1614, and in the months before the Estates General met, France experienced one of the worst harvests in its history. Citizens rioted in the street clamoring for bread as widespread starvation swept the countryside.

When the Estates General finally did meet in June 1789, the commons, composed mainly of middle-class merchants, took control of the meeting. They had never exercised power, but now named themselves a National Assembly and claimed to represent the entire country. Afraid of losing his power, Louis ordered the Royal Guard to make a show of force on the streets of Paris. Meanwhile, the poorest citizens of Paris began to riot and soon formed their own army, the National Guard, to protect and defend the Assembly. News of the revolution spread through the countryside and before long angry peasants were storming the luxurious homes of the nobility, burning records of debts and taxes owed and occasionally the houses themselves.

In August, the National Assembly, renamed the Constitutional Assembly, created a document called the Declaration of the Rights of Man and Citizen, much like the Declaration of Independence created by Thomas Jefferson. The French declaration declared a constitutional monarchy under which the nobility would keep their property but lose their rights of taxation.

Louis withheld his support of the declaration and remained at his splendid Palace of Versailles. During a banquet, however, twenty thousand hungry peasants stormed the palace and ordered the royal family back to Paris. Louis had no choice but to be escorted back to the city by thousands of armed peasants.

The Death of a King

Factions of the National Assembly formed clubs with differing political beliefs. One of the most influential was the Jacobin Club, comprising middle-class professionals, one of whom was a lawyer named Maximilien Robespierre. The Jacobin Club believed that its ideals of liberty at any cost could save France. Its message became very popular, and Jacobin clubs formed in cities across France. Before long, the Jacobins were the most powerful faction in the French Revolution.

Under the new freedoms, the number of newspapers and pamphlets increased exponentially. Without royal censorship some six hundred new newspapers represented all sides of the political spectrum.

The new assembly began reforms in education and government, and dealt with the problem of government bankruptcy by seizing the huge landholdings of the Catholic Church. This paid off the national debt, but angered many in the strongly religious regions of southern France.

The kings of Prussia and Austria feared that the French Revolution might spread beyond its borders and envelop their countries. In the summer of 1792, an allied army of Austrians and Prussians invaded France with the intention of restoring royal authority to Louis. A hastily assembled Revolutionary Army, however, turned back the Austrian invaders. A new assembly was called, which outlawed the monarchy.

In November, charges were made that Louis had planned the previous summer's Austrian invasion to restore his power. The king was put on trial for treason, found guilty, and executed. The queen, Marie Antoinette, met the same fate.

The Reign of Terror

Emboldened by their new power, the assembly, now known as the National Convention, declared that France should expand its borders throughout Europe. It declared war on Britain, Holland, and Spain, but when ill-trained revolutionary armies invaded neighboring countries they were quickly subdued. Embarrassed, the National Convention ordered the conscription of 650,000 men into the army.

France was now at war, and any opposition was considered treason. The government set up dozens of revolutionary tribunals in major cities to seek out and prosecute traitors. The committees filled the jails with people suspected of counterrevolutionary activities. As the terror increased, the term *traitor* was applied to almost anyone who spoke out against the government madness. Led by Robespierre, the Jacobins, who held the most power, began to execute their opponents in the assembly. With those enemies gone, the Jacobins turned on one another, and those who had helped Robespierre gain power were also executed. Within a year, 35,000 people lost their heads to the guillotine. In Paris alone, during one seven-week period, 1,376 people were beheaded.

In 1794, when Robespierre demanded yet another purge of enemies, he too went to the guillotine and the Reign of Terror ended. A new group, called the Thermidorians, took the reins of power. The nobility who had survived the Reign of Terror held a majority in this new government and many revolutionary laws were repealed. A young general by the name of Napoléon Bonaparte turned the government's guns on the hostile mobs protesting in the streets. In the following years, Napoléon led the French armies on campaigns across Europe and Egypt. In 1799, the Jacobins were driven from assembly chambers by Napoléon's troops, and the French Revolution was over. Within weeks, Napoléon named himself emperor of France, and once again France was ruled by a single man.

The Industrial Revolution

The eighteenth century was a time of scientific as well as political revolution. At the beginning of the 1700s, most people lived as their ancestors had lived, but by the end of the century, advances such as James Watt's steam engine had transformed the way people worked and the way people traveled.

The first crude steam engine had been invented in 1712. But Watt, working in the 1760s and 1770s, improved the design and produced an engine capable of powering riverboats, railroad trains, and industrial machinery. This discovery led to the other far-reaching revolution of the eighteenth century, the Industrial Revolution.

Until the last third of the eighteenth century, commercial products were generally manufactured by artisans either in their homes or in small workplaces. The steam engine, and other inventions, allowed a dramatic increase in production by mechanizing production processes. This quickly transformed agricultural-based culture into an industrialized urban society awash in commercially manufactured products.

The factory system, the hallmark of the Industrial Revolution, exacted high social costs. Factory workers were expected to work up to sixteen hours a day in dark, dirty factories at repetitive and sometimes hazardous tasks. Women and children as young as six years old were exploited by the system. Steam engines ran on coal, and the cities of England were bathed in filth as the skies blackened with a non-stop stream of air pollution.

There was, of course, a positive side to the Industrial Revolution. The economy was transformed when thousands of formerly poor farmers began to draw steady paychecks from the factories. The demand for goods and services increased and roads, canals, and railroads were built to supply the countryside with new products. As the nineteenth century dawned, the per capita income of the average citizen began a slow steady rise that would help transform Britain into a modern industrial power.

A Different World

At the beginning of the eighteenth century, the Western world was divided into small kingdoms ruled by powerful European kings and queens. At the end of the century, ideals of democracy and freedom had spread throughout the world because of the American Revolution. Although it would take many more years, the theories of personal liberty, democracy, and freedom that were spawned in the ancient kingdoms of Europe would grow into a worldwide movement that would envelop the globe. And the eighteenth-century ideas of Jefferson, Voltaire, Hamilton, and Franklin hold their mark on the world today.

Notes

1. Quoted in Will and Ariel Durant, *The Age of Louis XIV,* vol. 8 of *The Story of Civilization.* New York: Simon & Schuster, 1963, p. 15.
2. George R. Havens, *The Age of Ideas.* New York: Free Press, 1965, p. 9.
3. Peter Gay, *Age of Enlightenment.* New York: Time-Life Books, 1966, p. 40.
4. Nancy Mitford, *The Sun King.* New York: Harper & Row, 1966, p. 209.
5. Will and Ariel Durant, *The Age of Louis XIV,* p. 700.
6. Gay, *Age of Enlightenment,* p. 165.
7. Will and Ariel Durant, *The Age of Voltaire,* vol. 9 of *The Story of Civilization.* New York: Simon & Schuster, 1965, p. 24.
8. Will and Ariel Durant, *The Age of Voltaire,* pp. 60–61.
9. D.W. Meinig, *The Shaping of America,* vol. 1, *Atlantic America 1492–1800.* New Haven, CT: Yale University Press, 1986, pp. 205–206.
10. Donald R. Wright, *African Americans in the Colonial Era.* Arlington Heights, IL: Harlan Davidson, 1990, p. 68.
11. George Washington, *George Washington Writings.* New York: Literary Classics, 1997, p. 58.
12. Quoted in David Horowitz, *The First Frontier: The Indian Wars and America's Origins 1607–1776.* New York: Simon & Schuster, 1978, pp. 185–86.

Chapter

1

1700–1720

PREFACE

The early years of the eighteenth century were dominated by the European rulers of England, France, Spain, Russia, and Prussia. The main concern of these monarchs was consolidating their power and using their country's treasuries to extend their reach into foreign lands from India to the Americas. Without a system of democracy to replace kings and queens when they died, major wars, such as the War of the Spanish Succession, were fought to decide who would ascend the throne. It was business as usual to find Austria, Prussia, England, and France warring over who would become king of Spain.

While soldiers fought and died and treasuries were drained to stoke the machines of war, average people lived in what was commonly described as "water and mud." Small windowless hovels with thatched roofs housed the typical peasant family while disease, starvation, and death stalked young and old alike. Most people lived in the countryside and spent their lives wresting subsistence from the soil. The nobility who owned the land exacted a large percentage of the peasant's toil in the form of duties, taxes, and rents.

In France, the powerful nobility was granted the right of taxation by the "Sun King," Louis XIV. In return, the nobles granted Louis absolute power to rule the most populous country in Europe. Louis used his power to live a life of lavish abundance beyond the imagination of most of his subjects. In fact, Louis spent the equivalent of $2 billion to build his luxurious Palace of Versailles, while his countrymen suffered through bad harvests, epidemics, and some of the coldest winters in history.

In Russia, Peter the Great, whose power was as vast as that of the French king, ruled a country that, by European standards, was mired in the Middle Ages. Peter ordered several hundred thousand of his countrymen to build a capital city in his honor on the mouth of the Neva River. Often using nothing but their bare hands, Russian laborers constructed the shining jewel of St. Petersburg. Cynics said the foundation of the city was built on bones as up to forty thousand workers died in the process.

Far to the west, an uncontrolled experiment in colonialism was taking place on the Atlantic coast of North America. The English pilgrims who founded Massachusetts Bay Colony in the seventeenth century had passed into history. In their wake came 250,000 immigrants from Scotland, Ireland, the Netherlands, Germany, and elsewhere. Lured to America by the promise of cheap land and unlimited riches, the ancient hardwood forests fell to the settlers' axes and cities such as Charleston, Philadelphia, New York, and Boston sprang up in the wilderness. The Native Americans who had lived in the region for millennia were pushed west or wiped out by European diseases such as smallpox.

As the farms in the southern colonies grew in size and number, white Americans discovered that a gift they had received from the Native Americans—tobacco—was the key to their economic success. As the popularity of tobacco grew, planters imported a growing number of black slaves from Africa to farm the labor-intensive cash crop. Each year, a larger percentage of the population was composed of slaves who had been cruelly kidnapped in their homelands and forced to labor in a strange land.

With little past history to draw on and a hodgepodge of cultures landing on eastern shores every day, America could only look to the future to find its purpose in a changing world.

The Absolutist Rulers of Europe

Alfred Cobban

Although power had been concentrated in the hands of kings and queens for centuries, the 1700s is known for its absolutist monarchs, despotic kings who ruled with unconditional authority. Louis XIV, king of France, is probably the most famous absolutist but he was certainly not the only one. Frederick the Great of Prussia and Peter the Great of Russia also single-handedly controlled their vast empires. To gain such great power, the absolutist monarchs had to wrest it from the church and the nobility. Louis did this by bribing the nobility with land and wealth in exchange for political power. Little concern was shown for the average citizen who lived in dire poverty, and little thought given to concern that this disparity in wealth would lead to the French Revolution in 1789. In the following excerpt Alfred Cobban, professor of French history at University College, London, describes the techniques absolutist kings used to maintain power in the eighteenth century.

That the . . . Age of Enlightenment, of toleration, increasing humanity and liberalism, should have been born in the second half of the 17th century, at the time of the absolutism of Louis XIV and the barbaric tyranny of Peter the Great, may seem a paradox. The . . . paradox cannot be denied, nor can it be explained away by underestimating the importance of politics. The 18th century believed and, making all allowances for the extensive areas of life which were outside political control, rightly believed in the influence of government. When [agricultural writer] Arthur Young, on the first of his travels in France, in 1787, returned after a journey into Spain . . . , he wrote:

> Here we take leave of Spain and re-enter France: the contrast is striking. . . . From the natural and miserable roads of Catalonia you tread at once on a noble causeway, made with all the solidity and magnificence that distinguishes the highways of France. Instead of beds of torrents you have well built bridges; and from a country wild, desert and poor, we found ourselves in the midst of cultivation and improvement. Every other circumstance spoke the same language, and told us by signs not to be mistaken, and some great and operating cause worked an effect too clear to be misunderstood. The more one sees, the more I believe we shall be led to think, that there is but one all-powerful cause that instigates mankind, and that is GOVERNMENT!

Even if this is not true, the fact that the 18th century believed it to be true is important. . . .

Enlightenment and Absolutism

The paradox of Enlightenment and Absolutism runs throughout the 18th century. Its pattern of government was set by the absolute monarchy of France, whose language and culture dominated Europe. In 1660, when Louis XIV, young and yet untried, came to the throne, France for the first time in a hundred years . . . had a King who was capable of personal rule. This was what she needed, for it had been repeatedly demonstrated that the turbulent French nobility would not accept any other authority. Autocracy was the lesson that was drawn from a century of civil wars, and Louis inherited . . . founders of mighty bureaucratic dynasties—through whom he was able to put it into practice.

These were the ministers who laid the foundations of the first centralized bureaucratic régime in Europe. A necessary corollary was that the King should have his own agents throughout the country. The provinces being too closely bound up with the old aristocratic order, the newer administrative division of France into *généralités,* originally used for tax collecting, took the place of them. . . . Even under Louis XIV the extent of autocracy and bureaucratic centralization was never as unqualified as critics . . . suggested or as historians have sometimes believed. The limitations on the power of the central government will have to be dealt with subsequently, but at the outset, it must be emphasized that Louis XIV, and his many imitators, had to manage, use and in a sense buy off the nobles, usually by increasing their social privileges, as the price of the diminution of their political power. Louis XIV set the pattern in the concessions he made to privilege as well as in his assertion of monarchical sovereignty.

The Glory of Versailles

The fusion of noble privilege with royal power was made possible because they both met in the most personal of Louis' achievements, his Court. This explains the importance of [the royal residence of] Versailles. The physical environment is an essential element in the functioning of all institutions. The absolutism of Louis XIV could never have developed in the Renaissance charm of the old [former royal residence at the] Louvre, emerging like a surprising jewel from the confusion of medieval Paris. Its rooms and audience chambers were far too few and too small to hold all those whom duty or pleasure or the hope of gain brought to the Court of the *roi soleil* [sun king]. It could provide no adequate accommodation for the swelling new bureaucracy. It was surrounded by narrow, winding streets and a teeming populace in which riot and revolution might be bred. . . . The city was also the breeding place of an even more dangerous enemy, plague. Health and the royal pleasures of the hunt had to be sought in the countryside. These were some of the reasons why the Louvre was abandoned, and a new palace built at Versailles on a larger, grander scale. Here ministers and mistresses, high nobles and lackeys formed a world apart, yet one which through its daily Councils, and the regular reports of the royal emissaries and agents, kept the whole life of France and the policy of the Crown under constant review. . . .

At Versailles all aspects of national life and all possible centres of power were brought under royal control. Towns and provinces gradually lost most of the autonomy which they had once possessed. The [governing body of the] *Parlements,* those venal and hereditary law courts which had so often played the game of the enemies of royal authority, even when they did not challenge it in their own right, were reduced to passivity. The Assemblies of the Clergy, controlled by the King's nominee, the Archbishop of Paris, performed only the royal will. The army became for the first time truly the King's army. The financiers and war contractors made greater fortunes than ever, but they were no longer practically a state within a state. . . . Royal manufactories were set up to promote industries; the crafts in the towns were compulsorily organized into guilds, which were created in far greater numbers than ever the Middle Ages had known. Overseas trade was regulated by royal companies. Academies were created to discipline the arts. And at the centre of the whole machine was *le roi soleil,* both the symbol of the unity of the State and—so far as one man could be—its actual ruler, the first of a long series of despots who straddle what has been called, as well as the Age of Enlightenment, the Age of Absolutism.

It would be misleading, on the other hand, to suggest that Louis XIV, great as was the example he set, was the model from whom European monarchs learnt to be despots. Mostly they did not require teaching. In Louis' own day Peter the Great was struggling to civilize his backward empire by the methods of barbarism. [Peter] required no teaching in the ways of arbitrary despotism. Soon after, Frederick William I, the 'Sergeant King' was ruling the small but rising state of Prussia like a military camp. Habsburg Spain had set Europe lessons in civil and religious intolerance before France. The little Italian princes had long abandoned even the pretence of popular liberties. Yet, after all this has been said, it remains true that Louis XIV stands apart. When [philosopher Baron de] Montesquieu wanted to condemn despotism it was of the oriental despotism of the Ottoman Empire that he wrote, but the monarchy of Louis XIV that he had in mind. The image of the great King spread through Europe with the French tongue and French culture. Even the Huguenot refugees served as unwilling propagandists for the France that had persecuted and driven them into exile. It is true that what was copied was what was more superficial, the external appearances rather than the essence of society and government, and that as we penetrate deeper the differences from one country to another appear more clearly; but this must not lead us to refuse to see influences and similarities. . . .

The French Nobles

So far I have stressed the absolutism of the age that extended from 1660 to 1789. This is the accepted picture, but taken by itself it is a misleading one. The role of aristocracy in European society had changed, but as has already been implied, the nobility still remained a potent factor. Here again France provides the model which other aristocracies tried to copy. The French [nobleman] . . . still imagined himself the representative of feudal chivalry—instead of, as he frequently was, the descendant only a few generations removed of an ennobled financier or lawyer who had bought his entry into the ranks of the nobility. His only expertise was in getting himself killed, bravely but often very incompetently, on the battlefield. Abstention from productive work of almost any kind was the one essential condition of preserving his status and privileges. His economic survival therefore depended primarily upon two sources of income—the exploitation of his estates, and this meant in the main the extraction of rents in kind or money . . . from the peasants; and, with luck . . . intriguing for sinecures and pensions from State and Church. Their legal status united the members of the order of *noblesse* in a single interest, though their possessions ranged in France, as in most other countries, from the vast riches of the princes of the blood to the poverty of the landless country gentleman whose standard of life might be below that of the struggling peasants, working their little farms on what might well have formerly been his own estates, who provided him with the pittance on which he lived. The social centre of the nobility had also changed. . . . They were becoming urbanized. When a great minister like the Duc de Choiseul fell from power and was sent to his ancient château, this was banishment. On the other hand, lawyers and financiers, in the process of making themselves into gentlemen, were building houses in the country.

While its privileges remained as great as ever, and even increased, the French nobility was clearly a declining order in the 17th and 18th centuries. Its political power had gradually been whittled down to negligible proportions. Except for the greatest nobles, its wealth was being overtaken by the riches of merchants and lawyers. The ownership of land had gradually been passing into the hands of bourgeois and peasants. Even war, when it brought only a succession of defeats, was no longer as satisfactory an occupation as it had once been. . . . Economic pressure, in the course of the 18th century, was producing a large body of discontented lesser nobility; while exclusion from the functions of government made the higher nobility restless to the point of rebellion. Put together, these two factors produced the aristocratic revolution which undermined the authority of the Crown and opened the door to the revolution of the Third Estate [average citizens] in 1789. . . .

The *noblesse* of the robe and the sword, formerly rivals, were now united in defence of their privileges; and the *Parlements* not only provided a constitutional basis for aristocratic ambitions, but also stirred up popular agitation in the towns. It is now a platitude to say that the French monarchy fell not because of its despotism but because of its weakness. The aristocracy took advantage of this weakness to overthrow the absolute monarchy, and in doing so destroyed itself.

Bourbon Monarchies

In most other countries in Europe, monarchy and aristocracy were mixed in different proportions, and a regime compounded of the two survived into the 19th and even the 20th centuries. Spain, which became a Bourbon monarchy [ruled by members of the Bourbon family] as a result of the War of the Spanish Succession, was the country in which one would have expected to see the French pattern of government most closely repeated; and so far as the Bourbon kings were able to do so, this was what they aimed at. The first Bourbon king [Spanish king], Philip V, introduced the system of government through ministers in place of the Habsburg conciliar system, though without robbing the councils of all their functions. . . . Charles III, who ruled from 1758 to 1788, continued the same trend, bringing into his service able professional administrators, under whom Spain seemed to be in the process of reversing the current of her national history and to offer the promise of returning to her greater days. It was an illusion. The success of all the European monarchies was bound up with the personality of the ruler. When Charles III, conscientious and capable of choosing able servants, was replaced by the weak-willed and stupid Charles IV, with his stronger but equally stupid consort, Maria Luisa . . . , the whole achievement of Bourbon kingship in Spain collapsed, all the more easily because the fundamental social evils of the Spanish *ancien régime* [ancient regime of previous monarchs] remained, as they were long to remain, unremedied. Nothing had been done to remove the older forms of provincial privilege and noble exemptions from taxation and prohibition from productive work. The grandees of the Court and the hordes of poverty-stricken gentry in the country were equally useless to the State, but they preserved within the husk of monarchical absolutism the seeds of aristocratic anarchy.

There were also Bourbon rulers in Italy, in Naples and Parma, who achieved no more permanent results than they did in Spain. Italy was a collection of different types of government. There were Habsburgs in Lombardy and Tuscany; Sardinia was a kingdom, Venice and Genoa fossil republics and the Papal States a medieval relic. Sardinia had a comparatively modern centralized administration and the future Emperor Leopold III gave Tuscany a reforming government. But elsewhere the Italian states remained internally what Italy was as a whole, a mosaic of petty privileges in which the pattern of the modern State had hardly begun to appear. Power and privilege everywhere resided in the hands of the noble landowners and there was little effective challenge to them from above or below. Politically, a great part of Italy seems to have skipped the 18th century and remained in the 17th until circumstances flung it headlong into the 19th.

The House of Habsburg

If in the Iberian [Spanish] and Italian peninsulas the past weighed so heavily on the present, the Austrian Empire might seem even more incapable of being adapted to 18th-century absolutism. It was an heterogeneous collection of provinces, united only by allegiance to the Austrian Crown. A description of them cannot be other than a catalogue. The lands of Austria proper stretched from the Alpine valleys to the Danubian plain and included the Tyrol, Breisgau and Burgen, Upper and Lower Austria, Carniola, Carinthia, Styria. These were mainly Catholic and German. The lands of the former Bohemian Crown, Bohemia, Moravia and Silesia, were Slav in race and language and in parts still retained memories of their Hussite [Protestant] past. Prince Eugene of Savoy had driven the Turks back to Belgrade in

1716 and by the Peace of Passerowitz in 1718 completed the emancipation of the Hungarian plain from the Turks; while about the same time the opposition of the Hungarian nobles to Austrian rule had been brought to an end by a compromise. But the Magyar [Hungarian] nobles and the Slav peasants under them had nothing in common with the other peoples of the Empire. South of the Alps Austria had the purely Italian province of Lombardy; and finally she ruled the former Spanish and now Austrian Netherlands. To add to the complication, the Austrian Emperor was also Holy Roman Emperor, a position which brought with it no power but some potentially dangerous responsibilities. To bring all these varied territories into the kind of administrative centralization that the 18th-century monarchies admired more often than they could achieve it, was an impossible task.

To think of the government of the Habsburg Empire in terms of absolute monarchy is however something of an illusion. It should rather be seen as yet one more variation, or rather a series of variations, on the general theme of aristocracy and monarchy. The direct personal control of the sovereign was at its height in the Austrian and Bohemian lands, where the Emperor ruling through his Privy Council and its Secretary was least restricted by aristocratic opposition. That imperial authority should be strongest in the hereditary Habsburg lands of Austria was natural; its strength in the lands of the Bohemian Crown is attributable to the passivity which had descended on them after the crushing defeat and reconquest at the battle of the White Mountain in 1620. . . .

Under Charles VI, who ruled from 1705 to 1740, little progress in centralization was to be expected. The Emperor being primarily concerned to secure the inheritance of the whole of the imperial possessions for his daughter Maria Theresa, could not afford to antagonize the lands which still retained some of their local autonomy. In particular this meant Hungary. For their part, the Magyar nobles were still too conscious of the Turkish menace not to be willing to accept a compromise, especially if the terms were favourable to themselves. The result was that government in Hungary remained essentially aristocratic, in the hands of Estates dominated by the great nobles, who were prepared to recognize imperial authority on condition of retaining their own privileges. When, by virtue of the Pragmatic Sanction, Maria Theresa succeeded to the dominions of Charles VI and to an inheritance threatened with partition by the rapacious powers around her, she appealed to the Hungarian Estates for support. She obtained it, but again at a price, in the form of the preservation of the aristocratic Hungarian constitution and the continuance of noble exemption from taxation.

Extraordinarily, Maria Theresa emerged from the War of the Austrian Succession with only the major loss of Silesia. The lesson drawn from this war and the subsequent Seven Years' War was the need for reforms which would enable Austria to resist the Prussian threat and recover the lost province. After the conclusion of peace in 1748 a general reorganization of government, setting up specialized ministries, and of taxation, removing it largely from the control of the Estates, was undertaken in Austria and Bohemia, which now came to correspond much more closely to the ideal pattern of 18th-century autocracy, with rather fewer concessions to the noblesse than had been made in France. In Hungary, on the other hand, it might be said that the situation was reversed and it was the nobles who condescended to make some concessions to the Crown. The best that Maria Theresa could do with the great Hungarian magnates was to adopt the policy that Louis XIV had used with his greater nobles. By attracting them to the Court at Vienna, they were tied more closely to the Habsburg house, which in its turn was committed to the preservation of aristocratic privileges.

Under Maria Theresa's heir, Joseph II, a more intensive policy of centralization was attempted, combined with the promotion of Germanization through the educational system. Widespread unrest throughout the Austrian dominions, culminating in the revolt of the Austrian Netherlands, and the failure of the ambitious foreign policy which Joseph's internal measures had been intended to promote, proved that Maria Theresa had been correct in limiting her administrative changes to what she believed the different provinces of her Empire would accept peacefully.

Prussian Despotism

If the supposed absolutism, or enlightened despotism, of the Austrian Empire was so limited in its achievement and concealed so much variation within a single state, how much greater variety was to be expected in patterns of government throughout the whole of Europe. We have still not reached the heights of absolutism or the extremes of aristocracy. The kingdom of Prussia might seem to carry us a long way towards absolutism. In fact, what we discover is a simultaneous development towards a centralized absolutism and an increasingly privileged aristocracy. Brandenburg-Prussia was, like the Habsburg Empire though on a much smaller scale, a conglomeration of provinces. . . . With the revenue . . . assured to the State a standing army, disproportionately large in relation to the size of the State, was built up. In other European countries the army was created to serve the State; in Prussia it might almost be said that the State was created in the service of the army. It has been pointed out that Frederick William I was the first European ruler habitually to be seen in uniform. . . . The whole success of the government . . . depended on the ability of the ruler. This was common to all the absolutisms but even the ablest and most hard-working of the 18th-century despots could only achieve a limited success. Frederick II governed from Potsdam on the basis of reports sent to him by ministers, who were no more than officials, from Berlin. The profound distrust with which he regarded them was met by the evasion and deceit which they employed towards him. Under a weak successor, after the death of Frederick, disaster struck the Prussian State.

. . . As almost everywhere, the ruler had purchased autocracy by guaranteeing and even increasing the social and economic privileges of the nobility. Also as elsewhere, the officer class in the army was recruited from the nobles. Where a marked difference is revealed is that in the absence of a middle class and given the comparative lack of wealth of even the higher nobility, the nobles and gentry were prepared, and needed, to play an active and not merely an honorific role in the higher ranks of the bureaucracy and at the head of local administrations, as well as in the army. When the central government collapsed, therefore, before the Napoleonic Empire [in 1799], the aristocratic foundations remained intact for the reconstruction of a centralized military State.

The variations of government in the other German states are too great to be gone into here. For the most part they combined, in different proportions, most of the vices of aristocracy and monarchy with few of their virtues.

Russia: Absolutism Supreme

To see absolutism at its height we must move east to Russia. Two powerful and ruthless aristocrats, Peter at the beginning and Catherine at the end, dominate the century. In between, women or children were set up as supreme rulers by Court factions and the Imperial Guard, or overthrown by palace revolutions. This was the despotism of the degenerate [ancient] Roman Empire. Nevertheless what Peter and Catherine did, or tried to do, is not irrelevant to the general pattern of government, for it represents yet another variation on the theme of aristocracy and monarchy. Like Prussia, Russia in the 17th century was a military State, with an administration organized for defence or conquest. Under Peter the Great, and again under Catherine, extensive changes were made in both the central government and local administration. Their effectiveness is doubtful and their duration was limited. Essentially the government was and remained a pure despotism, exercised by the arbitrary will of the ruler. If there was one institution which was necessary to it this was the secret police, whose power was well established during the 18th century.

As in every other country, the basic problem of government in Russia was the relation between the sovereign and the nobility. Peter's solution had been to accelerate, sometimes by rather drastic means, the decline of the old class of boyars [aristocrats] and replace it with a serving nobility. The theory was that after a cumpulsory education, from the age of 10 to 15, the young noble entered either the bureaucracy or the army, and continued in these for the rest of his active life, slowly working his way up through fourteen grades. The weaker successors to Peter found it impossible to maintain this system. In 1736 the term of service was limited to twenty-five years; and in 1762 compulsory service was abolished. In fact it still remained customary for many nobles to serve in the army or bureaucracy, largely for economic reasons. Their support for the tsardom was ensured not only by the reduction of their obligations but also by the increase in their privileges. This was particularly the work of the German princess, Catherine, who emerged as Empress in 1762 as the result of a military coup and the murder of her husband. Like her immediate predecessors, she multiplied the privileges of the nobles, though she kept political authority strictly in her own hands. The masses of the peasantry were consequently thrust into the depths of serfdom and the tyranny of the ruler was founded on the innumerable petty tyrannies of the class of landowners.

The War of the Spanish Succession

Maurice Ashley

The following excerpt explains why the War of the Spanish Succession was fought, who the key players were, how the war was carried out, and how it was concluded. The war was fought by hundreds of thousands of soldiers in almost every European kingdom west of Poland. The instigators, especially Louis XIV, expected to win the war quickly. Instead it dragged on for years. As tens of thousands of military and civilian casualties mounted, and the treasuries of France and other countries were drained, the war was finally concluded with little change on the political landscape.

Maurice Ashley has written several books about the seventeenth century as well as biographies of Spanish king Charles II and French king Louis XIV.

The first partition treaty [drawn by Britain's King William III in 1698] was . . . concluded in secret; but the second [drawn in 1700] was an open treaty, since in order to make it workable it was necessary for the Spanish and Austrian Habsburg rulers to consent to its terms. The [Holy Roman] Emperor Leopold, who in 1699 at last concluded a treaty of peace with the Turks and thereby ensured his dominion over the whole of Hungary and Transylvania, was in

Excerpted from *The Age of Absolutism: 1648–1775* (Springfield, MA: G&C Merriam, 1974) by Maurice Ashley.

no mood to accede to the treaty. Nor was the King of Spain. Spanish pride demanded that its empire (already shorn of the northern Netherlands and Portugal) should not be cut up. [Spanish king] Carlos II therefore made a will. . . . By his [will] he bequeathed [his possessions] not to Louis XIV's heir, the Dauphin [future French king], but to the Dauphin's second son, Philip of Anjou. If Philip refused this magnificent gift, it was to be offered to the Archduke Charles of Austria. Thus—in theory at least—whatever happened, the Spanish empire would remain intact and independent. Such was the belief that glowed in the cloudy mind of Carlos, who was at last really dying. He signed his second will in October 1700 and a month later 'the Sufferer', as he was called, expired.

Louis XIV had now to decide whether he should attempt to abide by the terms of the partition treaty or acquiesce in the will. The question was urgently debated in Versailles and who exactly said what is still disputed. . . . The Dauphin, who was fat and usually apathetic, insisted that the will should be accepted: he was content to be the son of a great king and the father of a great king. Louis XIV himself was convinced that whatever else he did he would be obliged to fight against the Austrian Habsburgs again, for they were unlikely to accept meekly either a partition or the accession of a French Bourbon prince to the throne of Madrid. Moreover, however the new King of Spain behaved, a Bourbon alliance was surely likely in the future. . . .

A Ruinous War for France

For a few months it seemed as if the French decision to accept the testament of Carlos II was the right one. 'Some very wise men believe', wrote Madame de Maintenon, Louis XIV's . . . wife, 'that there will not have to be a war and that we should have had a long and difficult one, ruinous to France, if Louis had insisted on the execution of the treaty.' French historians have supported her view, maintaining that the war of the Spanish succession, which began in full force in 1702, was the result of unscrupulous propaganda by interested parties such as the exiled French Huguenots. The only government which immediately thought of war was that at Vienna, where the Emperor Leopold had refused to agree to the two partition treaties on the ground that his family were the legitimate heirs to the whole of the Spanish inheritance. Nevertheless, there was the possibility that unless he could acquire allies the Emperor might have to agree to some compromise and that even if he would not, the war might be confined to northern Italy. Both the English and Dutch governments recognized Philip of Anjou, named Philip V of Spain, as heir. In business circles the hope was expressed that Philip would not prove himself to be a tool of France and that his succession might even be helpful to the expansion of trade.

William III, a sick and petulant man, had no such faith in the coming independence of Spain nor in the altruism of France. He had been disappointed . . . that Louis XIV had become a chastened and reasonable ruler ready to accept a balance of power in Europe. He told his friend, Heinsius, that they had been duped and regarded war as unavoidable. But he proceeded cautiously, anticipating correctly that public opinion in England and in the Dutch Republic might change when the significance of events dawned on them. Thus although he sent John Churchill, the Earl of Marlborough, an experienced diplomat and proved military commander, to The Hague to conclude another Grand Alliance with the Dutch and the Austrians, this was not, on the surface, a signal for war against France. It allowed for negotiations and it did not commit the maritime powers to obtaining the entire Spanish heritage for the Austrian Habsburgs. It was envisaged that the Emperor should acquire all the Spanish possessions in neighbouring Italy, that the Dutch should receive a barrier of fortresses in the southern Netherlands and that the maritime powers should gain commercial and colonial advantages. Louis himself seems to have been prepared to make concessions to avert another war. It is indeed ironical that after twelve years of fierce fighting a compromise, based on the idea of partition, was eventually to be reached.

Political Blunders

Decisions taken in France and Spain in 1701 which, French historians maintain, were misunderstood and distorted by unscrupulous propagandists finally brought about the war. Shortly after the signature of the treaty of the Grand Alliance against him (7 September) Louis recognized [the exiled] James III as the legitimate King of England, which naturally angered William [who was the king]. . . . Permission was obtained from Spain for French soldiers to occupy the fortresses held by Dutch troops in the Spanish Netherlands. Swift action followed; the Dutch were surprised, disarmed and sent home. In Italy a French force was ordered to seize the duchy of Milan in the name of the new Spanish King. Furthermore, two diplomatic blunders of the first magnitude were committed. It was announced both in Madrid and in Versailles that Philip of Anjou had not renounced his right to succeed ultimately to the French throne: this was explained to be a mere statement of fact because constitutionally he could not do so. The other blunder was that the Spanish Regency, while awaiting the arrival of their new young King, invited Louis XIV to direct the government in his name. Fuel was added to the fire when the French were given exclusive trading privileges in Spanish overseas possessions.

All this meant—as William had expected—that effective public opinion in the two Protestant countries which he ruled, already largely antagonistic to France for historical reasons, became extremely hostile and militant. The English [political party known as the] Whigs, who had asserted that William had acted unconstitutionally and foolishly in negotiating the partition treaties, were won over to the idea of war. In fact to a large extent the coming war was for these two countries one strongly influenced by economic considerations, for merchants did not relish the notion of the French winning a trading monopoly both in the Mediterranean and across the Atlantic. So an undeclared war began in 1701. In September [Austrian commander] Prince Eugene inflicted an important defeat on the French expeditionary force at Chiavi in the duchy of Milan. This put the allies in good heart. On 15 May 1702 they officially declared war on France.

Nations Choose Sides

The French appeared at first to enjoy several advantages in the coming war. Their army was well trained with some experienced generals who had emerged since the death of the Duke of Luxembourg. Initially it amounted to over two hundred thousand men and soon rose to a quarter of a million. Again, Louis XIV had unity of command and could operate defensively on inner lines. This time the French had the Spaniards for allies instead of enemies; though they did not have much to offer in the way of troops or equipment, the loyalty of the bulk of the Spanish people to their new king was to prove a useful asset. The French also persuaded the Portuguese to become their allies. Thus the French had access to a large number of naval bases in the Mediterranean and the Atlantic and also, after their army had occupied the southern Netherlands, in the North Sea. Although the French navy was inferior to that of the English and Dutch combined, throughout the war much damage was inflicted on allied trade by French privateers [pirates, working for the government]. French diplomacy also enlisted the alliance of the Duke of Savoy. . . . However, his alliance facilitated their operations in Italy. Finally, the French obtained the alliances of the two Wittelsbach brothers (the Elector of Bavaria and the Elector of Cologne) who had always been envious of the Habsburgs. The Elector of Bavaria's accession to the French side constituted a threat to Vienna while his brother gave French troops manoeuvring power on the Lower Rhine. Furthermore the French encouraged and supported Francis Rakoczi, a proud Magyar [Hungarian] magnate who had inherited a Hungarian nationalist tradition and enmity towards Austria. In 1703 he was to head a rebellion which was to distract the attention of Leopold I and his successors from the western theatre of war. Though the French were in no position to seek help in the Baltic, the fact that the Swedes were already engaged in fighting the Danes, the Poles

and the Russians meant that the danger of the Grand Alliance finding active assistance from northern Europe was relatively small.

The Grand Alliance

On the allied side an impressive accumulation of strategic resources
was steadily built up. The Dutch and English rapidly raised large
armies because they could afford to hire mercenaries from Denmark
and the smaller German states. Brandenburg had a substantial army
which was joined to the allied forces; for the Elector was anxious to
please the Emperor who agreed to recognize him as King Frederick
I in Prussia. In fact most of the German principalities consented to
fight under the banner of the Holy Roman Emperor because they had
been provoked by French aggression in two previous wars. But some
of their soldiers proved pretty useless. Moreover the Emperor's attention was often distracted from the theatres of war in the Netherlands and in Spain because of the nearer problems he had to face in
the Balkans and in Italy. However, he had a fine general in Eugene,
just as the British had in Marlborough, while Heinsius was the diplomatic heir of William III, who died in March 1702. Queen Anne, his
sister-in-law, who succeeded as queen, boasted of her 'English heart'
and proved more popular than Dutch William, whom the English political nation had never fully trusted. The wealth of the English kingdom and the Dutch Republic, deriving from commerce, industry and
banking (the Bank of England, which lent money to the government,
was founded in 1694) made them the paymasters of the Grand Alliance which was able finally to bring the Bourbons to heel.

A War Across the Continent

The war of the Spanish succession ranged over much of Europe; it
was fought in the southern Netherlands, in Germany, in Italy and in
Spain. The French, although profiting from their inner lines of communication and their unity of command, were handicapped by their
inferiority at sea, particularly in the Mediterranean. In the first two
years of the war the allies pushed back the French defensive lines on
the Meuse and the Lower Rhine. On the other hand, in 1703 the Marquis of Villars, a boastful and quarrelsome man, who proved himself
to be easily the best of the French commanders, broke through the
fortified lines of Stollhofen, which had been constructed by Prince
Louis of Baden, one of the Emperor's generals, and which were intended to prevent the French from advancing north between the
Black Forest and the Upper Rhine. Meanwhile in Italy the French
had made progress in the duchy of Milan after a drawn battle fought
at Luzzara in August 1702 between Marshal Vendôme, France's second best general, and Prince Eugene. In Spain, the allies had done

well through the exertion of sea power. Cadiz was attacked and a Spanish silver fleet destroyed off north-west Spain at Vigo, the French escort squadron being destroyed. This episode made a profound impression on both Portugal and Savoy and induced them both to change sides. By the treaty with Portugal, signed in May 1703, the allies gained a valuable base at Lisbon. At the same time the Portuguese, who did not wish for a French prince as king in Madrid, insisted that no peace should be made without the Austrian candidate becoming the ruler of Spain. This commitment in fact prolonged the war, since it delayed the peace treaty being concluded on the basis of a division of the Spanish empire. The accession of Savoy to the alliance opened the opportunity for an attack on France from the south. But French troops immediately occupied both Savoy and Piedmont so the Austrians fighting in Italy became bogged down, to the disappointment of the Vienna government which sought territorial gains in Italy rather than in Spain.

Villars's success in southern Germany (for which he was created marshal) and the seizure of the city of Ulm on the Danube by the French ally, the Elector Maximilian Emmanuel of Bavaria, opened up for the French a real offensive opportunity by allowing them to advance into Austria itself and by defeating the Emperor compel him to agree to peace. The scheme was that Villars should march through the Tyrol and link up with Maximilian Emmanuel, while Vendôme, leaving some forces to contain the Austrians in Italy, should join up with them through the Brenner pass. Meanwhile the rebel Hungarians, subsidized from Paris, would threaten Vienna from the east. Another French army under Marshal Tallard was sent to replace that of Villars in Alsace. However the scheme fell to pieces: Maximilian Emmanuel had ambitions of his own in the Tyrol; Vendôme was afraid to leave Italy; Villars quarrelled with Maximilian Emmanuel, who, as a prince, was his superior in rank. Nevertheless the French were not unsuccessful in 1703. The veteran Marshal Vauban captured the town of Breisach in Alsace, thus opening the long lines of communication between France and Bavaria. Prince Louis of Baden was defeated by the French at the battle of Höchstadt and the town of Augsburg on the river Lech, a tributary of the Danube, was occupied. Augsburg was on the route to Vienna so that the threat became obvious. But Louis made one fatal mistake. He recalled Villars and replaced him by an inferior marshal, Marsin.

French Losses

The danger to the Grand Alliance was grave enough for the allies, led by Marlborough (who had been given a dukedom on account of his successes in 1702) and Prince Eugene, who had been recalled from Italy to the Bavarian front, to concert a campaign to relieve the pressure on Austria. Marlborough skilfully led an army of twenty thousand (later to be swollen by German contingents to fifty thousand) from the Meuse to the Danube, a distance of two hundred and fifty miles, deceiving the French about his ultimate destination. Prince Eugene, who joined Marlborough fifty miles west of Ulm early in June, soon established a good relationship with him. It was agreed that Eugene should go west to prevent the French under Tallard from coming to the Danube, but in this he was unsuccessful, and Tallard met Marsin and the Elector of Bavaria at Augsburg on 5 August. On 13 August 1704 the two groups of armies confronted each other at Höchstadt, where Villars had won a victory for the French the year before. To distinguish the two battles the second one is known as the battle of Blenheim (Blindheim was a village not far from Höchstadt). Although the French and the Bavarians outnumbered the allies, a great victory was won by Marlborough and Eugene. Thus Bavaria, which had been systematically devastated before the battle, was knocked out of the war. The Elector Maximilian Emmanuel went back to his profitable post as governor of the Spanish Netherlands. The French lost over twenty thousand men in the battle and Marshal Tallard was taken prisoner. The blow to French military prestige was incalculable. Marlborough returned to the Moselle from whence he planned to invade France in the following year. Shortly before the victory at Blenheim an English admiral, Sir George Rooke, captured the Rock of Gibraltar and had the better of the French and Spanish fleets, which aimed to retake Gibraltar, in an engagement off Malaga. Never again did the French fleet seek battle with the allies nor were attempts to recapture Gibraltar effective.

Rejected Peace Plan

1705 was another crucial year in the war. Marlborough's plan to advance into Lorraine from the Moselle was frustrated by the vigilance of Marshal Villars, who had been restored to command. In Italy, to which Prince Eugene had returned, his attempt to link up with the turncoat Duke of Savoy was withstood by Vendôme at the battle of Cassano in August. The only allied success was the capture of Barcelona, where the Catalans had rallied to the cause of the Archduke Charles. Next year, however, was a disaster for the French. On 23 May Marlborough won a big victory at Ramillies, north of Namur, which was more pregnant in its consequences even than Blenheim. For the whole of the Spanish Netherlands fell almost without resistance into the allied hands. In August the allies laid siege to Menin, a frontier fortress in France itself. A month later the Archduke Charles, who had landed at Lisbon in March 1704, marched into Spain and was crowned as Carlos III in Madrid. In September Prince Eugene, assisted by the Duke of Savoy, won another big victory over the French at Turin; Marshal Marsin was killed and the French field army was forced to retreat across the Alps.

It looked as if the war was at an end. Louis XIV put out peace feelers in the Netherlands, expressing himself as willing to concede the same kind of terms as those he had agreed with William III in the second partition treaty. The Dutch, who might have been willing to treat if promised a barrier of fortresses in the southern Netherlands, however, remained loyal to their allies. The new Habsburg Emperor, Joseph I, who had succeeded his father in 1705, wanted the entire Spanish inheritance for his younger brother (except for Milan which he intended to keep for himself). The English, committed by the treaty of 1703 with Portugal and fearful of a French predominance in southern Italy which might harm their Mediterranean trade, were adamantly opposed to any concession whatever. Thus the opportunity passed. Next year Archduke Charles was driven out of Spain after an allied army had been defeated by the French at the battle of Almanza. In 1708 the French began a counter-offensive in the southern Netherlands, but Vendôme was defeated at the battle of Oudenarde. However, stalemate developed. In the previous year a big allied operation against Toulon was a failure, while the Emperor, greedy for territorial gains in Italy, agreed to the convention of Milan with the French, enabling them to evacuate northern Italy and use the troops thus released to reinforce the other fronts. In 1709 the battle of Malplaquet, fought by Villars to stave off the threat of invasion of France from the north-east, was a murderous battle in which the Duke of Marlborough, though nominally victorious, had to sustain heavy casualties which deeply distressed him. Though he remained in command for two more years he did not fight another battle. In fact from 1709 onwards it was simply a question of negotiating a peace. As at Ryswick over twelve years earlier, the bargaining was long and complicated. But at last in April 1713 the maritime powers concluded a treaty at Utrecht in Holland with France, while the Emperor somewhat reluctantly came to terms with the French at Rastatt a year later.

The Peace of Utrecht

The peace of Utrecht brought to an end the period which is usually called that of the ascendancy of France or the age of Louis XIV. The French King was now seventy-five years old and had seen his heirs dying off one after another until his great-grandson (the youngest son of the Duke of Burgundy), who was only two years old, was left as the direct heir. Louis believed that the loss of his grandchildren and his defeat in the war were punishments imposed upon him by God. Yet Jean-Baptiste Colbert Torcy, the son of Colbert and the grandson of a cloth merchant in Rheims, who was mainly responsible for the negotiation of the treaty, could write: 'God has crowned the Christian courage of the King in maintaining Philip V, his grandson, on the Spanish throne in spite of the efforts of a formidable league. . . .' Philip had to swear that he renounced his claims to the French succession before the *Cortes* in Madrid—for what that was worth. He retained not only the throne of Spain but all Spain's overseas possessions in the Americas and the West Indies. . . . France itself was by no means shattered territorially by the conclusion of the prolonged wars. It kept Strasbourg, Franche-Comté and Alsace, though it was obliged to give up its conquests on the right bank of the Rhine such as Breisach, Kehl and Frieburg, and it did not lose all its colonies overseas.

Benefits to the Grand Alliance

What did the allies gain? The Duke of Savoy, who had changed sides at a fortunate time, was among the best-off. He was given Sicily to add to his dominions of Savoy and Piedmont, while Nice was restored to him. He was also allowed to adopt the title of king, as, on the other side of Europe, was Frederick I, confirmed as King in Prussia. The Portuguese position in Brazil was strengthened at the expense of both the Spaniards and the French. The Emperor, who was now that very Archduke Charles who had aspired to the Spanish throne and who was known as the Emperor Charles VI, though he regretted not having achieved his full ambitions, did not do badly out of the peace, for as a result of it the southern Netherlands were added to his empire as was also much of Italy including the duchy of Milan and the island of Sardinia. Upper or Spanish Gelderland, however, was detached from the southern Netherlands and awarded to Prussia. The Wittelsbachs were restored to their Electorates in Germany. Henceforward the authority of the Habsburgs as the suzerains of Germany began to be steadily eroded.

What of the maritime powers? The Dutch gained remarkably little from a war in which they had expended so much money and so many lives. They had, it is true, realized William III's ambition of preventing the Spanish Netherlands from falling into the hands of the French and they had obtained a barrier of fortresses—though it excluded Lille—in that area to obstruct further French aggression. The barrier was not as comprehensive as they wished because the English who after a Tory victory in the general election of 1710 had reached a separate peace with France were not prepared to allow the Dutch all that the Whigs had promised them in a treaty of 1709, while the commercial advantages they won were small. They had to negotiate the details of their fortresses with the Emperor Charles VI. But in any case the whole idea of a barrier was a delusion. Never in the history of the Western world were the Dutch able by the mere

possession of fortifications to stop invasion by more powerful enemies. Utrecht, wrote the distinguished Dutch historian, Pieter Geyl,
ended the period of Dutch greatness, although, as has been noticed
already, other historians do not agree with him.

England, or rather Great Britain, for the union with Scotland had
at last been agreed to in 1707, benefited most from the war. It was
given, much to the annoyance of the Dutch, a virtual monopoly of
the slave trade with Spain, being permitted by what was known as
the *'asiento'* to carry some five thousand slaves a year to the Spanish Indies. A ship was also allowed to carry goods to South America once a year and under the cover of that concession a busy smuggling trade grew up. England gained Gibraltar and Minorca, thus
strengthening its naval superiority in the Mediterranean. Queen
Anne (who died in 1714) was recognized as the legitimate Protestant Queen; this was necessary because the French and Spaniards
had naturally backed the exiled Roman Catholic Stuarts during the
war. Finally England made substantial gains overseas. Hudson Bay,
Newfoundland and Acadia (Nova Scotia) were all recognized as
British; St Kitts was added to the British West Indies; certain fishing rights in the neighbourhood of Newfoundland were all that were
retained by the French. The French still ruled Canada and Louisiana
in the north and south of the North American continent, but the
colonies there were sparsely populated and had been neglected by
Louis XIV. Thus the settlement at Utrecht not only presaged the
building of the first British empire, but also the continuing expansion of the Western world across the Atlantic.

The French Rout in Flanders

Louis de Rouvroy, duke of Saint-Simon

By 1708, the French had won a few battles in the War of the Spanish Succession but had lost most of the Spanish Netherlands, Gibraltar, and Bavaria to the English and all of Italy to the Austrians. At that point, French general Louis Joseph, duc de Vendôme, was transferred from Italy to Flanders (the region north of France) to stop the British, who were rapidly advancing onto French soil.

Vendôme was an unusual character in the court of Louis XIV. At the age of fifty-four, he was incredibly rich, but he was overweight, refused to bathe, and ridden with syphilis. Because of his wealth, however, Vendôme was the favorite of Louis, and was allowed to treat the king in a disrespectful manner as no one else dared. Louis made Vendôme a general and sent him to command French soldiers against the British near the city of Oudenarde in Flanders. Because Vendôme was famous for his eating, drinking, and philandering, the king sent Louis de France, duc de Bourgogne (Burgundy), to keep an eye on the general.

The operation quickly turned into a catastrophe. Although the British commander, John Churchill, first duke of Marlborough, was advancing on Oudenarde, Vendôme did not want to move from his comfortable quarters to the battlefield. The conflict turned into a rout against the French, and Vendôme tried to blame Bourgogne for its failure.

In this excerpt, Louis de Rouvroy, duke of Saint-Simon, describes the disastrous French loss to British troops in the War of the Spanish Succession. The duke was a member of the court of Louis XIV. Like many royal courtiers, Saint-Simon wrote memoirs, which have left a vivid record of the long reign of the Sun King.

Excerpted from *Memoirs of Louis XIV and His Court of His Regency* (New York: P.F. Collier, 1910) by Louis de Rouvroy, duke of Saint-Simon. Copyright © 1910 by P.F. Collier & Son.

Early in July, we [the French army] took Ghent and Bruges [in present-day Belgium] by surprise, and the news of these successes was received with the most unbridled joy at [the royal residence Chateau de] Fontainebleau. It appeared easy to profit by these two conquests, obtained without difficulty, by passing the Escaut [River], burning [the city of] Oudenarde, closing the country to the enemies, and cutting them off from all supplies. Ours were very abundant, and came by water, with a camp that could not be attacked. [Monsieur Louis Joseph Duc] de Vendôme [French general and duke of Savoy] agreed to all this, and alleged nothing against it. There was only one difficulty in the way,—his idleness and unwillingness to move from quarters where he was comfortable. He wished to enjoy those quarters as long as possible, and maintained, therefore, that these movements would be just as good if delayed. Monseigneur le Duc de Bourgogne maintained on the contrary, with all the army—even the favourites of M. de Vendôme—that it would be better to execute the operation at once, that there was no reason for delay, and that delay might prove disastrous. He argued in vain. Vendôme disliked fatigue and change of quarters. They interfered with the daily life he was accustomed to lead. . . . He would not move.

"The Work of the Devil"

[Captain general of the English land forces, John Churchill, the duke of] Marlborough clearly seeing that M. de Vendôme did not at once take advantage of his position, determined to put it out of his power to do so. To reach Oudenarde, Marlborough had a journey to make of twenty-five leagues [one league equals about three miles]. Vendôme was so placed that he could have gained it in six leagues at the most. Marlborough put himself in motion with so much diligence that he stole three forced marches before Vendôme had the slightest suspicion or information of them. The news reached him in time, but he treated it with contempt according to his custom, assuring himself that he should outstrip the enemy by setting out the next morning. Monseigneur le Duc de Bourgogne [Louis de France, duke of Burgundy] pressed him to start that evening; such as dared represented to him the necessity and the importance of doing so. All was vain—in spite of repeated information of the enemy's march. The neglect was such that bridges had not been thought of for a little brook at the head of the camp, which it was necessary to cross.

On the next day, Wednesday, the 11th of July, a party of our troops, under the command of [Louis] Biron, which had been sent on in advance to the Escaut, discovered, after passing it as they could, for the bridges were not yet made, all the army of the enemy bending round towards them, the rear of their columns touching at Oudenarde, where they also had crossed. Biron at once despatched a messenger to the Princes and to M. de Vendôme to inform them of this, and to ask for orders. Vendôme, annoyed by information so different to what he expected, maintained that it could not be true. As he was disputing, an officer arrived from Biron to confirm the news; but this only irritated Vendôme anew, and made him more obstinate. A third messenger arrived, and then M. de Vendôme, still affecting disbelief of the news sent him, flew in a passion, but nevertheless mounted his horse, saying that all this was the work of the devil, and that such diligence was impossible. He sent orders to Biron to attack the enemy, promising to support him immediately. . . .

Outflanked by the Enemy

Biron meanwhile placed his troops as well as he could, on ground very unequal and much cut up. He wished to execute the order he had received, less from any hopes of success in a combat so vastly disproportioned than to secure himself from the blame of a general so ready to censure those who did not follow his instructions. But he was advised so strongly not to take so hazardous a step, that he refrained. . . .

While this was passing, Biron heard sharp firing on his left, beyond the village. He hastened there, and found an encounter of infantry going on. He sustained it as well as he could, whilst the enemy were gaining ground on the left, and, the ground being difficult (there was a ravine there), the enemy were kept at bay until M. de Vendôme came up. The troops he brought were all out of breath. As soon as they arrived, they threw themselves amidst the hedges, nearly all in columns, and sustained thus the attacks of the enemies, and an engagement which every moment grew hotter, without having the means to arrange themselves in any order. The columns that arrived from time to time to the relief of these were as out of breath as the others, and were at once sharply charged by the enemies, who, being extended in lines and in order, knew well how to profit by our disorder. The confusion was very great: the new-comers had no time to rally; there was a long interval between the platoons engaged and those meant to sustain them; the cavalry and the household troops were mixed up pell-mell with the infantry, which increased the disorder to such a point that our troops no longer recognised each other. This enabled the enemy to fill up the ravine with fascines [bundles of sticks used for fortification] sufficient to enable them to pass it, and allowed the rear of their army to make a grand tour by our right to gain the head of the ravine, and take us in flank there.

Mass Confusion

Towards this same right were the Princes [Louis III de Condé and François-Louis Conti], who for some time had been looking from a mill at so strange a combat, so disadvantageously commenced. As soon as our troops saw pouring down upon them others much more numerous, they gave way towards their left with so much promptitude that the attendants of the Princes became mixed up with their masters, and all were hurried away towards the thick of the fight, with a rapidity and confusion that were indecent. The Princes showed themselves everywhere, and in places the most exposed, displaying much valour and coolness, encouraging the men, praising the officers, asking the principal officers what was to be done, and telling M. de Vendôme what they thought.

The inequality of the ground that the enemies found in advancing, after having driven in our right, enabled our men to rally and to resist. But this resistance was of short duration. Every one had been engaged in hand-to-hand combats; every one was worn out with lassitude and despair of success, and a confusion so general and so unheard-of. The household troops owed their escape to the mistake of one of the enemy's officers, who carried an order to the red coats [French soldiers], thinking them his own men. He was taken, and seeing that he was about to share the peril with our troops, warned them that they were going to be surrounded. They retired in some disorder, and so avoided this.

The disorder increased, however, every moment. Nobody recognised his troop. All were pell-mell—cavalry, infantry, dragoons; not a battalion, not a squadron together, and all in confusion, one upon the other.

Intoxicated on Anger

Night came. We had lost much ground, one-half of the army had not finished arriving. In this sad situation the Princes consulted with M. de Vendôme as to what was to be done. He, furious at being so terribly out of his reckoning, affronted everybody. Monseigneur le Duc de Bourgogne wished to speak; but Vendôme, intoxicated with choler [anger] and authority, closed his mouth, by saying to him in an imperious voice before everybody, "That he came to the army only on condition of obeying him." These enormous words, pronounced at a moment in which everybody felt so terribly the weight of the obedience rendered to his idleness and obstinacy, made everybody tremble with indignation. The young Prince to whom they were addressed, hesitated, mastered himself, and kept silence. Vendôme went on declaring that the battle was not lost—that it could be recommenced the next morning, when the rest of the army had arrived, and so on. No one of consequence cared to reply.

From every side soon came information, however, that the disorder was extreme. . . . Vendôme, seeing that it was useless to resist all this testimony, and beside himself with rage, cried, "Oh, very well, gentlemen! I see clearly what you wish. We must retire, then;" and looking at Monseigneur le Duc de Bourgogne, he added, "I know you have long wished to do so, Monseigneur."

These words, which could not fail to be taken in a double sense, were pronounced exactly as I relate them, and were emphasized in a manner to leave no doubt as to their signification. Monseigneur le Duc de Bourgogne remained silent as before, and for some time the silence was unbroken. At last, Puységur interrupted it, by asking how the retreat was to be executed. Each, then, spoke confusedly. Vendôme, in his turn, kept silence from vexation or embarrassment; then he said they must march to Ghent, without adding how, or anything else.

A Difficult Retreat

The day had been very fatiguing; the retreat was long and perilous. The Princes mounted their horses, and took the road to Ghent. Vendôme set out without giving any orders, or seeing to anything. The general officers returned to their posts, and of themselves gave the order to retreat. Yet so great was the confusion, that the Chevalier Rosel, lieutenant-general, at the head of a hundred squadrons, received no orders. In the morning he found himself with his hundred squadrons, which had been utterly forgotten. He at once commenced his march; but to retreat in full daylight was very difficult, as he soon found. He had to sustain the attacks of the enemy during several hours of his march.

Elsewhere, also, the difficulty of retreating was great. Fighting went on at various points all night, and the enemy were on the alert. Some of the troops of our right, while debating as to the means of retreat, found they were about to be surrounded by the enemy. The Vidame of Amiens saw that not a moment was to be lost. He cried to the light horse, of which he was captain, "Follow me," and pierced his way through a line of the enemy's cavalry. He then found himself in front of a line of infantry, which fired upon him, but opened to give him passage. At the same moment, the household troops and others, profiting by a movement so bold, followed the Vidame and his men, and all escaped together to Ghent, led on by the Vidame, to whose sense and courage the safety of these troops was owing.

M. de Vendôme arrived at Ghent, between seven and eight o'clock in the morning. Even at this moment he did not forget his disgusting habits, and as soon as he set foot to ground . . . in sight of all the troops as they came by,—then at once went to bed, without giving any orders, or seeing to anything, and remained more than thirty hours without rising, in order to repose himself after his fatigues. He learnt that Monseigneur de Bourgogne and the army had pushed on to Lawendeghem; but he paid no attention to it, and continued to sup and to sleep at Ghent several days running, without attending to anything.

A Day in the Life of Louis XIV

Gilette Ziegler

The following excerpt tells of daily life in the sumptuous court of Louis XIV, which was attended by dozens of nobles who had surrendered their political power to the absolutist monarch in exchange for land, lavish lifestyles, and royal favor. Many of these educated aristocrats wrote memoirs of their days with the Sun King, which were compiled by French historian Gilette Ziegler.

Primi Visconti, *who lived at the Court from 1673 onwards, recorded with amazement the sight of the King and his suite setting out on . . . a journey:*

It is a fine spectacle to see Louis XIV setting out, surrounded by his Royal Guard, carriages, horses, courtiers, valets and a great throng of people, all in a state of complete confusion, running and shouting around him. It is exactly like the queen bee leaving her hive accompanied by her swarm.

Visconti *goes on to describe the daily routine involved in the King's life at Versailles:*

All his daily actions are strictly regulated. He always arises at eight o'clock, and remains with his Council from ten o'clock until midday, when he and the Queen attend Mass, accompanied by members of the royal family. At one o'clock, after hearing Mass, he visits his favourites until two o'clock, at which hour he dines, always with the Queen and always in public. The rest of the afternoon he spends hunting or taking the air, and very often he holds another Council. From nightfall until ten o'clock he converses with the ladies, or plays cards, or attends a play or a ball. At eleven o'clock, after supper, he returns once more to the apartments of his favourites. He always sleeps with the Queen. Thus he divides the hours of his day and his night between his public affairs, his pleasures, his devotions and his duties. . . .

Mass was celebrated in the Chapel. La Bruyère *has described the scene, with the King kneeling down on a velvet cushion, in the Royal Tribune facing the altar:*

The great ones of the nation assemble each day, at a certain hour, in a temple which they call a church. At the far end of this temple is an altar consecrated to their God, at which a priest celebrates sacred and redoubtable mysteries named saints. The great ones form a vast circle at the foot of this altar and remain standing, their backs turned to the priest and the holy mysteries, and their faces lifted towards their king, who is to be seen on his knees in a tribune; and it seems that their minds and their hearts are concentrated on him alone. This procedure would seem to indicate a sort of subordination, for the people appear to adore the prince and the prince to adore God.

Eating with the King

Then came the main meal, an important affair if we are to judge by the number of employees of the Service de la Bouche (the royal table) which totalled 498. The King had a robust appetite, and according to the Princess Palatine:

I have often seen the King eat four plates of soup of different kinds, a whole pheasant, a partridge, a large plate of salad, two thick slices of ham, a dish of mutton in a garlic-flavoured sauce, a plateful of pastries and then fruit and hard-boiled eggs. Both the King and Monsieur are exceedingly fond of hard-boiled eggs.

And, in a later observation, she speaks of the royal table manners:

The Duc de Bourgogne [the [queen's] son] and his two brothers had been taught the polite innovation of using a fork while eating. But when they were invited to the King's table at supper, he would have none of it and forbade them to use such a tool. He would never have had occasion to reproach me in that matter, for I have never in my life used anything to eat with but my knife and my fingers.

[Louis de Rouvroy, Duke of] Saint-Simon has described the ceremonial surrounding the service of dinner:

The dinner was always *à petit couvert,* that is to say by himself in his room, at a square table . . . . The meal was fairly substantial, for in the morning he ordered either a *petit couvert* or a *très petit couvert* to be prepared, though even the latter comprised a number of dishes, and three separate courses, not counting fruit. When the table had been set, the principal courtiers entered the room, followed by others who had permission to attend. Then the First Gentleman of the Chamber went to inform the King that the meal was ready to be served, and served the meal himself, if the Grand Chamberlain was not there. . . .

I have often seen Monsieur, either just arrived from Saint-Cloud to see the King, or else coming from the *conseil des dépêches* [council meeting], enter the room alone, hand the King his napkin and remain standing. A little later, the King, noticing that he was not going away again, would ask him if he would not like to be seated, whereupon Monsieur would bow and the King would order a chair to be brought. A *tabouret* [small stool] was then placed behind him. A few moments later the King would say to him: 'Brother, be seated.' Monsieur would bow again, and remain seated until the King had finished his meal, continuing to present the napkin to him. . . .

Except when with the Army, the King never ate in company with any other man, wherever he may have been, not even with the Princes of the Blood, although when one of the princes married, the King sometimes arranged a wedding banquet and then might join him at table.

Travels of Louis XIV

After his meal, the King often decided to go on an outing, usually in his carriage and far from the Château, since, according to the Princess Palatine:

Although Versailles possesses the loveliest promenades in the world, no one except myself ever walks in them. The King is always telling me: 'You are the only one who enjoys the beauties of Versailles.'

The occasional moves to [the royal residences at] *Saint-Germain or Fontainebleau involved certain discomforts* en route, *if we are to believe* Saint-Simon, *writing at a later date:*

During these journeys, there was always a vast store of provisions of various kinds, including meats, pastries and fruits. The expedition would not have covered a quarter of a league before the King would be asking the ladies in his carriage whether they did not care to eat something. . . . Then they were all obliged to say how hungry they were, put on an air of jollity, and set to with good appetite and willingness, otherwise the King became displeased and would show his resentment openly. . . . As for the needs of nature, they could never be mentioned, and in any case, any such needs would have proved most embarrassing to the ladies in the party, with the carriage preceded and followed by detachments of the Household cavalry and the Royal Guards, and equerries riding by the doors, raising a dust that covered everyone in the carriage. The King liked fresh air and insisted on having all the windows lowered; he would have been extremely displeased had any lady had the temerity to draw one of the curtains to keep out the sun, the wind or the cold. There was no alternative but to pretend not to notice that, nor any other kind of discomfort. . . . To feel sick was an unforgivable crime.

In fact, the courtiers were subject to an iron discipline. Ezechiel Spanheim *notes that at Versailles:*

Everything is more stiff, more reserved, more constrained and also less free than is typical of the nation's general character. Even the entertainments and fêtes which the King often arranges for the principal ladies of the Court seem to lack spontaneity and appear stiff and formal, with a sense of constraint reigning over the pleasures.

Games and Gambling

But happily, everyone was able to relax at the gaming tables, playing frantically for high stakes in an atmosphere which was not only tolerated, but approved of, by the King. In a letter to her daughter dated October 9th, 1675, Mme de Sévigné *comments:*

They play for enormous sums at Versailles. In Paris *hoca* [a board game] is forbidden, under pain of death, and yet the King and his Court play it: for [huge sums of money] to change hands in a single morning is nothing.

The Princess Palatine *adds confirmation:*

The players behave like madmen, one screaming aloud, another striking the table so hard with his fist that the whole room echoes with the sound, a third uttering blasphemous oaths so terrible as to make one's hair stand on end; they all appear to be completely out of their minds.

And the young Marquis de Feuquières *writes to his father:*

Mme de Montespan's gaming has reached such excessive proportions that [huge] losses . . . are common. . . .

Certain courtiers, such as the Marquis de Dangeau, lived from their gambling. Saint-Maurice asserted that Dangeau's entire existence was bound up with the fortunes of the gaming table. . . . Primi Visconti *comments wrily on the gambling mania:*

The Queen's favourite game is *hombre,* but she is so simple-minded that she loses continuously, and the Queen's losses provide the poor Princesse d'Elbeuf with her sole means of support. This gaming, if it continues at the present intensity, will be the Court's finest source of revenue. It is a general fault in France, especially among the ladies. The art of conversation is a finished thing; nowadays people are simply concerned with making some money one way or another. The money they win is not hoarded, it is needed to cover the vast cost of feeding and dressing themselves.

It was, indeed, absolutely necessary to have a constant flow of money coming one's way, in order to maintain a ruinously extravagant way of life. Courtiers often wheedled favours for their friends in return for substantial cash payments. In the view of Mme de Motteville:

The King's establishment is like a vast market, where there is no choice but to go and bargain, both to maintain one's own existence and to protect the interests of those to whom we are attached by duty or friendship.

But gambling often gave way to ballets and various divertissements *given in the gardens, to which the general public were admitted, for, in the words of* Louis XIV, *in his* Mémoires:

The people enjoy pageantry and display. In this way we retain their loyalty and devotion, sometimes more effectively, perhaps, than by just rewards and benefits.

But on most occasions, the King spent the hour between seven and eight o'clock playing billiards in the Salon de Diane, with refreshments being served in the Salon de Vénus. These rooms were known collectively as 'l'appartement'. The Princess Palatine *confessed to being bored to distraction in that atmosphere:*

The *appartement* is an absolutely intolerable experience. We all troop into the billiard room and lie on our stomachs or squat, no one uttering a word, until the King has finished his game. Then we all get up and go to the music room where someone is singing an aria from some old opera which we have heard a hundred times already. After that, we go to the ball, which lasts from eight to ten o'clock. Those who, like me, do not dance have to sit there for hours without budging for an instant, and can neither see nor hear anything except an interminable minuet. At a quarter to ten, we all follow one another in a quadrille, like children reciting the catechism, and then the ball is finally over.

Three times a week, plays were performed, but many members of the public of that era would have agreed with the Duchesse d'Osnabrück *(aunt of the Princess Palatine), who, on a visit to Versailles, declared:*

I found so many people to occupy my time and thoughts that I took very little notice of the plays. There was terrible overcrowding in the audience, and the heat was unbelievable; I came to the conclusion that the pleasures of the Court of France are mingled with many inconveniences. We refreshed ourselves by drinking lemonade.

The French Peasant's Life

Henri Sée

Even as Louis XIV was finishing his royal residence at Versailles at a cost of over 200 million francs in 1690 (the equivalent of several billion dollars in modern terms), most French citizens were living in hovels and nearly starving to death. Bad harvests, unusually cold winters, and disease left most peasants in a perpetual state of misery in the early eighteenth century. The government offered nothing for their troubles, as it was bogged down in the costly War of the Spanish Succession.

This excerpt, originally published in France in 1927 by Henri Sée, an author and expert in French history, details the hardships faced by French peasants during the early 1700s.

T he material existence of the peasants was still quite miserable, even at the end of the *ancien régime* [the political system of the French monarchy]. Their dwelling-places were altogether inadequate. Most of them were built of mud, covered with thatch, and having only a single low room without a ceiling. The windows were small and had no glass. In Brittany [western France], and especially in Lower Brittany, it has been said that the peasants lived "in the water and in the mud." This is one of the principal causes for the epidemics that were still so frequent. However, as today, living conditions varied in different regions. In northern France the peasants seemed to have the most comfortable homes.

Furthermore, we must never fail to distinguish between the peasants in comfortable circumstances and the poor ones, particularly

Excerpted from *Economic and Social Conditions in France During the Eighteenth Century* (New York: Cooper Square Publishers, 1968) by Henri Sée.

when we consider furniture and clothing. The former had furnishings that were simple, primitive and suitable, sufficient dishes and linen, as well as enough clothing. The poor, on the other hand, could hardly satisfy their most elementary requirements. Among the well-to-do the inventory after death—our principal source of information—sometimes estimates the furnishings at over one thousand francs; among the poor they are frequently worth no more than 50 or even 20 livres [$500 or $200]. The poor dispose of only one or two trunks, a table, a kneading-trough, a bench, and a roughly hewn bed. Among the farmers in good circumstances we find well made beds, wardrobes, all sorts of household utensils, bowls of wood or earthenware, pottery, and glasses. In clothing we also find great variety, from very good to very poor. Working clothes were almost always of canvas. Many peasants had only wooden shoes, or went barefoot, especially in the south. Heavy taxes on skins made shoes very expensive.

A Basic Diet

The food of the peasants was always coarse, and often insufficient. Meat appeared on the table but rarely. Sometimes they ate bacon. Except in sections where wine was plentiful, water was the usual beverage. In Brittany cider was drunk only in years of abundance. The basic foods were bread, soup, dairy products, and butter. Wheat bread was quite rare; only bread of rye and oats, and that frequently of poor quality, was known. In the poorest regions the peasants ate biscuits and porridge of buckwheat, or even of chestnuts or maize. Wheat and even rye served largely to pay the taxes and farm-rent, or were sold for export when this was permitted. Potatoes, which later became a staple food-product among the farmers, were grown only in a few particularly fertile regions, as for example in certain parts of the coastal region of Brittany.

Clothes were often wretched. The description of Besnard in "Souvenirs d'un nonagénaire" probably is accurate:

> The clothing of the poor peasants—and they were almost all poor—was even more pitiful, for they had only one outfit for winter and summer, regardless of the quality of the material. And their single pair of shoes, very thin and cleated with nails, which they procured at the time of their marriage, had to serve them the rest of their lives, or at least as long as the shoes lasted.

The women "wore a short cloak of coarse material or black caddis, to which was attached a hood for enveloping the head and neck in case of rain or cold." This description agrees pretty well with the reports of the inventories.

Great Suffering

If we would form an idea of the mode of life of the peasants, we must also distinguish between normal periods and critical times caused by foreign wars or bad crops.

In the eighteenth century the crises were less grave but no less frequent than in the seventeenth century. Certain provinces had directly borne the brunt of war, as for example Lorraine and Burgundy, which suffered terrible ravages, especially during the first half of the seventeenth century. Around Dijon . . . entire villages were depopulated and the fields were left uncultivated. . . .

During the last fifteen years of the reign of Louis XIV [1700–1715] the misery grew more serious. The winter of 1709 witnessed a veritable famine.

All these facts must be taken into consideration if we would realize that during the last twenty-four years of the *ancien régime* there was, so far as these matters are concerned, undeniable improvement. During the eighteenth century the theatre of hostilities was almost always located beyond the frontiers, and there were fewer wars than during the era of the Great King. Nevertheless, there were great crises in 1725, 1740, 1759, from 1766 to 1768, from 1772 to 1776, in 1784 and 1785, and in 1789. Prices of food increased enormously. In 1785 the great drought compelled the farmers to sell a part of their cattle. In 1774 and again in 1789 the farmers had to live from turnips, milk, and even grass. In these critical years the day-laborers especially were affected, since they had nothing but the strength of their arms to depend upon.

"Agriculture and Progress"

But perhaps we should not paint the picture in too lurid colors. There were regions where agriculture was more prosperous, such as Flanders, Picardy, Normandy and Beauce, where the peasants were better off. This will be better understood when new monographs have been published. At present the best impression of this condition is given by Arthur Young's "Travels in France." This English economist observes the contrast that exists between the various regions. He notes the prosperity of sections where the land is cultivated mostly by small proprietors. Coming from Spain to France, he admires the prosperity of Béarn:

> Here, without passing a city, a barrier, or even a wall, we enter a new world. From the poor, miserable roads of Catalonia we suddenly reach a splendid highway built with all the substantial quality and excellence that characterize the great highways of France. In place of beds of torrents, there are well constructed bridges. From a rude desert region we come suddenly into a country of agriculture and progress.

All in all, we may say that there was more prosperity, relatively at least, in the rural sections, especially after 1750. And yet the peasant at the time of the outbreak of the Revolution [in 1789] had a keener feeling for his suffering. The reason is perhaps, as has been well said, that "the very alleviation of his misery made him feel all the more acutely what remained of it. Perhaps he was disgusted with the present by the new ideas and hopes that had made their way even into the rural sections."

Epidemics and Disease

A consequence of the misery and bad living conditions are the frequent epidemics, which, although less dreadful than those of the Middle Ages, were none the less quite fatal. Measles and especially small-pox, typhus and typhoid fever claimed thousands of victims. In Brittany alone, during the year 1741, there were 80,000 deaths. It is a curious fact that the epidemics were more frequent and more formidable in the rural sections than in the cities. This is commented upon by the physicians of the period, and particularly by Dr. Bagot of Saint-Brieuc, in his "Observations médicinales" (Medical Observations). The peasants were almost entirely without medical attention. Only toward the end of the *ancien régime* did the government organize medical assistance, distributing remedies and appointing physicians in charge of epidemics.

Mendicity [begging] and vagrancy became veritable scourges against which the government was powerless. Especially in the rural sections the beggars and tramps were numerous. At critical times the day-laborers, reduced to misery, increased the number of these unfortunates. Many sought refuge in the cities, thinking that they would secure aid there. But the cities were no better off than the country.

In the face of this misery private charity was of no avail. Public assistance, organized in the cities, became increasingly inefficient in the country. Hospitals and charitable institutions, until then rather common, gradually disappeared. For example, in the section of Rennes, Fougères, and Vitré [in Paris], at the end of the *ancien régime,* there remained hospitals in only three out of 140 parishes. For feeding the poor there were, generally speaking, only small foundations. The parish clergy took pity on the unfortunates, but generally there were no resources available. The rich abbeys did not respond as much as might have been expected. Hence the state was obliged to do what it could. . . . Charitable workshops were established to help the poor, and stations for distributing alms. But at the approach of the Revolution only insignificant results had been achieved, and the question, now having assumed serious proportions, was brought before the Constituent Assembly, which elected a Committee on Mendicity.

The Age of the Composer

Yehudi Menuhin and Curtis Wheeler Davis

In the early eighteenth century classical music became an important part of European culture. In earlier years this music was commissioned by and performed for royalty and the nobility and religious elites. But the rise in popularity of individual composers such as Antonio Vivaldi and Johann Sebastian Bach meant that more music was being written and made available to common people via the relatively new music publishing business. The development of keyboard instruments such as organs, harpsichords, and pianos also allowed individual musicians to take their music out of the royal courts and play for people in churches and recital halls.

In this excerpt, renowned violinist, conductor, and composer Yehudi Menuhin examines the importance of eighteenth-century composers such as J.S. Bach. His coauthor, Curtis Wheeler Davis, is a television writer and producer who has won three Emmy and two Peabody Awards.

A s we enter the eighteenth century, in music as in world affairs, the period of Western exploration and exploitation of new territories was beginning to give way to a consolidation of knowledge gained and battles won. It was also a time when the many voices of the people began to demand a hearing. England had established the principle of a constitutional monarchy with her Glorious Revolution of 1688, and some one hundred years later France and America were to abolish and repudiate monarchy altogether. The composer began to speak increasingly for the larger mass of the people throughout this period, whether in the noble, unifying voice of Bach or the proud, defiant one of Beethoven. It is also in this century that we leave behind a society built around the great courts and kingdoms, moving toward one which relies on individual initiative. It is natural enough that the composer should be part and parcel of this gradual transformation.

The seeds of change can be seen in Venice, for this city of wealth and diversity, founded upon the sea and its commerce, was a symbol of Italy's dominance over Western music during most of the Renaissance [of the fifteenth and sixteenth centuries]. Toward the end of the seventeenth century, as the Baroque era was dawning, power was moving north and Venice was in the sunset of her world influence. Here in 1678 one of the last of the long line of outstanding Venetian musician-composers was born, Antonio Vivaldi.

Of all my illustrious predecessors, perhaps none was more gifted or enviable than the Venetian violinist, Antonio Vivaldi. The son of a brilliant and well-known violinist, he started his virtuoso career at an early age. He was an ordained priest at the age of twenty-five, known as the "Red Priest," in those days a benign title referring only to the color of his hair. He was entrusted with a musical seminary for young, orphaned illegitimate girls, the Ospedale Santa Maria de la Pieta. These young women became the most proficient and well-known instrumentalists and singers of their day. They even played the bassoon and the double bass, not to speak of conducting the orchestra with elegance and precision. For these inspiring young women, Vivaldi composed no less than five hundred concertos and symphonies, and innumerable other works of a musicality and verve, charm and warmth which delight us today as much as they did his devoted wards and his enthusiastic audiences.

The Harpsichord Changes Music

Vivaldi, a Venetian, inevitably composed a great many operas as well, which are today virtually forgotten, though one or two have finally appeared on recordings. Toward the end of his life, as his music was fading from favor in Venice, and hearing that he was known to the [Austrian] Hapsburg emperor, Charles VI, Vivaldi travelled to Vienna hoping to find fresh employment. Soon after he arrived, the Emperor died, and the next year, in 1741, Vivaldi also died and was buried in Vienna, far from the scene of his triumphs. His music was to lie neglected for two hundred years, until the response to passion tempered by order brought him back to public favor. It was a rebirth which would have surprised nobody more than Vivaldi himself, for he wrote his music for immediate consumption rather than

Johann Sebastian Bach

for posterity, a point of view which only began to change with Beethoven [at the end of the eighteenth century].

The violin and the singing voice were Vivaldi's chief means of expression, as they had been throughout the long evolution of Western music since the Middle Ages. Many composers owe a debt to Vivaldi, beginning with [Johann Sebastian] Bach, who adapted and rewrote many of his concertos. Later, [Wolfgang Amadeus] Mozart and [Felix] Mendelssohn acknowledged his influence. Vivaldi is the champion of emotion immediately translated into pure melody. But the violin was also nearing the end of its leadership role in Western music.

Although the violin dominated the music of the Baroque, as the voice had done in the Renaissance, the keyboard represented a unique resource for the composer. It was a research tool, a means of testing and measuring musical ideas. In the seventeenth century, it also became an instrument for highly skilled improvisation, espe-

cially in the hands of such northern organists as Pachelbel and Bux-
tehude. In the eighteenth century, the harpsichord began to take over
from the violin as leader, determining dynamics, tempo and harmony. Within the compass of ten fingers, the keyboard performer
held the whole gamut of separate melodic lines, counterpoint and
rhythm—little wonder that the Western composer usually has been
a pianist also. With the advent of the keyboard, the violinist was de-
moted, intellectually and creatively; and as political and musical influence moved north, the keyboard was on the rise, along with the
music of the Germanic culture, a music of discipline and order, pre-
meditation and power.

By now, music in the West had become an interchangeable commodity, with musicians and composers everywhere adopting each
other's style. [The English composer born in Germany George Fred-
erick] Handel's music is a consummate blend of German, Italian,
English and even French idioms. It was in its popular forms that music in German lands retained a local flavor, a quaint turn of phrase,
which varied like the dialects from area to area. It seems to have
been a way of holding onto the past, even as a national spirit was beginning to emerge. We can hear it still in the traditional dance music of such districts of Switzerland. . . .

The Passion of J.S. Bach

We have seen that the concept of harmony evolved slowly out of rules
for the agreement of separate voices. No manifestation of harmony is
more impressive than the resonance of a great church organ. . . .

This is the great Western musical achievement, a multitude of
voices each carrying its own melody, yet sounding together as one.
Perhaps the origins of that harmony lie far back in the medley of
races moving across the Eurasian continent, following the setting
sun, only to find themselves trapped in the European peninsula, each
clamoring to be heard in its own tongue, yet having also to learn
how to coexist. Not for a long time had such a diversity of cultures
met in so small a space. For Western music it meant that sooner or
later a truly universal spokesman would appear, and for me that man
is Johann Sebastian Bach, composer, organist, violinist, teacher, the-
orist, and servant of God.

Bach has passion as well as serenity, for in his day religion was
the center of the life of sentiment. Biblical events were seen as symbols, replicas of events in the daily lives of people who were truly
in love with the life of Christ. The birth of every child was to be
compared with [Christ's] pain and sorrow, His exaltation and resur-
rection, His love. The passion of Bach's music is the passion of humanity. It is not music which says, "I feel, I hurt, I suffer"; it says,
"We feel, we hurt, we suffer—and we accept."

In the same way that language was becoming a unifying factor amongst the Germanic peoples, composers like Johann Sebastian Bach were narrowing the gap between the music of their church and that of the people. The *Brandenburg* Concerti, evolving largely from folk dances, are a good example of that evolution. Bach was a German, a devout Lutheran, but if ever there was music in the world that can be described as belonging to all time, to my mind that of Bach is first in line. He is a servant of music, but he is also its sovereign.

One might say that the Bachs were almost the *griots* [respected African master musician and storyteller] of northern Germany. What other family has produced a larger number of eminent composer-performers over so long a period? The family was of pure German stock, although some of its members may have lived in Hungary during the Middle Ages. [Distinguished Spanish composer] Pablo Casals used to say he was sure there was gypsy blood in Bach, such is the inspired passion in his improvised fantasies. The father, uncles, grandfather and great uncles were all musicians, as were Bach's cousins, sons, nephews. Only nine of his twenty children survived him. The influence of the Bach family lies at the heart of the formation of German musical taste, reflecting the time when the name of Bach had become almost synonymous with music throughout northern Germany.

The Illustrious Bach Family

Johann Sebastian Bach was the clan's greatest product. . . . He was a complete all-round musician. He . . . started as a choirboy, reputedly possessing one of the finest, truest soprano voices anywhere in Saxony. By the time he was eighteen he was making his living as a violinist and organist. His life is actually rather uneventful. There were none of the scenes of triumph, as with Handel in England. He was a hired court musician for twenty years, applying at last for the post of head of music and education at St. Thomas School in Leipzig. Bach won the job, but he was the third choice, selected only after two others had turned it down. He kept the job for the rest of his life. For his acceptance test he had offered the city fathers no less than his *St. John Passion,* which they considered a little stodgy and old-fashioned. In a way they were right, for Bach knew and admired the music of many older composers. . . .

We have the benefit of hindsight; we know that with Bach we are dealing with a giant. We must not blame the good burghers of Leipzig for failing to recognize a miracle. For one thing, in his day Bach's style was considered heavy compared to the Italian and French. And when he came to the St. Thomas School, much of his greatest work was still to come. Besides, he was famous as a performer and scholar, but as a teacher he was an unknown quantity. What could he do with five dozen boys, aged eleven to seventeen, with whom he was expected to provide the music for Sunday services the year round in four churches? Actually, the city fathers need not have looked further than the job Bach was doing with his own sons. Nowhere is his teaching skill more evident. He gave them a profession with which they could make an honest living and bring pleasure to their employers, a life of service in the best sense. Karl Philipp Emmanuel Bach, the second son, became attached to the court of Frederick the Great in Berlin. Despite his fame and wealth, he remained devoted to his father's memory, and it is thanks to his care that a great many of Sebastian's scores have survived. Johann Christian Bach, the youngest son, became the darling of London after Handel. When Mozart first speaks of the Great Mr. Bach, it is to Johann Christian he is referring, for as a boy he sat on his knee to play duets. Christian Bach was ruined trying to maintain the production of his operas, unfortunately not possessing Handel's superior flair for wise speculation in the market.

The sons of Johann Sebastian Bach helped to train another generation of musicians, as the father had trained them and so many of their peers. The impact of Bach's teaching is only now being fully recognized. Bach is a perfect example of what Western music had been moving towards for five hundred years. Here is a composer-performer who can do anything with his material that he pleases. He can take simple dance rhythms and turn them into elaborate suites or variations. He can turn his themes upside down, inside out, backwards and sideways, as he delights to do in the fugues. He can combine many independent voices, each heard clearly, as in the opening chorus of the *St. Matthew Passion*. He can test the skill of the best players on every instrument, as in the *Brandenburg* Concerti. He can turn the organ into a match for the finest orchestra. He did his best to pass these skills along to his boys, in the school and at home.

The Primeval Powers of the Universe

When our Western music began to grow in medieval times, composers were mainly content to add a layer of melody at a time, usually over and under a basic chant taken from plainsong, or blending a dance rhythm with a lyric to produce a two-part song. The procedure is not unknown elsewhere; you find its counterpart in Africa, the Near East, Indonesia. In the West it led to a different result. By the time we come to Bach, the process had undergone a striking development. Not only is each separate part beautiful in its own right . . . , but Bach interlinks them all so as to form a complete harmonious whole. In this respect it is difficult to compare Bach to anybody else, for his ability is so far superior to others.

Bach's musical structures seem dictated by the primeval powers of the universe—almost like the earth's own landscapes which are fashioned by the opposition of elements and temperatures. To me, Bach represents the ideal toward which Western music had been striving for a thousand years. Bach is a rule to himself, virtually self-taught, and the creator within an established convention of an unmistakable personal language. The quality of his mind is dazzling. We can reproduce what he wrote down but we cannot duplicate, much less surpass, his feats of invention. There is that troublesome word again, invention. Did Bach invent, did he create, or discover and combine? He did more than this, for he made music which joined art and science, thereby moving people's hearts and disciplining their minds in a compelling, living experience *in time,* such as had never been achieved on such a scale or intensity before.

We can see this clearly in a Bach fugue, one of his most rigorous and at the same time most ingenious disciplines. In a fugue the theme appears again and again in different registers and keys, sometimes moving from major to minor or the reverse. In its classic form, the main thematic idea is most often introduced four times in succession, once each in voices equivalent to soprano, alto, tenor and bass. Once launched, each of these voices continues independently while complementing the others as they enter. The theme can also be inverted or reversed, given at half or double speed. The other voices fill out the harmonic pattern while retaining their separate identity, as if each voice had a will of its own. The form does not originate with Bach, for many composers had been developing it for nearly two centuries. The fugue owes something to the idea of theme and variations as in the *tientos* of Cabezon, but still more to the canon, that form made popular among singers even before "Sumer Is Icumen In."

To me a fugue is like our own process of thought. We think by comparison, by analogy, by going back over our tracks, by reversal, parallel, by comparing angles and speeds. We say, "If this is true, then that must follow." We obtain results by experiment. We remember and we think ahead. A fugue is like that. The various episodes are developed according to principles of logic and brought to a closing climax or result. The wonderful thing with Bach is how natural all this was to him. He was such a master of the form that he could improvise his fugues, tossing them off on the spot even on themes suggested by others. Among those Bach committed to paper there were many in which he introduces two or even three separate musical themes, all fitting with each other, and developing simultaneously. His last and greatest set is called *The Art of Fugue* and is his master's thesis on this form of music. It is as universal, true and inevitable as the motions of the stars. Such pure music is not conceived for any one instrument in particular. It is an exercise in construction, testing whether indeed it is inhabited by life. Repetition of the theme offers a security, but the form is not rigid, it can contain the personal and spontaneous, as in chess. The theme can be presented in double time, half time, like the many speeds of our heartbeat. Its nature corresponds to human biology, as it does to human thought.

The Accomplishment of Peter the Great

Will and Ariel Durant

Peter the Great was the czar of Russia from 1682 to his death in 1725. Previous Russian leaders had hated and feared influence from foreigners and outsiders from western Europe. Peter, however, was fascinated by the West and wanted to wrest his country from Asian and Eastern influences and progress in modern European standards. To facilitate his plans, Peter traveled in Europe from 1697 to 1698. As the first Russian czar to make such a trip, Peter studied the latest scientific advances and recruited architects, engineers, and military experts to help him renovate Russia. He later built the city of St. Petersburg, modernized the Russian alphabet and calendar, and ordered Russian citizens to adopt Western clothing styles.

Through it all, Peter remained a hard-drinking, cruel, and crude man. The bloody, iron-fisted reforms he forced on his people, however, Westernized Russia's government, army, and society, and laid the foundation of modern Russia.

This excerpt by Will and Ariel Durant examines the life and rule of Peter I, or Peter the Great, one of the few European monarchs who rivaled Louis XIV in absolutist ruling style.

Will Durant was born in 1885 and, after teaching college in New York, began working up to fourteen hours a day to write his acclaimed ten-volume *The Story of Civilization* with his wife and coauthor, Ariel Durant. Beginning in 1927, the Durants traveled around the world for forty years until the last volume was completed in 1967.

Voltaire wanted "to know what were the steps by which men passed from barbarism to civilization." No wonder he was interested in Peter, for Peter embodied, if not that process, at least that effort, in his flesh and soul and people. Or hear another "Great," Frederick II of Prussia, writing about Peter to Voltaire, a bit confusedly:

> He was the only truly educated prince. He was not only the legislator of his country, but he understood perfectly all naval science. He was an architect, an anatomist, a surgeon, . . . an expert soldier, a consummate economist. . . . To make him the model of all princes he only needed an education less barbarous and ferocious.

[There was a great deal of] barbarous and ferocious education, [and] violence and bloodshed that surrounded Peter's childhood, shocking his nervous system and accustoming him to brutality. Even in youth he suffered from a nervous tic, which may have been aggravated later by heavy drinking and venereal disease. "He is subject to convulsions all over his body," reported [clergyman Thomas] Burnet after visiting him in England in 1698. "It is well known," said an eighteenth-century Russian, "that this monarch . . . was subject to short but frequent brain attacks, of a somewhat violent kind. A sort of convulsion seized him, which for a certain time, and sometimes even for hours, threw him into such a distressing condition that he could not bear the sight of anyone, not even his nearest friends. This paroxysm was always preceded by a strong contortion of the neck towards the left side, and by a violent contraction of the muscles of the face." Yet he was robust and powerful. We are told that when he and [king of Poland] Augustus II met they rivaled each other in crumpling silver plate in their hands. [Painter Sir Godfrey] Kneller in 1698 pictured him as a youth in arms and regalia, quite incredibly gentle and innocent; later we find him more realistically portrayed as a stooping giant, six feet eight and a half inches tall, with full round face, large eyes and nose, and brown hair falling in curls rarely cut. His look of stern command hardly harmonized with his careless and untidy dress, his coarse, darned socks, his rudely cobbled shoes. While he put a nation in order he left his immediate surroundings in disorder wherever he went. He was so immersed in large endeavors that he grudged all time given to little things.

A Coarse and Cruel King

His manners, like his dress, were so informal that he might have been taken for a peasant rather than a king—except that he had none of the muzhik's [peasant's] stolid patience. Sometimes his manners were worse than a peasant's, because unrestrained by fear of a master or the law. Seeing a phallus in a collection of antiquities at Berlin, he ordered his wife to kiss it; when Catherine refused he threatened to have her beheaded; she still refused, and he was calmed only by receiving the object as a present to adorn his private room. In his conversation and correspondence he allowed himself the crudest obscenities. Time and again he reproved his closest friends with blows of his massive fist; he gave [Prince Aleksandr] Menshikov a bloody nose, and kicked [General François] Lefort. His fondness for practical jokes occasionally took cruel forms; so he forced one of his aides to eat tortoises, another to drink a whole flask of vinegar, and young girls to down a soldier's ration of brandy. He took undue pleasure in practicing dentistry, and those near him had to guard against the slightest complaint of a toothache; his forceps were always at hand. When his valet complained that his wife, on the score of pretended toothache, refused him the consolations of matrimony, he sent for her, forcibly extracted a sound tooth, and told her that more would be forthcoming if she continued celibate.

His lawless cruelty exceeded the degree in which it might be excused as normal or necessary in his time and land. The Russians were accustomed to cruelty, and were probably less sensitive to pain than persons of a subtler nervous organization; they may have needed a harsh discipline; but Peter's almost personal massacre of the Streltsi [disloyal soldiers of the Moscow garrison] suggests a sadistic pleasure in cruelty, an orgasm of blood; and no need of the state required to have two conspirators sliced to death inch by inch. Peter was immune to pity or sentiment, and lacked the sense of justice that checked the whims of Louis XIV or Frederick the Great. His violations of his solemn word, however, were fully in the manner of the age.

Like the muzhik, Peter thought intoxication was a reasonable vacation from reality. He had taken upon himself all the burdens of the state, and the far greater task of transforming an Oriental people into Western civilization; festive drinking with his friends seemed a merited relief from these undertakings. He heartily accepted the peasant adage that drinking is the Russian's joy. The ability to hold liquor was one of his measures of a man. When he was in Paris he wagered that his priest-confessor could drink more and remain stable than the priest-secretary of the French ministry; the contest went on for an hour; when the abbé rolled under the table Peter hugged his priest for having "saved the honor of Russia." About 1690 Peter and his intimates formed a band called the "Most Drunken Assembly [*sobor*] of Fools and Jesters." Prince Feodor Romodanovsky was elected czar of the *sobor;* Peter accepted a subordinate position (as he did in the army and navy), and often in real life he pretended that Romodanovsky was Czar of Russia. The *sobor* of drunkards was formally dedicated to the worship of [Greek deities] Bacchus and Venus; it had an elaborate ritual, mimicking with grossness and obscenity those of the Russian Orthodox and Roman Catholic churches; and much of this mock ritual was composed by Peter himself. The *sobor* took part in many official state celebrations. When its mock patriarch, Nikita Zatov, aged eighty-four, married a bride of sixty, Peter designed and commanded an ornate ribald ceremonial (1715), in which the dignitaries and ladies of the court were to take part along with bears and stags and goats, and ambassadors playing flutes or the hurdy-gurdy, and Peter beating a drum.

His sense of humor was hilarious and unrestrained, often stooping to buffoonery. His court was crowded with jesters and dwarfs, who seemed indispensable to every ceremony. Once the Czar, nearly seven feet tall, playing Gulliver to his Lilliputians [a reference to the giant stature of Gulliver in Swift's novel], rode in a procession at the head of twenty-four mounted dwarfs. At one time Peter had seventy-two dwarfs at his court, some of whom were served up at table in gigantic pies. There were giants too, but most of these were sent as gifts to Frederick William of Prussia to join his army. . . . Several Negroes were presented to Peter. He held them in high esteem, and sent some of them to Paris for an education. One of them became a Russian general, the great-grandfather of the poet Pushkin.

An Economical King

So far we picture Peter as still very much a barbarian, an Ivan the Terrible [former Russian king] but humorous; anxious to be civilized, but envying the West not for its graces and arts but for its armies and navies, its commerce and industry and wealth. His virtues were directed to these ends as the prerequisites of civilization. Hence his insatiable curiosity. Of everything he wanted to know how it worked, and then how it could be made to work better. On his travels he exhausted his aides by running about to see this and that, even through the night. He was swamped with ideas, thereby amazing [philosopher Baron Gottfried Wilhelm von] Leibniz, who had a swamp of his own; but Peter's ideas were frankly utilitarian. He had an open mind for anything that could make his country catch up to the West. In a nation gloomily religious and fanatically hostile to foreign creeds and ways, he was as unprejudiced as a child or a sage, sampling Catholicism, Protestantism, even free thought. He was rather imitative than original; he transplanted ideas rather than conceived them; but in attempting to raise his nation to a competitive level with the West it was wiser to absorb first the best that the West could teach, and then try to surpass it. Never had imitation been so original.

His indefatigable devotion to his purpose raised him out of barbarism to greatness. If he conscripted and consumed millions of Russians to his ends, he used himself up, too, in the effort to give Russia a modern army, a more efficient government, more varied and productive industries, wider commerce, and ports that could reach the world. He was economical of everything except human life, which was Russia's one abundant commodity. Almost his first measures on reaching power were to dismiss the horde of servants and palace officials that had cluttered the royal household; to sell three thousand horses from the royal stables; to sweep away three hundred cooks and kitchen boys; to reduce the royal table, even on feast days, to sixteen places at most; to dispense with formal receptions and balls; and to make over to the state the sums that had heretofore been allotted to these luxuries. His father, Alexis, had left him a personal property of 10,734 dessiatines (28,982 acres) of cultivated land and fifty thousand houses, bringing in a revenue of 200,000 rubles yearly [$4 to $6 million]; Peter turned nearly all this over to the state treasury. . . . In effect, and in sharp contrast to Louis XIV, the greatest of the czars reduced his court to a few friends, with an occasional festival, informal and sometimes hilarious, to brighten Moscow's monotony. Often his economy became parsimony [stinginess]. He underpaid his palace staff, meted out mathematically its daily allowance of food, invited his friends not to dinner but to picnics where each would pay his share; and when the prostitutes who served him bemoaned their modest honorariums he replied that he paid them as much as he paid a grenadier [soldier], whose services were far more valuable.

Peter's Women

Women, with one exception, were minor incidents in his life. He was not keenly sensitive to beauty. He had sexual needs, but he dispatched them without ritual. He did not like to sleep alone, but this had nothing to do with sex; usually he had a servant share his bed, probably he wanted someone near him in case he should have a convulsion during the night. At seventeen, to quiet his mother, he married Eudoxia Lopukhina, who was described as "beautiful but stupid"; finding one quality more lasting than the other, he neglected her, and went back to his friends and his ships. He took a succession of transient mistresses, nearly always of lowly origin and condition. When Frederick II of Denmark jested with him about having a mistress, Peter answered, "Brother, my harlots do not cost me much, but yours cost you thousands of crowns, which you could spend in a better way." Both Lefort and Menshikov served the Czar as procurers, and Menshikov surrendered his own mistress to be Peter's second wife. There must have been remarkable ability in her to raise her . . . from strumpet to empress.

The future [queen] Catherine I was born about 1685 in Livonia of humble stock. Left an orphan, she was brought up as a servant by the Lutheran Pastor Glück in Marienburg. He taught her the catechism but not the alphabet; she never learned to read. In 1702 a Russian army . . . besieged Marienburg. Despairing of defense, the commander of the garrison decided to blow up his fortress and himself. Pastor Glück, informed of his intention, took his family and his servant and fled to the Russian camp. He was sent on to Moscow, but Catherine was kept as a solace for the soldiers. She graduated through them to . . . Menshikov to Peter. In those wars and regions a simple woman had to be complaisant in order to eat. For a time Catherine seems to have served both Menshikov and the Czar. They liked her because she was neat, cheerful, kind, and understanding; for example, she did not insist on being sole mistress. Peter found her a gay relief after the alarums [alarms] of politics or war and the tantrums of jealous concubines. She accompanied him on campaigns, lived like a soldier, cut her hair, slept on the ground, and did not flinch when she saw men shot down at her side. When a convulsion seized Peter, and all others were afraid to touch him, she would speak to him soothingly, caress him, calm him, and let him sleep with his head on her breast. When they were apart he wrote to his "Katierinoushka" [as he called her] letters of playful and yet sincere tenderness. She became indispensable to him. By 1710 she was his wife in everything but law. She bore him several children. In 1711 she helped to save him at the Prut. In 1712 he publicly acknowledged her as his wife. In 1722 he crowned her empress.

Her influence over him was good in many ways. She, the peasant girl, improved the manners of the royal boor. She moderated his drinking; on several occasions she entered the room where he was carousing with friends, and quietly commanded him, *"Pora domoï, batioushka"* (Come home, little father), and he obeyed. She winked at his postmarital flirtations. She made no attempt to influence politics, but she saw to it that the Czar provided for her future, her relatives, and her friends. She overcame widespread resentment of her elevation by acting as an angel of mercy; in several instances she saved persons from the penalties to which Peter wished to condemn them; and when he insisted on severity he had to conceal it from her. She abused her power over him by [amassing] a secret fortune, part of which she judiciously invested under assumed names at Hamburg or Amsterdam. Shall we blame her for seeking some security at a time when everything depended upon one man's whim, and all Russia was in flux? . . .

Building St. Petersburg

[Peter] worked as hard as the simplest peasant in his realm. Normally he rose at five in the morning and labored fourteen hours a day. He slept only six hours at night, but took a siesta after noon. Such a program was not impracticable in the St. Petersburg summers, when daylight began at 3 A.M. and lasted till 10 P.M.; but in winter much of it had to go on during the night, which began about three in the afternoon and continued till nine the next morning.

St. Petersburg was the symbol . . . of his revolution. . . . The city . . . was founded in 1703, on the model of Amsterdam. Since much of the site was marshy . . . , St. Petersburg was built upon piles—or, as a sad Russian saying had it, upon the bones of the thousands of laborers who were conscripted to lay those foundations and rear the town. In 1708 some 40,000 men were sent to the task; in 1709 another 40,000; in 1711, 46,000; in 1713, 40,000 more. They were paid half a ruble per month, which they had to supplement with begging and thieving. Swedish prisoners of war employed in the construction died by the thousands. As there were no wheelbarrows, the men transported the materials in their uplifted caftans [ankle-length tunics]. Stone too was conscripted; a ukase [decree] of 1714 forbade the erection of stone houses anywhere in Russia except in St. Petersburg; but there every nobleman in the land was commanded to raise a dwelling of stone. The nobles did it under protest, hating the climate and not sharing Peter's love of the sea. For himself Peter had some Dutch artisans put together a cottage like those that he had seen at [the city of] Zaandam, with log walls, shingle roof, and small rooms. He disliked palaces, but allowed three at Peterhof (now Petrodvorets), on the southern outskirts of the city, for ceremonial occasions; this "Summer Palace" was destroyed in the Second World War. In a nearby suburb, Tsarskoe Selo (now Pushkin), he built a summer cottage for his Katierinoushka [Catherine I].

He did not at first intend to make St. Petersburg a capital as well as a port; it was too close to hostile Sweden; but after his victory over [Swedish king] Charles XII at Poltava he decided to make the change. He longed to get away from the somber ecclesiastical atmosphere of Moscow and its narrow nationalism, and he wanted the conservative nobles to feel progressive winds from the West. So in 1712 he made it his capital. . . . Peter was so anxious to Westernize Russia that he dragged it, so to speak, to the Baltic and bade it look through his "window on the West." To this purpose, and to have a base for his fleet and a port for foreign trade, he sacrificed all other considerations. The port would be icebound five months in the year, but it would face the West and touch the sea. . . .

The next step was to build a navy that would guard the lanes of Russian commerce through the Baltic to the West. Peter achieved this for a time by building in the course of his reign a thousand galleys; but they were hastily and badly constructed, their timbers rotted, their masts broke in the wind; and after his death Russia reconciled herself to being what geography had made it, a landlocked country shut off from the Atlantic, and waiting for the conquest of the air to overleap its barriers into the world. In this sense Moscow was right: Russia's power and defense had to be on land, through its armies and its space. So, in 1917, Moscow had its revenge, and became the capital again.

Transforming the Russian People

Peter's most permanent reform was the reorganization of the army. . . . He could not develop Russia without opening a way to the Baltic or the Mediterranean; he could not do this without a modern army; he could not maintain such an army without transforming the Russian economy and government; and he could not transform these without remaking the Russian people in manners, aims, and soul. It was too great a task for one man, or for one generation.

He began, in his whimsical impulsive way, with the beards and dress of the men around him. In 1698, soon after returning from the West, he had his own sparse beard shaved, and commanded all who wished to keep his favor to do the same, excepting only the Patriarch of the Orthodox Church. Soon an edict went throughout Russia that all laymen were to shave their chins; mustaches might remain. The beard had been almost a religious symbol in Russia; it had been worn by the Prophets and the Apostles; and the reigning Patriarch, Adrian, only eight years before, had condemned the shaving of the beard as irreligious and heretical. Peter accepted the challenge: beardlessness was to be a sign of modernity, of willingness to enter into Western civilization. Those laymen who felt a dire need of whiskers might keep them by paying an annual tax rising from one kopek for a peasant to a hundred rubles for a rich merchant. "There were many old Russians," says an old history, "who, after having their beards shaved off, saved them preciously, in order to have them placed in their coffins, fearing that they would not be allowed to enter heaven without them."

Next to go was the Russian costume. Here too Peter felt that internal resistance to Westernization would be reduced by wearing Western garb. He himself cut off the long sleeves of the army officers who appeared before him. "See," he said to one of them, "these things are in your way. You are safe nowhere with them. At one moment you upset a glass, then you forgetfully dip them in the sauce. Get gaiters made of them." So an order went forth (January, 1700) commanding all courtiers and officials in Russia to adopt Western dress. All persons entering or leaving Moscow had to choose between having their ankle-long caftans cut at the knees or paying a fine. The women were likewise urged to adopt Western costume; they resisted less than the men, for in dress women are annual revolutionists.

New Attitudes Toward Women

Not so much by decrees as by the example of his family, Peter ended the seclusion of Russia's women. His father, Alexis, and his mother, Natalia, had led the way; his half-sister Sophia had broadened it; now Peter invited women to social gatherings, encouraged them to remove their veils, to dance, to make music, and to seek education, even if only through tutors. He issued edicts forbidding parents to marry their children against their will, and requiring an interval of six weeks between betrothal and marriage; in that period the engaged couple should be allowed to see each other frequently, and to break off the engagement if they wished. The women were glad to emerge . . . ; they began a race to adopt new fashions; and some increase in illegitimate births gave the clergy a weapon against Peter's revolution.

The resistance of religion was his greatest obstacle. The clergy realized that his reforms would lessen their prestige and power. They bemoaned his toleration of Western faiths in Russia, and they suspected that he himself had no religious belief. They heard with horror of the parodies with which he and his intimates mocked the [Christian] Orthodox ritual. For his part Peter resented the diversion of manpower into the vast and innumerable monasteries, and he coveted the enormous revenues that these institutions enjoyed. . . .

A vast process of secularization changed the life and spirit of Russia from domination by priests and landlords to rule, almost regimentation, by the state. Peter subordinated the boyars [Russian aristocracy] to his will, made them serve the public, and reorganized social ranks according to the importance of the social service performed. . . .

Modernizing Russia

That transformation had to be economic as well as political, for no purely agricultural society could long maintain its independence against states enriched and armed by industry. . . . For agriculture, therefore, Peter did little. . . . By his own example he taught the peasants how to cut their corn, and he commanded the replacement of sickles with scythes. The Russians were accustomed to burn the woodlands to provide fertilizing ashes for the soil; Peter forbade this, needing lumber for his ships, trees for his masts. He introduced the cultivation of the tobacco plant, the mulberry, and the vine, and began the Russian breeding of horses and sheep.

But his chief aim was rapid industrialization. The first problem was to provide raw materials. He spurred the spread of mining; he gave stimulating rewards to men like Nikita Demidov and Aleksandr Stroganov who showed enterprise and skill in mining and metallurgy; he urged landowners to encourage or allow the extraction of minerals from their soils, and decreed that if they neglected to do this their soil might be mined by others by paying them merely a nominal fee. By 1710 Russia ceased to import iron; before Peter's death it was exporting it.

He brought in foreign artisans and managers, and prodded the Russians of every rank to learn the industrial arts. An Englishman opened in Moscow a factory for treating hides and making shoes; Peter commanded every town in Russia to send a delegation of cobblers to Moscow to learn the latest methods of making boots and shoes, and held the galleys as a threat over shoemakers who clung to their old ways. To encourage the Russian textile industry he wore, after this was functioning, only native-made cloth, and forbade the Muscovites to buy imported stockings. Soon the Russians were making good textiles. An admiral shocked tradition and delighted the Czar by manufacturing silk brocades. A muzhik developed a lacquer superior to any similar product in "Europe" except the Venetian. Before the reign was over there were 233 factories in Russia. Some were quite large: the Moscow manufacture of sailcloth employed 1,162 workers; one textile mill used 742 men; another, 730; one metallurgical establishment had 683 employees. There had been factories in Russia before Peter, but not on this scale. Many of the new plants were started by the government and were later sold to private management; but even then they received state subsidies, and were subject to detailed supervision by the government. . . .

To man the factories Peter resorted to conscription. Since there were few free laborers available, peasants were converted, willy-nilly, into industrial workers. Manufacturers were empowered to buy serfs [agricultural workers] from landlords, and put them to work in the factories. Large-scale undertakings were supplied with peasants transferred from state lands and farms. As in most governmental attempts at rapid industrialization, the leaders could not wait for the acquisitive [desire for monetary gain] instinct to overcome habit and tradition and lead workers from old fields and ways to new tasks and disciplines. An industrial serfdom was developed, more or less reluctantly by Peter, deliberately by his successors. Peter apologized in an edict of 1723:

> Is not everything done [at first] by compulsion? That there are few people willing to go into business [industry] is true, for our people are like children, who never want to begin the alphabet unless they are compelled by their teachers. It seems very hard to them at first, but when they have learnt it they are thankful. Already much thanksgiving is heard for what has already borne fruit. . . . So in manufacturing affairs we must act and compel, and help by teaching.

Slavery in New England

Lorenzo Johnston Greene

The first black African slaves to arrive in America landed in Jamestown, Virginia, in 1619. As the colonies became more prosperous and the climate proved beneficial for cultivating tobacco, rice, cotton, and sugar cane a large commercial slave trade began to grow. By the eighteenth century, slave dealers had perfected a system known as the "triangular trade." This scheme allowed slavers to leave Europe in ships loaded with liquor, guns, cloth, and other European trade goods. The merchants sailed south to Africa where the goods were exchanged for African men, women, and children who were sold into slavery, often by African tribal chiefs. The slaves were then packed tightly into the filthy cargo holds of the ships and taken on the notorious Middle Passage either to the West Indies or Britain's American colonies. Here the slaves were traded for sugar, molasses, rum, and other products of the New World. The slave dealers then returned to England with these valuable goods and began the triangular trade once again.

This lucrative trade in human misery grew very quickly, with 8 to 15 million Africans brought to the Americas between the sixteenth and the nineteenth century. Close to 7 million people were sold into slavery in the eighteenth century alone. In the following excerpt, Lorenzo Johnston Greene explains the impact of the slave trade on colonies in New England.

Greene, a professor of history at Lincoln University in Missouri and a member of the NAACP, served on the Missouri Advisory Committee to the U.S. Civil Rights Commission.

On August 3, 1713 the stepbrother of Benjamin Franklin advertised in the columns of the *Boston News Letter:*

> Three Negro Men and two Women to be Sold and to be seen at the House of Mr. Josiah Franklin . . . in Union Street, Boston.

Josiah Franklin was a prosperous merchant, who not only sold Negroes at his tavern, but also permitted other slave dealers to use his place as a show room for human chattels [slaves]. The sale of Negroes by Franklin should not have been surprising to the casual reader of the *News Letter* in 1713. By this time Bostonians had grown accustomed to the auctioning of slaves, for advertisements listing them for sale had become commonplace—as commonplace, in fact, as the appearance of Negroes on the bustling streets of New England towns. . . .

Although blacks had been sold in Boston for some time, it is not definitely known when the first Negro slaves were brought into New England. Slavery, like indentured servitude [contract labor], is said to have existed in New England before the settlement of the Massachusetts Bay Colony in 1629 and was first identified with Massachusetts. Samuel Maverick, apparently New England's first slaveholder, arrived in Massachusetts in 1624 and . . . owned two Negroes before John Winthrop, who later became governor of that colony, arrived in 1630. . . . The beginnings of New England Negro slavery would [in this case] fall somewhere between 1624 and 1630. . . .

By 1676 Bay Colony merchants were bringing slaves from the distant island of Madagascar. Two years later John Endicott and John Saffin of Boston were selling these Negroes in Virginia. In 1681 Saffin, merchant and jurist, was smuggling slaves overland through Rhode Island into Massachusetts. By 1700, Boston traders were supplying the other New England colonies with Negroes. In short, the New England slave trade of the seventeenth century seems to have been centered almost wholly in Massachusetts, with Boston the chief, if not the only, slave port. If New Hampshire, Connecticut and Rhode Island engaged in the Negro trade before 1700, they officially denied it. . . .

A Legal Slave Trade

Although New England's share in the slave trade was small in the seventeenth century, her merchants had by 1700 laid the foundations of a lucrative commerce. They had already begun the . . . slave voyages and had learned that the West Indies offered the best market for Negroes. As comparatively few Negroes were brought to New England in the seventeenth century, the traders in these colonies made their profits as carriers rather than as exploiters of Negro labor. In 1700 there were probably not more than a thousand Negroes in all the Puritan colonies.

The New England slave trade attained its greatest development in the eighteenth century. Several factors stimulated its growth. The revocation by the British Parliament in 1696 of the monopoly held by the Royal African Company made it possible for all Englishmen to engage legally in the slave trade. Equally important was the *Assiento* [treaty agreement] of 1713, by which England wrested from Spain the privilege of supplying 4800 Negroes a year to Spanish America for thirty years. In the execution of this huge contract the participation of colonial merchants was essential. Increasing demand for Negroes in the sugar islands of the British and "foreign" West Indies, together with the growing employment of blacks in the tobacco and rice growing colonies of the South, also furthered the growth of the New England slave trade. The British government, furthermore, encouraged and protected the traffic and vetoed every attempt of the colonists to hinder or to abolish it. Increasing well-being in the colonies, and particularly in New England, gave added impetus to the slave trade. Geographic conditions also played an important role, since the New Englanders, prevented by climate and soil from reaping rich returns from agriculture, had to look elsewhere if they were to match the wealth of the landed aristocracy of the South. For this reason, the thrifty New Englanders, attracted by the prospect of far greater profits than could possibly be drawn from the land, early began to engage in commerce, the fishing industry and in the trade in [African slaves].

A Triangular Journey

As a result of these factors the New England colonies in the eighteenth century became the greatest slave-trading section of America. There came into vogue the famous triangular slave trade, with New England, Africa and the West Indies as its focal points. From New England's many ports trim, sturdy ships, built from her own forests, carried to the West Indies much needed food and other commodities, such as surplus beans, peas, hay, corn, staves, lumber, low-grade fish, horses, dairy products and a miscellaneous assortment of goods. When the captains of these vessels were able to exchange their cargoes for rum, they would next proceed directly to Africa. There they bartered their rum for slaves whom they transported to the West Indies, where they disposed of them for rum, sugar, molasses and other tropical products or for bills of exchange. But there were necessary variations from this procedure. When rum was unobtainable in the islands, the Yankee captains gladly bartered their wares for sugar, cocoa, molasses or other products. The sugar and molasses were carried to New England, distilled into rum, and along with trinkets, bar iron, beads and light-colored cloth taken to Africa and exchanged for Negroes. The slaves who survived the terrible ordeal of the Middle

Passage—as the crossing between Africa and America was called—were sold in the West Indies for more rum, sugar and molasses, or for bills of exchange.

Vital to the slave trade as well as to New England's economy were sugar, rum and molasses. The distillation of millions of gallons of molasses brought from the British islands, or smuggled from the foreign West Indies, was the basis of a liquor industry of such proportions that the making of rum became New England's largest manufacturing business before the Revolution. The number of distilleries was almost incredible, with more than thirty in Rhode Island, twenty-two of them in Newport, and in Massachusetts sixty-three, which alone produced 2,700,000 gallons of rum in 1774. Little Newburyport, a bustling ship-building and commercial town on the Merrimac River, had ten distilleries. Of Boston's eight distilleries the most modern one was credited with producing a large amount of rum of remarkable cheapness. Although vast quantities of this rum were consumed at home, it was by no means all intended for domestic consumption. It was an almost indispensable article aboard fishing and whaling vessels, in lumber camps and for the fur industry. But primarily rum was linked with the Negro trade, and immense quantities of the raw liquor were sent to Africa and exchanged for slaves. So important was rum on the Guinea Coast that by 1723 it had surpassed French and Holland brandy, English gin, trinkets and dry goods as a medium of barter.

Profiting from Human Misery

Merchants spared no effort to make the slave trade as profitable as possible. Slaves and commodities were carried in small undermanned ships with crews rarely exceeding eighteen men, while some vessels, like the *Nancy* and the *Betsy*, carried only six. According to Mason, most of the slave vessels ranged between forty and fifty tons until 1750, when ships up to 200 tons were used. In the early years of the trade a space three feet ten inches high was reserved between decks for the slaves, but later, by reducing its dimensions to three feet three inches, additional room was made available for carrying Negroes. Men, women and children were separated by bulkheads. With only ten to thirteen inches of surface room alloted each slave the Negroes, packed spoon-fashion and unable to stand, suffered cruelly on the trip to America. With this extreme economy in ships and men, it is remarkable that mortality on the slave ships, great as it was, failed to reach an even higher figure.

Among the New England slave trading colonies, Massachusetts and Rhode Island ranked first, with Connecticut and New Hampshire playing relatively minor roles in the traffic. Boston was preeminent as the port of departure for slave ships, with Newport,

Rhode Island as its closest rival. . . . In these towns there grew up a privileged class of slave-trading merchants whose wealth was drawn largely from the Negro traffic. They enjoyed the highest social position and held public offices of the greatest trust and responsibility. The Belchers, Waldos, Fanueils, and Cabots of Boston; the Royalls of Charlestown; the Pepperells of Kittery; and the Crowninshields of Salem, Massachusetts, were but a few of the leading slave merchants of the Bay Colony. . . .

The Role of Newspapers

New England merchants sold most of their slaves in the West Indies and in the southern colonies, areas in which the great demand for Negroes to work the plantations resulted in high profits. Slaves, costing the equivalent of £4–£5 [$200 –$250] in rum or bar iron in Africa, were sold in the West Indies in 1746 at prices ranging from £30 to £88 [$1500–$4400]. It is not surprising, therefore, that the original destination of virtually every cargo of slaves was the sugar, or tobacco or rice colonies. . . .

During the eighteenth century the expansion of New England industries, with a corresponding shortage of labor, as well as the phenomenal growth of the slave trade, stimulated the sale of Negroes in New England. The advent of the newspaper in 1704 also proved a boon to slave merchants, by affording them the opportunity to advertise their chattels more widely. The New Englanders were the first to employ the newspaper for this purpose, and the *Boston News Letter,* the first permanent newspaper published in America, almost from its beginning on April 24, 1704, carried advertising of slaves. It listed for sale on June 1, "Two Negro Men and one Negro Woman and Child."

As newspapers increased in number and circulation, slave merchants, like other business men, regularly advertised their wares. So common was the practice, that it is almost impossible to find an eighteenth century newspaper not containing such notices. Prospective Boston buyers, for example, might purchase according to their fancy: "three likely negro men and two women" from Mr. John and James Alford, as "a parcel of fine negro boys and girls" from William Clark, Esq. In Newport, Rhode Island, in 1740, "men women and boys" were offered for sale by Josiah Bagley; or "a parcel of likely negro men women boys and girls," might be purchased from Channing and Chaloner. Connecticut and New Hampshire slave dealers advertised in a similar manner. John Bannister, a Newport merchant, was gratified to place on the Middletown, Connecticut market in 1752 what he considered to be the "finest cargo of negro men, women, boys and girls" ever imported into New England. In Hartford, prospective purchasers might buy "a very likely *NEGRO*

BOY", or a "Negro man about 47 years of age." New Hampshire dealers were no less active. In Portsmouth one could buy a "Negro man about 20 years of age . . . and one Negro girl about 17 years old"; or a "fine Negro man about 20 years of age."

The source of most of these slaves cannot be definitely stated. Negroes were brought from Africa, the West Indies, and the southern colonies, but in what proportion is a matter of speculation. The advertisements fail to give this information, although frequently describing the Negroes as "lately imported," "just imported," "lately arrived" or "just arrived." Of 125 advertisements of slaves in newspapers examined by the author, 80 gave no indication of the source of the supply, 19 gave the West Indies and 26 Africa as the point of origin.

It is probably true, as these figures seem to indicate, that more Negroes were imported into New England from Africa than from the West Indies, but nearly every cargo of slaves brought from Africa went first to the sugar islands. Many Negroes, ostensibly brought to New England from the West Indies, were sickly or "refuse" Negroes, who had been taken there first and had been found unsalable. Sometimes, however, ship captains were expressly ordered to reserve some "likely" slaves for the home market, but New England, as a rule, does not appear to have received prime, robust slaves. These were kept for the West Indies and plantation colonies, where they sold for higher prices. New England masters could afford to buy less able-bodied Negroes, for their slaves, generally speaking, were never subjected to the exacting toil demanded of those in the West Indies. Many New England Negroes, therefore, were recruited from the off-scourings of the slave ships—"refuse" persons—who sold for what they would bring. Governor Dudley of Massachusetts called the attention of the Board of Trade to this situation in 1708, when he informed its members that "the Negroes . . . brought in from the West Indies, are usually the worst servants they have," which accounted for their being sold in New England. Prices indicated their quality for, according to Dudley, "they usually brought between fifteen and twenty-five pounds per head."

Negroes from Africa were conspicuously "played up" in the advertising columns of the newspapers. Illustrative of these advertisements are: "very likely, agreeable and healthy negro boys and girls lately imported from Guinea," and "prime young slaves" just "imported from Africa." Gold Coast Negroes, because of their vigor and intelligence, were considered of highest quality in New England as well as in South Carolina and the West Indies. It is not surprising, therefore, that in 1726 a dealer announced the arrival of several "choice Gold Coast Negroes," or that in 1748, Robert Hall, a Charlestown merchant, rhapsodized over "four fine likely Gold

Coast Negroes" whom he had intended to sell South but later decided to offer to his fellow New Englanders. In 1762 an anonymous merchant was offering "a few prime men and boy slaves from the Gold Coast."

High-Pressure Selling

Negroes who had spent some time in the West Indies, or in the South, seem to have been found preferable to the "raw," turbulent Negroes brought directly from Africa. To New England buyers they possessed advantages over the natives, for often they had been "seasoned"; that is, they had become acclimated, were more accustomed to regular labor, could speak some English and, to some degree, were familiar with [Western] customs. These qualities were especially desirable, because the New England slave . . . came into unusually close contact with the master's family. For this reason, men like Peter Fanueil and Sir William Pepperell sometimes sent to the West Indies for slaves. Alert traders never failed to inform prospective buyers that their Negroes had been "lately imported from the West Indies"; and were therefore "fit for town or country service." Other advertisements gave prominence to the fact that the "slaves could speak English," had been brought up to do housework or were skilled in the trades.

Dealers frequently resorted to high pressure salesmanship. Black merchandise was most commonly labelled with the vague description of "likely" or "very likely." Physical characteristics were prominently described. Slaves were often recommended as: "healthy," "likely healthy," "strong healthy," "well-limbed," "stout," "lusty" or "lusty strong." Likewise merchants frequently directed attention to the personality or to some moral quality of the slave, and often advertised their Negroes as: "agreeable," "good," "honest," or as abstaining from "strong drink." At times slaves were cited as possessing a combination of desirable qualities such as "likely, agreeable, and healthy" or "strong healthy (and) ingenious." Gambia and the Gold Coast denoted quality, and Negroes born there were frequently advertised as "Choice Gold Coast or Gambia Negroes." Since smallpox was a common scourge among slaves and often raged with deadly virulence among the whites in colonial New England, slave dealers found that their Negroes sold more easily if they had already had this disease and had become immune. In such cases the master need not fear that his bondman might contract the malady and communicate it to him or to members of his family. As a result, it was not unusual for advertisements to state that the Negro "hath had the small pox." The first notice of this nature to come to the writer's attention was one issued in 1738, but such statements may have been employed before that date. If the Negro spoke English, was born in

Slaves who spoke English or who were born in America often commanded a higher price at slave auctions.

New England, or even in America, or had been in the country long enough to learn to serve efficiently the master class, his salability was also increased. Slave dealers and private individuals accordingly placed emphasis upon the fact that the Negro spoke "good English" or was "born in this town," "was born in the country" or "has been sometime in the country."

In addition to the external trade, a spirited domestic or internal slave traffic was carried on. Compared to that of the antebellum South, however, the local New England trade in Negroes was small. It was engaged in by persons who, for various reasons, such as urgent need of money, lack of employment for or dissatisfaction with their Negroes, desired to get rid of their chattels, just as one today disposes of a used automobile. The New England internal slave trade, however, lacked entirely the drama and spectacular brutality of certain phases of the Southern overland trade. Nevertheless, prospective buyers were literally bombarded with slave advertisements. One master placed on the market "a very likely young Negro girl fit for service either in town or country"; another, "A likely Negro maid aged about sixteen years fit for any service either in town or country . . . ; a third, "a young Negro woman . . . who has been ten years in the country" and a fourth, a "female Negro child, about seven years old," who was born in Boston.

Selling Whites and Indians

These advertisements did not diminish in number after the Revolution; rather, they seemed to increase through the stimulus of hard times and the increasing insecurity of slave property. In 1772 a Newport master offered to sell his "Negro girl about nine years old" and in 1780 Dr. William Jepson of Hartford was trying to find a buyer for a "likely Negro boy." In 1784, the very year that slavery was abolished in Rhode Island, a slaveholder in that state was seeking to dispose of a "likely stout Negro fellow about 23 years of Age . . . who understands the farming business exceedingly well."

Throughout the eighteenth century, whites and Indians, as well as Negroes, were offered for sale. A purchaser was not limited by race in his choice of a bondman, for he was free to buy a red, white or black slave. Let us assume that a Bostonian of the period had decided to buy a servant or a slave. He would naturally peruse the newspapers, where the following notice might engage his attention:

> A Lusty Indian Man-Servant, aged about 20 years, that speaks very good English, and fit for any service in Town or Country to be sold on reasonable Terms by *Mr. Jonathan Williams* over against the Post Office in Cornhill, Boston.

If his fancy ran to a black slave, he had only to glance over the following:

> To be Sold on reasonable Terms a Negro Man aged about 26 years, and a Negro Boy aged about 14 years, and a Negro Woman aged about 24 years and her child, to be seen at *Mr. James Pecher's* House in Salem Street Boston.

Finally, if the prospective purchaser preferred a person of his own race, he would pay particular attention to an advertisement of this type:

> Just imported from Ireland and to be sold on Board the Ship Virtue, John Seymour, Master, now in the Harbour of Boston, a parcel of healthy men Servants chiefly Tradesmen.

Occasionally Negroes and whites and Negroes and Indians were sold from the same auction block. Such a scene took place in 1714, when Samuel Sewall, a prominent Boston merchant, announced the sale at his warehouse of

> several Irish Maid Servants time most of them for Five Years one Irish Man Servant who is a good Barber and Wiggmaker, also Four or Five Likely Negro Boys.

Five months earlier an anonymous dealer had advertised:

> An Indian Boy aged about sixteen Years, and a Negro man aged about twenty both of them very likely and fit for any Service, they speak very good English: to be sold: Enquire at the Post Office in Boston.

Negroes were often sold for reasons which not only suggest a sense of humor or exasperation in the master but also shed light on the character of the slave. In 1742 a Boston owner was naively trying to dispose of a Negro "whose master vice is laziness, for which fault" alone he was to be sold. Plagued by his garrulous slave, another master in 1767 wanted to sell the Negro because he had "too long a tongue." Eight years later a Connecticut man sought to rid himself of a slave who expressed "too great fondness for a particular Negro wench in his old neighborhood."

1721–1750

A s the eighteenth century progressed, the intellectual movement known as the Age of Enlightenment swept across Europe. Based on recent discoveries in science, Enlightenment philosophers wrote tracts on democratic government, human liberty, freedom of religion, and other concepts that would have been considered blasphemous in earlier centuries. To avoid strict censorship laws in France, philosophers such as Baron de Montesquieu, Jean-Jacques Rousseau, Voltaire, and others often disguised their radical beliefs as humorous tracts, plays, and biting satires.

Although their books were sometimes banned, and their careers stifled by censorship and exile, Voltaire and others became legends in their own time. Their writings were widely disseminated and later influenced revolutionaries in America and France.

The eighteenth-century philosophers based their work on seventeenth-century writers and scientists such as Francis Bacon, Galileo, Descartes, Isaac Newton, and John Locke. These men believed in the laws of science and nature as opposed to the laws of religion and government, and they held the hope that scientific inquiry might reveal the meaning of life to humanity.

Philosophers of the Enlightenment

George Rudé

The abuses of power by European absolutist monarchs in the 1700s influenced writers and philosophers to question the the basis of such rule. In previous centuries, no one dared question the decrees of king or church. Those who did might be tortured or burned at the stake. But along with stunning advances in science and technology, philosophers began to see the world as governed by natural laws such as gravity and motion. Just as scientists questioned all manner of physical phenomena, philosophers began to question the basic workings of government and society. This inquiry gave rise to the period known as the Age of Enlightenment.

George Rudé, the author of more than a half-dozen books on French and English history, is professor of history at Sir George Williams University, Montreal, Canada.

If some doubt remains about the artistic and literary achievements of the eighteenth century, there can be none whatever about its importance in the history of ideas. It was, in fact, an age of outstanding intellectual vigour, which extended over the greater part of Europe—an age of Enlightenment, that the French have called *'le siècle des lumières'*, the Germans *'die Aufklärung'*, the Italians *'i lumi'* and the Spanish *'el siglo de las lucas'*. In its wider context, the Enlightenment reached into almost every brand of knowledge: into philosophy, and the natural, physical and social sciences, and into their

Excerpted from *Europe in the Eighteenth Century*, by George Rudé. Copyright © 1972 by George Rudé. Reprinted with permission from Greenwood Publishing Group, Inc., Westport, CT.

application in technology, education, penology [study of prison management], government and international law. In the physical sciences it was the age of [mathematician Leonhard] Euler in Switzerland, of [scientist Mikhail Vasilevich] Lomonosov (also a poet) in Russia, of [Benjamin] Franklin's lightning conductor in America, of [physicist Joseph Louis] Lagrange's *Mécanique analytique,* a work second only to [Isaac] Newton's *Principia* in the history of mechanics; and of [Luigi] Galvani's and [physicist Alessandro] Volta's experiments (1783), that led, a dozen years later, to the discovery of current electricity. In chemistry Joseph Black discovered 'latent heat' (and later 'fixed air') which helped James Watt to make his separate condenser [which led to the steam engine]; while [Henry] Cavendish discovered hydrogen (1760) and [Joseph] Priestley oxygen (1774), and [French chemist Antoine Laurent] Lavoisier combined the two by revealing the properties of air and water. . . . In philosophy, [David] Hume wrote the *Treatise on Human Nature* (1739–40); Voltaire issued his *Dictionnaire philosophique* in 1764; and, at Königsberg in Prussia, [Immanuel] Kant wrote in succession the *Metaphysics of Morals* in 1775, the *Critique of Pure Reason* in 1781, the *Critique of Practical Reason* in 1788 and the *Critique of Judgement* in 1790. . . .

Among these writers and thinkers, there were many—though by no means all appearing on this list—who have been given the name of *philosophe,* or 'philosopher'. The term, of course, originated in France; and among the *philosophes* the most active and, in many respects, the most influential were Frenchmen. . . .

Rational Explanations of the World

The *philosophes* had certain distinctive qualities of thought in common. They all questioned the basic assumptions which their contemporaries had inherited from the past, whether these were philosophical, theological or political. They were generally hostile to organised or revealed religion, and they all rejected the churches' barbarous dogma of original sin. They gave a rational, non-mystical, non-theological explanation of the world and of man's existence and place in society; for (to quote Ernest Cassirer) they were convinced that 'human understanding is capable by its own power, and without recourse to supernatural assistance, of comprehending the system of the world'. Such being their basic optimism with regard to man's capacity to master nature and to comprehend the world and the society in which he lived, they tended to be optimistic too—though this was not . . . a quality shared by all—about man's future, his perfectibility and possibility of happiness. Moreover, while not practising politicians . . . , they were not armchair philosophers who engaged in abstract or metaphysical explanations: their 'philosophy' was practical and empirical and they used it as a weapon of social and political criticism and tried to persuade others, whether governors or governed, to think and act the same. The *philosophes* themselves were well aware of this empirical, didactic and crusading element in their thinking and behaviour and took pride in it. At Königsberg in 1784 Kant defined the *Aufklärung* as a 'revolt against superstition' and put forward the slogan, *Sapere aude,* 'Dare to know'. [Anne] Turgot wrote to Hume that *'les lumières'* meant the capacity to know 'true causes'. [Denis] Diderot believed that *philosophes* must be united by a common 'love of truth, a passion to do good to others, and a taste for truth, goodness and beauty'. To [Marquis de] Condorcet, the *philosophes* were men 'less concerned with discovering truth than with propagating it', who 'find their glory rather in destroying popular error than in pushing back the frontiers of knowledge'; and their battle-cry must be 'reason, toleration, humanity'.

So the *philosophes* were a self-conscious élite, a small band of enlightened and dedicated men, who set out to convert others of their kind both by their ideas and the force of their example. But being an élite, their philosophy had its social limitations: they had little message or comfort for the poor and, as [French revolutionary leader Maximilien] Robespierre later complained, they showed little concern for 'the right of the people'. 'It is not the labourers one should educate,' wrote Voltaire, 'but the good bourgeois, the tradesmen'; and [Paul Henri] Holbach and Diderot, too, admitted that they wrote only for an educated public. And Turgot (with Voltaire's support) put loyalty to Physiocratic principles before the provision of cheap bread for the poor.

Seventeenth-Century Philosophers

Like all thinkers, the *philosophes* had their intellectual forbears: their ideas, whether in philosophy, or in the physical or social sciences, derived in great measure from the writers and thinkers of the century before. A few of these were Frenchmen. [René] Descartes in his *Discours de la méthode* (1651) had taught . . . that truth is attainable by logical reasoning; but he had drawn a sharp division between intellect and faith; faith lay outside the realm of reason; so, to appease the Church, he had left religion and the Bible untouched. Pierre Bayle, however, a Frenchman living in Rotterdam, had taken up the argument where Descartes had left it off; and in his *Dictionnaire historique et critique* (1697) he had applied Cartesian scepticism and scientific method to a study of history and the Bible. So now the field lay wide open for further exploration, and with no holds barred. But it was their English forbears rather than the French who provided the *philosophes* with their major shot and shell. 'Without the English,' wrote [German diplomat Melchior] Grimm, 'reason and philosophy would still be in the most despicable infancy in France'; and he added that Montesquieu and Voltaire 'were the pupils and followers of England's philosophers and great men'. In the first place there was Francis Bacon, the great protagonist of inductive reasoning, experimental science and empirical research. 'The true and lawful goal of the sciences,' Bacon had written in words that might have been the *philosophes'* own manifesto, 'is none other than this: that human life be endowed with new discoveries and powers.' Equally important in this ancestry was Sir Isaac Newton, the mathematician and astronomer and author of the *Principia,* or *Mathematical Principles of Natural Philosophy* (1687), and the *Optics* (1704). In the *Principia,* Newton had propounded the laws governing the motions of the earth and heavenly bodies; in his law of gravitation, he showed that gravity was directly related to the density of matter and that bodies attracted one another in proportion to the quantity of the matter they contained. Thus the phenomena of nature and the mysteries of the universe were reduced to simple, universal principles of mathematics. The third great influence—this time, in the social sciences— was [John] Locke. Locke had published his two *Treatises on Civil Government* and his *Essay Concerning Human Understanding* in 1690. In his *Treatises* Locke took over from [Thomas] Hobbes the 'social contract' theory, whereby civil government was presumed to have evolved from a contract between the ruler and his subjects. But whereas Hobbes had argued that the contract implied the complete surrender of the subjects' rights to the ruler's undisputed sovereignty, to Locke the contract was a bargain with obligations on both sides: the subjects must respect the ruler's sovereignty, but he in turn must respect their liberties and rights of property; failing which, the contract might be dissolved. . . . Locke went on in his *Essay* to lay the foundations of modern sensational psychology. The mind, he taught, was a *tabula rasa* [blank tablet], on which all impressions and experiences were grafted by the senses, not by innate or inherited qualities or by the accidents of birth. Thus, it might be inferred, all men came into the world as potential equals, all equally subject to the formative influence of the environment in which they lived.

It was Voltaire who first popularised these works in France. Having been exiled from Paris in 1726, he returned two years later from a long stay in England and fed back to his countrymen, in his *Lettres philosophiques* (1734), what he had learned from Bacon, Newton, Locke and the English deists [who believed God reveals Himself in scientific laws]. Having meanwhile become a deist and a Newtonian himself, it was these ideas that he was most eager to propound.

Montesquieu's Thoughts on Government

Charles Louis de Brède, Baron de Montesquieu

French philosopher Montesquieu was born in 1689 to a wealthy family as Charles-Louis de Secondat. He inherited a huge sum of money, and the title of baron de La Brède et de Montesquieu, in 1716. His interest in philosophy, personal freedom, and liberty led him to write a satire on French institutions called *Persian Letters* in 1721. This book was so popular, Montesquieu was named to the prestigious French Academy literary society in 1725, though the king opposed his election.

Montesquieu soon began a research tour to study the people, customs, and legal institutions of Europe. While in England, Montesquieu observed Parliament in action, and saw how the English were granted many rights of liberty denied to the French. He began to write *Spirit of the Laws* in 1743 and finished it in 1747.

Spirit of the Laws compares three types of governments: monarchy, despotism, and republic. It analyzes democracy, criminal laws, commerce, poverty, election, and government bodies under each system of government. Montesquieu's book was widely read in France and was also picked up by Thomas Jefferson, Benjamin Franklin, and other Americans who used the philosopher's theories as a basis for the U.S. Constitution.

Idea of this Book. Men are governed by several kinds of laws; by the law of nature; by the divine law, which is that of religion; by

Excerpted from *Spirit of the Laws*, by Baron de Montesquieu, 1747.

ecclesiastical, otherwise called canon law, which is that of religious polity; by the law of nations, which may be considered as the civil law of the whole globe, in which sense every nation is a citizen; by the general political law, which relates to that human wisdom whence all societies derive their origin; by the particular political law, the object of which is each society; by the law of conquest founded on this, that one nation has been willing and able, or has had a right to offer violence to another; by the civil law of every society, by which a citizen may defend his possessions and his life against the attacks of any other citizen; in fine, by domestic law, which proceeds from a society's being divided into several families, all which have need of a particular government.

There are therefore different orders of laws, and the sublimity [great worth] of human reason consists in perfectly knowing to which of these orders the things that are to be determined ought to have a principal relation, and not to throw into confusion those principles which should govern mankind.

Of Laws Divine and Human

We ought not to decide by divine laws what should be decided by human laws; nor determine by human what should be determined by divine laws.

These two sorts of laws differ in their origin, in their object, and in their nature.

It is universally acknowledged, that human laws are, in their own nature, different from those of religion; this is an important principle: but this principle is itself subject to others, which must be inquired into.

It is in the nature of human laws to be subject to all the accidents which can happen, and to vary in proportion as the will of man changes; on the contrary, by the nature of the laws of religion, they are never to vary. Human laws appoint for some good; those of religion for the best: good may have another object, because there are many kinds of good; but the best is but one; it cannot therefore change. We may alter laws, because they are reputed no more than good; but the institutions of religion are always supposed to be the best.

There are kingdoms in which the laws are of no value as they depend only on the capricious and fickle humour of the sovereign. If in these kingdoms the laws of religion were of the same nature as the human institutions, the laws of religion too would be of no value. It is however, necessary to the society that it should have something fixed; and it is religion that has this stability.

The influence of religion proceeds from its being believed; that of human laws from their being feared. Antiquity accords with religion, because we have frequently a firmer belief in things in proportion to their distance; for we have no ideas annexed to them drawn from those times which can contradict them. Human laws, on the contrary, receive advantage from their novelty, which implies the actual and particular attention of the legislator to put them in execution.

The Philosophy of Rousseau

Diané Collinson

Jean-Jacques Rousseau was born in Geneva, Switzerland, in 1712. Rousseau was a leading thinker of the Enlightenment and a social critic whose writings influenced not only other philosophers but the leaders of the French Revolution in 1789. This excerpt analyzes the life and philosophy of Rousseau.

Diané Collinson is a senior lecturer and staff tutor in philosophy at the Open University in the United Kingdom.

One of the most quoted remarks in the whole of political philosophy is the sentence with which Rousseau opens Chapter 1 of *The social contract:* 'Man is born free and everywhere he is in chains.' The chains he refers to are not those of a particular despotic rule but of legitimate government in general and his chief concern is to discover a justification for submitting to this kind of bondage. Rousseau is popularly thought to be the champion of an attitude that saw virtue in natural things and 'the noble savage' as the ideal human being, but his mature thought rejected much of this view, recognised the benefits and advantages of civil society and considered its 'chains' justified so long as it enacted what the general will of the people decreed was for their real good. Freedom was supremely important to him and his whole theory was designed to secure it for everyone; not, however, in the form of a removal of all constraints but as a positive freedom to participate in the activity of legislating for the common good. For Rousseau it is law rather than anarchy that sets people free. In *The social contract* he investigates the principles underlying this freedom, examining 'men as they are' and 'laws as they can be'. He seeks to elucidate a form of political association which, he writes, 'will defend and protect with the whole common force the person and goods of each associate, and in which each, while uniting himself with all, may still obey himself alone, and remain as free as before'.

Condemned by Parlement

Rousseau was born at Geneva [Switzerland]. His upbringing and education were unconventional. His mother died when he was a few days old and his father's care of him was somewhat erratic. In 1728 he left Geneva and thereafter travelled and studied, tried his hand at tutoring and working on a new method of musical notation and met a number of interesting and influential people. He was, though only briefly, (because of a quarrel) secretary to the French Ambassador at Venice. The publication of his writings began in 1750 when he was awarded a prize by the Academy of Dijon [in France] for an essay on 'Whether the restoration of the Sciences and the Arts has had a purifying effect on morals', a work now known as his first *Discourse.* In 1755 he published a second, much longer work, the *Discourse on the origin of inequality*, again in response to a question set by the Academy of Dijon. His work reached a high peak in 1762 when *Emile,* his treatise on education, and then *The social contract* were published. *Emile* was condemned by the Paris Parlement and Rousseau fled to Neuchatel [in Switzerland] to live under the protection of the King of Prussia. In 1765 the Scottish philosopher, David Hume, invited Rousseau to England but the two quarrelled, largely because Rousseau became irrationally convinced that Hume wished to humiliate and vilify him. He returned to France in 1767 and for three years moved from place to place, eventually settling in Paris in 1770. He moved in 1778 to the estate of the Marquis de Girardin at Ermenonville but died there within two months of the move. In the last few years of his life he wrote about his personal and emotional life: some dialogues, an unfinished reverie, and the famous *Confessions,* published posthumously, which describe the first 53 years of his life.

A Part of the Whole

In *The social contract* Rousseau suggests that the structure of society in general is that of the family writ large. The ruler of a society is like the father of a family and people yield up their freedom to the ruler as children yield it to a father, in order to preserve their safety. Might, he says, does not create right. We obey only legitimate might. The contract that is made between ruler and people is a just one in that it entails reciprocal rights and obligations. Moreover, in Rousseau's scheme of things, it is citizens in association who constitute the sovereign ruler and who therefore determine legislation. His social contract works only if every individual gives up all rights. He says 'Each of us contributes to the group his person and the powers which he wields as a person, and we receive into the body politic each individual as forming an indivisible part of the whole.' Individuals together become a collective moral body, a kind of dispersed self which, in its wholeness, is the sovereign power. The sovereign is a moral concept, a rational abstraction which is the basis of the equality and freedom of the people it comprises. It transforms natural liberty into civil liberty and is that through which a moral will can be expressed. The social contract, too, is an abstraction: it is a concept that describes the kind of association that obtains in a state or civil society rather than any specific agreement drawn up at some particular time and place.

Jean-Jacques Rousseau

Rousseau distinguishes between what he calls 'the will of all' which is the totality of individual self-interested wishes and the General Will, which is arrived at only when each citizen reflects on what will produce the good of all. The General Will must be general not only in its origins but also in its application: 'What makes the will general is not the number of citizens concerned but the common interest by which they are united . . . the sovereign knows only the nation as a whole. Rousseau maintains that the General Will is always right. This is not to say that the actual deliberations of the people are always right but that when every citizen is adequately informed and deliberates rationally for the general good then the conclusions arrived at will be right. Moreover, the enactment of the General Will is a culmination and fulfilment of freedom, for the initial contract that establishes the collective sovereign person is freely entered into by its members who then put themselves under laws of their own making. As subject to the sovereign the citizen participates in the making of legislation; as an individual he or she is recipient of rights thereby allocated: 'Sovereign and subjects', Rousseau says, 'are simply the same people in different respects.' We compel ourselves to be free.

A Champion of Revolution

The problem of how the mass of the people together, however well intentioned, can actually determine the General Will troubled Rousseau greatly. 'How', he asks, 'can a blind multitude, which often does not know what it wills because it rarely knows what is good for it, carry out for itself so great and difficult an enterprise as a system of legislation?' His solution to the difficulty was the concept of the Legislator, someone who is neither magistrate nor sovereign but who has an intelligence that can articulate the objective good sought by the many for their society. The Legislator is completely outside the structure of the legislation he suggests. Yet he has a god-like quality that evokes the recognition in his utterances of ideals only half-sensed by most people but nevertheless sought by them. This curious concept in Rousseau's system has provoked much discussion. In particular he has been accused, in introducing the idea of Legislator, of producing a political theory that in the last analysis invites despotism. It is as if he suddenly loses faith in the unaided natural goodness of humanity and has to find some force to send it in the right direction. In a similar vein, towards the end of *The social contract,* he introduces the idea of a profession of allegiance to the state to which every citizen would be bound for life. This, too, has shocked liberal-minded readers. Others have regarded him as a champion of revolution, largely because of the tone of his earlier writings in which he rails against the decadence of the culture around him and the way in which, to his mind, it has corrupted human nature. Certainly, by 1791, thirteen years after his death and two years after the beginning of the French Revolution [in 1789], his name was on many lips in France and his ideas on egalitarianism and the General Will were common parlance.

In *Emile,* the treatise on education, Rousseau considers the development of a child growing up in the country and tries to analyse the principles underlying a natural process of maturing from infancy to adulthood. He affirms his belief in a natural human goodness, albeit one that is vulnerable to vice and error, and advocates a quiet and gentle nurturing that is related to the needs of each stage of a child's development and that is especially sympathetic to the thought that 'Nature wants children to be children before being men.' As the child matures, relationships with others begin to be more important; moral and political awareness follows and eventually the individual becomes a fully social human being who is well able, if his education has spared him unnatural stimulations and tensions, to exercise his natural powers to the full within a community of rational beings.

Rousseau's writing has an intense and personal quality that compellingly transmits his vision of a society in which each person is able to be fulfilled, happy and free. His views have been widely influential, in part because of their vitality and passion, but also because they focus on issues of freedom and human relationships that are of perennial interest as well as being difficult—perhaps impossible—to resolve. He traced the inspiration for all his ideas to the thoughts that flooded overwhelmingly into his mind when he contemplated the question set by the Dijon Academy about the influence of the arts and sciences on morals. In a letter to Malesherbes, written in 1762, he described how he sat beneath a tree, weeping over those thoughts. He wrote: 'All that I have been able to retain of those swarms of great truths that enlightened me under that tree have been scattered quite feebly in my main works.'

The Life and Times of Voltaire

George R. Havens

Voltaire, born François-Marie Arouet in Paris in 1694, was one of the most influential philosophers of the Enlightenment. A legend in his own time, Voltaire spoke out against abuses of power in the French monarchy, the Catholic Church, and the French criminal justice system. The writings of Voltaire influenced a generation of free thinkers who led the American Revolution in the 1770s and the French Revolution in 1789.

This excerpt by George R. Havens, an authority on French history prior to the 1789 revolution, is an essay on the life and times of Voltaire.

It was a frail child indeed who was born in the heart of Paris on November 21, 1694, in the midst of what are still the narrow twisting streets of the old parish known as Saint-André-des-Arts. Who, in this feeble infant, could have foreseen a long, combative, and colorful career of nearly eighty-four years?

His father was a businesslike notary of some distinction, what we should call a lawyer engaged in civil practice. The boy, François-Marie Arouet, as he was baptized the next day—the name Voltaire was to come later—belonged therefore to the prosperous upper *bourgeoisie* or middle-class. By his extraordinary wit, acumen, and literary ability, he was to step over the dividing line which sharply separated noble and commoner, getting himself more or less accepted as a member of that aristocracy to which his merit, if not his birth, entitled him. But the ascent was difficult, and the young man, if he

Excerpted from *The Age of Ideas: From Reaction to Revolution in Eighteenth Century France*, by George R. Havens. Copyright © 1955 by George R. Havens, renewed by Holt, Rinehart, and Winston. Reprinted with permission from Harcourt, Inc.

easily acquired a graceful and exquisite courtesy, lost none of his natural impudence on occasion or his mordant, critical spirit in regard to snobbery and ancient abuses.

The child's mother, Marguerite Daumard (or D'Aumard), was a descendant of the lesser nobility from the old province of Poitou in west-central France. From her the boy inherited, it seems, his keen taste for literature; from his father came that practical hardheaded business sense which is not often combined with authorship. But the mother died prematurely when the boy was seven, and we can only speculate in vain as to whether his life would have been notably different if he had longer enjoyed her vivid companionship and guidance.

Three years later the father, a busy man of affairs, unable no doubt longer to supervise effectively the upbringing of his precocious and self-willed son, placed him in the near-by Jesuit *collège* of Louis-le-Grand, adjacent to the Sorbonne in the ancient Latin Quarter of Paris. The institution still exists under the same name today as a state-supported *lycée* [secondary school]. Young Arouet was ten in 1704 when he entered the famous school; he was sixteen when he left it in 1711. Many sons of the nobility were to be found there. . . .

A Man of Letters

As he finished school in 1711, the question naturally came up of his plans for a career. With the self-confidence of youth, he replied: "I want none but that of a man of letters." All-too-conscious of the many uncertainties besetting such a profession, his practical father retorted: "That's the position of a man who wishes to be useless to society, a burden to his parents, and to die of hunger." With the advantage of our present hindsight, we can easily perceive now how wrong his father was on all three counts, but, in view of the unpredictability of genius and the hand-to-mouth existence of many a struggling writer in the eighteenth century, it did not look so then. The brash young boy was put to the study of law.

Like many another author, before and since, Arouet was infinitely bored by legal terminology and technicalities. He wanted none of what was to him a humdrum profession. Yet experience with the law sharpened his business sense, armed him with courtroom forms and procedure, made certain that he would be well able to increase and protect his later wealth—for he was by no means "to die of hunger," as his father had so sourly predicted.

Meanwhile, a freethinking, deistically-minded ecclesiastic, Abbé de Chateâuneuf, had introduced the lively youth to what was known as the "Society of the Temple," a group of men gathered about the Duc de Vendôme, Grand Prior of the Knights of Malta. It was a circle of distinguished *débauchés* [heavy drinkers] whose irreverent wit played gaily over all the seeming follies of Church or State. If

Arouet's frail physique left him little taste for the drinking bouts of these boon companions, he could soon vie with the best of them in quip, epigram, or light society verse. "Are we all princes or all poets?" he was to say later at supper to the Prince de Conti. His first classical tragedy of *Oedipus* was here read aloud and respectfully polished under the counsel of these arbiters of literary fame. The young author took eagerly to this worldly schooling, so different from the Jesuit *collège,* so fitted to his taste. We can sympathize, too, with the long-suffering father, sure that his riotous son was going completely to the dogs.

For a change of scene, the notary snatched up his troublesome offspring and packed him off in haste to Holland. It bespeaks the elder Arouet's considerable influence that he was able to put him under the charge of the French ambassador at The Hague. But the busy envoy had little time, no doubt, to watch over and check the rising ardor of youth. The boy promptly imagined himself in love with a certain Mademoiselle Dunoyer, "Pimpette," as she was nicknamed. With a useful veneer of piety he plotted the conversion of this girl of a dubious Protestantism, even planned an elopement to Paris. The harassed ambassador returned his disturbing protégé home, where the angry father thought of banishing the son to "America," that is, to the far-off islands of the French West Indies. What a different and probably obscure career if this hot-tempered impulse had been followed! But the father relented and some kind of a treaty of peace was made. Young Arouet went back by day to the musty law office of Maître Allain, while continuing his gay career by night with the dangerous *habitués* [regular attendees] of the Temple. With such a compromise, neither side could be happy, but the son had the better of the arrangement, for he managed still to neglect the law to his heart's content, while devoting his plentiful leisure to literature and the roistering companions who pleased him.

Imprisoned in the Bastille

In 1715, the irrepressible boy burst forth with satirical verses against the then well-known author [Jean-Marie] La Motte. The much-tried father sent his nuisance of a son into prudent exile at the château of Saint-Ange with the elderly noble, Monsieur de Caumartin. This was a most important experience, as it turned out, since the memory of Monsieur de Caumartin was well stored with significant and interesting anecdotes direct from the preceding seventeenth century. Here, at first hand, young Arouet was unconsciously preparing himself for what became his long-famous epic poem on Henry IV and his much more important history of the *Age of Louis XIV.*

Back in Paris, the son of the notary went on his merry way. But this time he aimed his shafts too high. A new satirical poem was leveled audaciously at the Regent of France, the dissolute [drunken] Duke of Orleans himself. The result was prompt imprisonment in the gloomy fortress of the Bastille which, until the Revolution [in 1789], continued to frown menacingly over the teeming eastern quarters of Paris. For eleven dragging months in 1717 and 1718, the young man remained behind these thick walls. The experience was not exactly painful, but it was boresome, an unhappy contrast to the joyous, varied life outside. There is a tradition that the budding poet contrived to write much of his future epic, the *Henriade,* between the lines of a book he had managed to get his hands on in default of paper. In the eighteenth century, such imprisonment in the Bastille for political, religious, or other defiance of censorship, was generally not too harsh and carried with it indeed a certain distinction. Nevertheless, we can be sure that young Arouet was not loath to be at last released. Wittily, he paid his court to the Regent in that best of coins at the time by begging him gaily in the future to provide his board, if he wished, but not his lodging!

A Successful Author

A successful series of performances of his play, *Oedipus,* at the Comédie-Française [theater] made the young author famous at twenty-four. He was hailed widely as the promising successor to the great Sophocles and Corneille. It was a heady diet for one in no way noted for prudence or restraint. The time seemed appropriate to adopt a new and more distinguished name. The dramatist signed himself Arouet de Voltaire. Of the different theories as to the origin of this name, perhaps the most plausible is that it comes from inverting and respelling the syllables of Airvault, a little village in the province of Poitou where the family owned property. . . . In any event, it was to be some time before the emerging writer could get his aristocratic name completely accepted by society.

Several uneasy years followed. The young author was not able immediately to duplicate the striking success of his tragedy of *Oedipus.* His next plays were failures. In 1722, Voltaire returned to Holland, this time in his greater maturity to be much impressed by the prosperous world trade and the extraordinary freedom which the little country enjoyed. The experience was a kind of preparation for the more important journey to England a short while later.

Beaten by a Nobleman

In 1725 the young man's new name and his self-assurance again got him into trouble. The Chevalier de Rohan-Chabot belonged to a haughty and illustrious family. Deciding no doubt to take down the upstart young author with a bit of studied insolence, the nobleman eyed him contemptuously one evening at the Opera and, alluding to his unauthorized change of name, addressed him with obvious sarcasm: "Monsieur de Voltaire, Monsieur Arouet, what is your name anyway?" Voltaire's exact reply is not certainly known. Perhaps he said, as was reported many years later by Abbé du Vernet, who is supposed to have drawn much of his information from [Nicolas Claude] Thieriot, the friend of Voltaire, that he did not dishonor a great name, and that he knew how to honor the one he did bear; perhaps he observed that he was beginning his line while on the contrary the Chevalier de Chabot was bringing his to a close. Little doubt that Voltaire's ready wit did not leave him at a loss.

Two days later at the Comédie-Française, the Chevalier renewed the quarrel. Voltaire answered that he had already made his reply at the Opera. The nobleman raised his cane as though to strike down this impudence, whereupon the celebrated actress, Mademoiselle Lecouvreur, conveniently fainted and, by thus diverting attention, put an end to the dispute for the moment. Two or three days later, Voltaire was dining in distinguished company at the table of the Duc de Sully. A lackey brought a message that someone was inquiring for him below. The author went downstairs, suspecting nothing. Outside the door, three lackeys promptly began belaboring him on the back and shoulders with rods, while the Chevalier de Rohan-Chabot, it is said, directed the affair from a neighboring carriage. There is a story from the diary of the contemporary Marquis d'Argenson that the brave Chevalier called out: "Don't hit him on the head; something good may come out of that yet!" Onlookers exclaimed ironically. "Oh, the kind nobleman!"

In this outrageous assault, the Duc de Sully refused to intervene. The Prince de Conti, who had praised the author of *Oedipus* as worthy . . . , dismissed the blows as "well received and badly delivered." Even Abbé de Caumartin, of the family with whom Voltaire had been so intimate at Saint-Ange, observed: "We should be most unfortunate if poets had no shoulders." The lawyer Marais reported simply and brutally: "The poor recipient of the blows shows himself, as much as he can, at the Court and in the city, but no one sympathizes with him, and those whom he thought his friends, have turned their backs on him."

Arrested Once Again

It was a bitter lesson in the great gulf which still yawned between noble and commoner. In spite of his witty sallies and striking success as a dramatist, in spite of his seeming equality at table with dukes and princes, Voltaire found himself relegated to the position of a clever entertainer with no rights which a degenerate scion of a noble house was bound to respect. In the effort to restore his wounded honor, the poet took lessons in fencing to prepare himself for a duel. But the Chevalier de Rohan-Chabot had no great reputation for courage. Besides, he would not lower his noble self to fight with a mere *bourgeois,* who if beaten by lackeys had received only his just deserts! The powerful Rohan family no doubt spoke a word to the government. An order was given for Voltaire's arrest and, during the night of April 17, 1726, he was hustled away a second time to the Bastille. More schooling in the capricious tyranny of the Old Régime!

While in the Bastille, Voltaire had English books brought him by his friend Thieriot. Since the imprisonment this time lasted but two weeks, they are significant, however, only as an indication of the way his mind was turning. Shortly the offended author received permission to exchange his walled cell for exile in England. Early in May he was released, on the fifth he was at Calais, and sometime during the month he

arrived in London. His stay in the country across the Channel is a very important period in his life. Perhaps he would have gone there sooner or later, anyhow, perhaps not. In any case, the Rohan-Chabot quarrel had far-reaching consequences. The empty-headed Chevalier had started a chain of events the ultimate importance of which he little knew. Voltaire was to become an important medium for the spread of ideas of English liberty over the Continent.

The Revocation of the Edict of Nantes in 1685 [which had allowed religious freedom in France] . . . had driven large numbers of Protestant refugees into difficult exile in England. Many

Voltaire

of them were educated pastors who, in their new-found asylum, made themselves into journalists eager to write in French periodicals about English liberty, English tolerance, and English literature. These periodicals generally circulated from Holland, thus avoiding censorship. Louis XIV, with his ill-conceived aim of religious unity based on force, had thus unwittingly set in motion forces destined to further the rise of the very freedom which he so much feared and hated.

It was no accident therefore that Voltaire chose in 1726 to go to

England as the condition of his release from the Bastille. England was the one country, at the time, which could best contribute to his education and experience. With all its human imperfections, the known bribery of many members of Parliament at the time, the violence of its political quarrels, England nevertheless offered the rare spectacle of a large measure of religious tolerance, of free debate over government policies, of arrest only on a warrant showing cause, of an early trial by jury guaranteed by the famous writ of *habeas corpus*. What a contrast to Voltaire's own two arbitrary imprisonments in France! Who better prepared than he to appreciate the lesson and its meaning!

Wisely, Voltaire set himself promptly to learn English. With many of the aristocracy and his literary confrères in Britain, he could of course have made shift to converse in his native French. Lord Bolingbroke, indeed, whom Voltaire had known in France since 1722 and at whose house he spent part of his time in London, had a French wife and spoke her language with a vigor and facility which astonished his guest. But Voltaire saw how much is closed to a traveler confined to his own tongue in a foreign country. He wished to be able to enjoy the theater, to read the literature of the past and present, to understand people in the street, to witness Parliamentary debates, to follow the course of events in the daily newspapers, in short, to steep himself to the full in English life.

In pursuance of his goal, Voltaire withdrew to the country for a period of quiet study at Wandsworth in the company of a distinguished merchant, [Everand] Falkener. At the startling performances of Shakespeare, so different from the classic [Jean] Racine, Voltaire sat with text of the play in hand, prepared to some degree in advance for the bold flights of Elizabethan poetry and vigorous action on the stage. He even argued baptism with a young Quaker, Edward Higginson. Legend has it that, when reviled in the street as "a French dog," Voltaire, in an impromptu speech regretting that he did not have the honor to be born an Englishman, quickly won the cheers of his hostile audience.

Thus Voltaire learned English well, even came soon to write it with force and a high degree of correctness as is evidenced by his unrevised letters to his friend, Thieriot. Naturally, however, since he was thirty-two years old at the time of his arrival across the Channel, he always retained a strong foreign accent and never quite mastered the intricacies of prepositions, those little demons which in all languages lie in wait for the unwary. Like a good Frenchman, for example, he spoke of obeying "to" the laws. Yet thirty-five years after his return to France he could still speak English with a readiness which amazed the visiting Boswell at Ferney. He even "swore bloodily as was the fashion when he was in England," commented the young interviewer as his aged host let fly with the out-of-date oaths of a former generation.

Hostility Towards Authority

One of the chief results of this important voyage was a little book known as the *Philosophical Letters,* sometimes called also more accurately Letters on the English. The adjective "philosophical" was itself provocative as it would not be today. It carried with it an idea of freethinking, of radicalism, of hostility to the conventional in government, religion, science, or literature. Moreover, it was the first work of Voltaire to be written in his characteristic prose with its short, crisp sentences, its brilliant concision, its biting irony, its effective challenge to the Old Régime. No wonder the work fell like a bombshell, as Gustave Lanson says, among the reading public of the day! No wonder it was officially burned by the hangman while the author, back in France since 1729, found it convenient for a time to remain away from Paris in the far-off South!

Fittingly, by August of 1733, the book had appeared first in English translation at London. The French version came out in Paris during the last week of April, 1734. Fearing the uproar it would create, the author had the work printed surreptitiously at Rouen, prudently withheld it for a time, and trickily denied responsibility for its final release. Making war upon governmental censorship and repression, Voltaire was never overscrupulous about the means used. He fought fire with fire. Stratagem and brash denial of authorship were his ready weapons against arbitrary force and tyranny. The government in turn often half-cooperated by pretending to believe such assertions. Printers and booksellers used similar methods in the effort to escape imprisonment or financial ruin. It required a bold spirit to spread new ideas under the Old Régime.

Birth of the Paris Art Salon

Thomas E. Crow

Before the eighteenth century great art was the province of royalty and aristocratic or religious elites. Public artwork existed in some cities, such as Florence, Italy, but for the average citizen art was one more luxury enjoyed only by the rich. These attitudes began to change during the Age of Enlightenment. As ideas of freedom, democracy, and liberty began to spread in the political world, they also took hold in the realm of everyday life, especially for people in large cities like Paris.

Beginning in 1737, the grand displays of art sponsored by the Academy of Painting and Sculpture in Paris were some of the first public art exhibits of the time. Known as the Salon, these celebrations of art attracted tens of thousands of people to crowded galleries at the Louvre. Here, as never before, wealthy aristocrats rubbed elbows with street sweepers and farmers, sacrificing formalities in order to gaze on the canvases of Europe's finest painters.

These displays, however, were not without controversy. When art was removed from the palaces and villas of the rich and given over to the average person, great debates ensued over what the public should be allowed to see. Much like the artistic controversies of modern times, the clash of religious beliefs, politics, and the will of the people often focused on works of art.

Thomas E. Crow is assistant professor of art and archaeology at Princeton University.

Excerpted from *Painters and Public Life in Eighteenth Century Paris,* by Thomas E. Crow. Copyright © 1985 by Yale University Press. Reprinted with permission from Yale University Press.

Ambitious painting most conspicuously entered the lives of eighteenth-century Parisians in the Salon exhibitions mounted by the Academy of Painting and Sculpture. These had begun as regular events in 1737; held in odd-numbered years, except for a brief early spell of annual exhibitions, they opened on the feast-day of St. Louis (25 August) and lasted from three to six weeks. During its run, the Salon was the dominant public entertainment in the city. As visual spectacle, it was dazzling: the *Salon carré* [square] of the Louvre— the vast box of a room which gave the exhibition its name—packed with pictures from eye-level to the distant ceiling, the overflow of still-life and genre pictures spilling down the stairwells that led to the gallery; an acre of color, gleaming varnish, and teeming imagery in the midst of the tumble-down capital (the dilapidation of the Louvre itself was the subject of much contemporary complaint). "Ceaseless waves" of spectators filled the room, so the contemporary accounts tell us, the crush at times blocking the door and making movement inside impossible. The Salon brought together a broad mix of classes and social types, many of whom were unused to sharing the same leisure-time diversions. Their awkward, jostling encounters provided constant material for satirical commentary.

The success of the Salon as a central Parisian institution, however, had been many decades in the making. Its actual origins lay in the later seventeenth century, but these had not been particularly auspicious. The Academy's initial efforts at public exhibition had been limited to a few cramped and irregular displays of pictures, first in its own meeting rooms and later in the open arcades of the adjoining Palais Royal. The disadvantage of the latter practice, according to an early account, was that the artists "had the constant worry of damage to the paintings by the weather, which pressed them often to withdraw the pictures before the curiosity of the public had been satisfied." By 1699 the Salon was more comfortably installed inside the Louvre, and Parisians were spared the sight of academicians hustling their canvases out of the rain. By all accounts, that exhibition was a popular success, but it was almost forty years before the Salon became a permanent fixture of French cultural life.

Art for the Masses

After 1737, however, its status was never in question, and its effects on the artistic life of Paris were immediate and dramatic. Painters found themselves being exhorted in the press and in art-critical tracts to address the needs and desires of the exhibition "public"; the journalists and critics who voiced this demand claimed to speak with the backing of this public; state officials responsible for the arts hastened to assert that their decisions had been taken in the public's interest; and collectors began to ask, rather ominously for the artists, which pictures had received the stamp of the public's approval. All those with a vested interest in the Salon exhibitions were thus faced with the task of defining what sort of public it had brought into being.

This proved to be no easy matter, for any of those involved. The Salon exhibition presented them with a collective space that was markedly different from those in which painting and sculpture had served a public function in the past. Visual art had of course always figured in the public life of the community that produced it: civic processions up the Athenian Acropolis, the massing of Easter penitents before the portal of Chartres cathedral, the assembly of Florentine patriots around Michelangelo's *David*—these would just begin the list of occasions in which art of the highest quality entered the life of the ordinary European citizen and did so in a vivid and compelling way. But prior to the eighteenth century, the popular experience of high art, however important and moving it may have been to the mass of people viewing it, was openly determined and administered from above. Artists operating at the highest levels of aesthetic ambition did not address their wider audience directly; they had first to satisfy, or at least resolve, the more immediate demands of elite individuals and groups. Whatever factors we might name which bear on the character of the art object, these were always refracted through the direct relationship between artists and patrons, that is, between artists and a circumscribed, privileged minority.

The broad public for painting and sculpture would thus have been defined in terms other than those of interest in the arts for their own sake. In the pre-eighteenth-century examples cited above, it was more or less identical with the ritualized assembly of the political and/or religious community as a whole—and it could be identified as such. The eighteenth-century Salon, however, marked a removal of art from the ritual hierarchies of earlier communal life. There the ordinary man or woman was encouraged to rehearse before works of art the kinds of pleasure and discrimination that once had been the exclusive prerogative of the patron and his intimates. There had been precedents for this kind of exhibition, of course, in France and elsewhere in Europe: displays of paintings often accompanied the [Christian] festival of Corpus Christi, for example, and there were moves underway in many places to make royal and noble collections available to a wider audience . But the Salon was the first regularly repeated, open, and free display of contemporary art in Europe to be offered in a completely secular setting and for the purpose of encouraging a primarily aesthetic response in large numbers of people.

Precious Liberty Is Visible

There was in this arrangement, however, an inherent tension between the part and the whole: the institution was collective in character, yet the experience it was meant to foster was an intimate and private one. In the

modern public exhibition, starting with the Salon, the audience is assumed to share in some community of interest, but what significant
commonality may actually exist has been a far more elusive question.
What was an aesthetic response when divorced from the small community of erudition, connoisseurship, and aristocratic culture that had
heretofore given it meaning? To call the Salon audience a "public" implies some meaningful degree of coherence in attitudes and expecta-
tions: could the crowd in the Louvre be described as anything more than
a temporary collection of hopelessly heterogeneous individuals? This
was the question facing the members of the art world of eighteenth-
century Paris. Many thought so, but the actual attempt caused them end-
less difficulty. Here is one representative effort, written in 1777 by a
veteran social commentator and art critic, Pidansat de Mairobert. He begins with his physical entry into the space of the exhibition:

> You emerge through a stairwell like a trapdoor, which is always choked
> despite its considerable width. Having escaped that painful gauntlet, you
> cannot catch your breath before being plunged into an abyss of heat and
> a whirlpool of dust. Air so pestilential and impregnated with the exha-
> lations of so many unhealthy persons should in the end produce either
> lightning or plague. Finally you are deafened by a continuous noise like
> that of the crashing waves in an angry sea. But here nevertheless is a thing
> to delight the eye of an Englishman: the mixing, men and women together,
> of all the orders and all the ranks of the state. . . . This is perhaps the only
> public place in France where he could find that precious liberty visible
> everywhere in London. This enchanting spectacle pleases me even more
> than the works displayed in this temple of the arts. Here the Savoyard odd-
> job man rubs shoulders with the great noble in his *cordon bleu* [Blue
> Ribbon—emblem of the highest order in France]; the fishwife trades her
> perfumes with those of a lady of quality, making the latter resort to hold-
> ing her nose to combat the strong odor of cheap brandy drifting her way;
> the rough artisan, guided only by natural feeling, comes out with a just ob-
> servation, at which an inept wit nearby bursts out laughing only because
> of the comical accent in which it was expressed; while an artist hiding in
> the crowd unravels the meaning of it all and turns it to his profit.

The source of this passage is Mairobert's clandestine news-sheet,
the "English Spy," hence the conspicuous English references. It appears as part of a lengthy and sober history of official art in France
and of the public exhibitions of the Academy (as good as any the
eighteenth century produced). His half-comic observations of the
Salon crowd are meant to carry serious meaning. . . .

Prejudices, Passions, and Jealousy

The rhetoric of the passage points up the degree to which the "public" in the Salon defied efforts at concrete description. In its choices

of metaphor it is positively at war with concreteness. Merely to enter the Salon requires a passage through a blinding vortex in which all the boundaries and distinctions which demarcate a ranked society are broken down. The result is a new social body which is seductive and enchanting in its liberated vitality, but at the same time mined with insidious hazards. Once barriers have been dissolved, social contact multiplies and expands uncontrollably like the invisible circulation of disease. The flux of the Salon crowd, likened to the commingling of heady and noxious gases, contains equal measures of vitality and peril. At the same time, this apparent chaos does in the end yield useful knowledge to the artist, knowledge free, as Mairobert states further on, from "prejudices, passions, jealousy, and servile conformity." Wisdom emerges from the most unexpected sources, and is easily misread by the complacent and shallow. But the artist, via saturation in the fluid mass of his public, does sort it all out, does come away with new information useful, indeed essential, to his art. . . .

It follows from this that the role of the new public space in the history of eighteenth-century French painting will be bound up with a struggle over representation, over language and symbols and who had the right to use them. The issue was never whether that problematic entity, the public, should be consulted in artistic matters, but who could be legitimately included in it, who spoke for its interests, and which or how many of the contending directions in artistic practice could claim its support. If the Salon as a social location seemed mystifyingly fluid and undefined, what other public spaces of assembly and shared discourse might it be like? In what ways did one's experience there overlap with those of the festival, fair, royal entry, marketplace, theater, salesroom, court of law, church, or political demonstration? A combination of historical factors made the conflict over such questions intense, and what might otherwise have been rather esoteric questions of artistic style and subject matter were often caught up in that struggle. One way therefore to begin an account of the place of painting in the social fabric of the city will be to trace the history of this argument, and in so doing, we will begin to understand something of the intensity with which it was fought out. . . .

Bringing Artists' Work to Light

Considering the casual hierarchy of the eighteenth-century debate over the Salon public, the most appropriate place to begin would be with the view of the state at the time of the revival of the Salon in 1737. The official responsible for its permanent reestablishment was the finance minister Philibert Orry. Newly appointed head of the arts administration (as *Directeur-général des bâtiments*), Orry seems to have carried a tendency to fiscal thinking over into his new responsibilities. The Salon, in his conception, would be like an annual public audit of artistic productivity. The official journal, the *Mercure de France,* endorsed Orry's proposal in just these terms:

> . . . the Academy does well to render a sort of accounting to the public of its work and to make known the progress achieved in the arts it nurtures by bringing to light the work of its most distinguished members in the diverse genres it embraces, so that each thereby submits himself to the judgement of informed persons gathered in the greatest possible number and receives the praise or blame due him. This will both encourage genuine talents and unmask the false fame of those who have progressed too little in their art, but, full of pride in their illustrious company, think themselves automatically as able as their fellows and neglect their calling.

This passage announces what will be an incessant theme in eighteenth-century discussions of art: that quality in art depends on public scrutiny, and that this quality is threatened or declines to the extent that artists restrict their audience, whether to a noble or moneyed elite or to a coterie [small, select group] of their fellow academicians. So declared that writer often cited as the first modern art critic, one La Font de Saint-Yenne. "It is only in the mouths of those firm and equitable men who compose the Public, who have no links whatever with the artists, . . . that we can find the language of truth," he wrote in defense of his critical pamphlet of 1747. That pamphlet, entitled *Reflections on Some Causes of the Current State of Painting in France,* contained a comprehensive discussion of the previous year's Salon and proposed for the first time that a museum be established in the Louvre to provide artists and public alike with a continuing education in art history. . . .

We could draw from all this an optimistic and affirmative picture of the new public sphere, one in which the audience (via the critics who spoke in its name) joined the Academy and the state in fundamental agreement on principles and the direction of needed reform. . . . The Salon as a public event had restored the mandate once provided by the aggressive cultural policies of Louis XIV. . . . In the process, direct subservience to the throne was muted and a more general notion of public service came to the fore. The engraver [Charles-Nicolas] Cochin, then first officer of the Academy, made the connection plainly in 1757: after the death of Louis XIV, he declared:

> . . . the art of painting languished without support or protection. . . . The custom of exhibitions at the Salon was not yet in force, and we can say confidently that this fortunate institution has saved painting by a prompt display of the most deserving talents and by inspiring with a love of the arts a good number of people who, without the exhibition, would never have given them a thought.

Morsels of Wisdom from Ben Franklin

Benjamin Franklin

Benjamin Franklin, one of the founders of the United States, was born in Boston in 1706. As a scientist, inventor, statesman, diplomat, and philosopher Franklin was a true student of the Enlightenment. Unlike French philosophers, however, whose weighty words were difficult for average citizens to understand, Franklin's aphorisms were simple, no-nonsense words to live by.

Franklin began his career as a printer in Philadelphia. Later he collected pithy sayings for publication in *Poor Richard's Almanack,* which was published annually from 1732 to 1757. Franklin stopped writing for the almanac in 1748 when he retired, but the income from is printing business and bookstore, operated by others, allowed him to pursue other interests. The excerpt below contains a few of the hundreds of witting sayings published in *Poor Richard's Almanack.*

With the old Almanack and the old Year, Leave thy old Vices, tho' ever so dear.

Ill Customs & bad Advice are seldom forgotten.

He that riseth late, must trot all day, and shall scarce overtake his business at night.

He that speaks ill of the Mare, will buy her.

Excerpted from *Poor Richard's Almanack* (Mount Vernon: Peter Pauper Press) by Benjamin Franklin.

Fish and Visitors stink after three days.

How few there are who have courage enough to own their Faults, or resolution enough to mend them!

A country man between two lawyers, is like a Fish between two cats.

There's many men forget their proper station
And still are meddling with the administration
Of government; that's wrong and this is right,
And such a law is out of reason quite;
Thus, spending too much thought on state affairs,
The business is neglected, which is theirs.
So some fond traveller gazing at the stars,
Slips in next ditch, and get a dirty arse.

He that can compose himself, is wiser than he that composes books.

Poor Dick eats like a well man, and drinks like a sick.

After crosses and losses, men grow humbler and wiser.

The worst wheel of the cart makes the most noise.

Well done is better than well said.

There are three faithful friends—an old wife, an old dog, and ready money.

Many of Benjamin Franklin's aphorisms from Poor Richard's Almanack *are still widely used today.*

He that can travel well afoot, keeps a good horse.

Who has deceiv'd thee so oft as thy self?

A traveller should have a hog's nose, a deer's legs, and an ass's back.

No better relation than a prudent and faithful friend.

There are no ugly loves, nor handsome prisons.

At the working man's house hunger looks in, but dares not enter.

A good lawyer, a bad neighbour.

Certainly these things agree, the priest, the lawyer and death, all
    three;
Death takes both the weak and the strong,
The lawyer takes from both right and wrong,
And the priest from the living and dead has his fee.

The Discoveries of Vitus Bering

William R. Hunt

In the 1700s, Russia was expanding its boundaries, both west into Europe and east into the frozen regions of Siberia. Because of the intense cold, the snow, and short summer seasons, few European explorers had ever journeyed to the far eastern edge of the Russian continent. Only the natives of the area knew that the Russian landmass almost touches North America near the Seward Peninsula.

In 1725, shortly before his death, the fierce Russian czar Peter the Great employed Danish explorer Vitus Jonassen Bering (1681–1741) to explore and map the lands that lay east of Siberia and discover a sea route to China. The men of the expedition journeyed to the Siberian city of Kamchatka, where they built ships and gathered supplies.

From the very beginning, Bering's expedition was badly organized, short of funds, and tortured by fog, snow, ice, and extremely cold temperatures. In spite of these hardships, Bering discovered the strait that would have his name (the Bering Strait), mapped the Siberian coast, and explored the southwest coast of Alaska and the Aleutian Islands. Bering was killed when his ship wrecked on the island that now bears his name. Out of several hundred original members, only a few survivors of Bering's expeditions made it back to St. Petersburg to report on their discoveries.

William R. Hunt, a professor of history at the University of Alaska, has been a miner, teacher, and journalist.

Peter the Great, a fierce titan, and something of a genius, who had forced the Russians to look to the West and at modernity, determined that the geographic mysteries of his eastern realm had to be solved. According to legend, Peter had been embarrassed on his European travels when geographers queried him about the extent of northeastern Siberia. Some map makers indicated that Siberia and North America were connected, while others showed a severance. . . . Thus, in 1725 Peter appointed Vitus Bering, a Dane with a distinguished record in the Russian navy, as commander of the expedition. Just five weeks before the czar died, he issued instructions to Bering:

1. You are to construct at [the Siberian city of] Kamchatka one or two boats with decks.

2. You are to proceed in these along the coast which extends to the north and which seems, in all probability (since we do not know where it ends), to be part of America.

3. With this in view you are to try to find where it is joined to America, and to reach some city in European possession, and to inquire what it is called, and to make note of it, and to secure exact information and to mark this on a map and then to return home.

Mark this on a map and then return home! Simple instructions indeed, but the task to be accomplished was a prodigious one. Transport was the major problem. There were no roads in eastern Siberia, yet men, provisions, and equipment for this major venture had to be taken to Kamchatka, where the discovery ships were then to be constructed. Hundreds of men and animals were to wear themselves out accomplishing this awesome task, but Peter's visionary scheme had to be carried through. Never mind the cost and the years of effort: the work must be done. There could be practical benefits too. Peter was aware of all the British and Dutch voyages in quest of a Northern Passage from the Atlantic to the Pacific Oceans. Perhaps the Russians could be successful in finding the passage from the Pacific Ocean side. This would be a great triumph. Great glory and possibly the domination of an important trade route would be the results of such a discovery.

Arrival of a Deadly Winter

The initial party of the first Kamchatka expedition left St. Petersburg [the Russian capital] in late January 1725. Several minor officers and technicians were selected on the way to the Siberian coast, including a surgeon, a geodesist [mathematician who calculates curve and shape of the earth], a quartermaster, four carpenters and three mechanics to build ships and boats, a priest, navigator, shipmaster, and clerk, plus soldiers and sailors. The men traveled across the Central Siberian Plains, floated down the Ob, Ketya, Yenisei, Tunguska, and Ilim Rivers and wintered in Ilimsk, about halfway across the great Asian continent. They built fourteen boats and eighteen barges for cargo and equipment and, in the following month of May, after many hardships, arrived in Yakutsk.

From Yakutsk they traveled in three companies, each of the principal officers heading the detachments, and arrived in Okhotsk in October. An early winter caused the death of many of the 200 horses, and so much suffering existed among the men that a mutinous spirit developed. With winter approaching, it was vitally important to build storage houses and living quarters as quickly as possible. Men deserted when they were not paid and some refused to search for the late-arriving party under Martin Spanberg, one of Bering's lieutenants. This company of Spanberg had over 200 men and much of the essential equipment for the expedition. The early winter had come upon them so swiftly that their boats froze fast in one of the rivers. They had to construct one hundred sleds to pull the cargo on to the village of Okhotsk.

Sailing into the Unknown

Months of anxious effort and adversity passed. It was a constant struggle to maintain progress. But Bering and his officers kept the work going and the men in line. Finally on April 4, 1728, the keel of the new boat was laid—the ship was to be sixty feet long with a beam of twenty feet—and on June 8, it was christened the *St. Gabriel.* Sealing tar had to be manufactured and this caused a month's delay before the *St. Gabriel,* with its forty-four officers and crew, was ready to sail into the unknown. Bering's men had done their work well.

Once at sea, Bering was in a more familiar element. He voyaged north cautiously in the fog-bound waters, making a wary reach toward the top of the world, vigilant, prudent, plodding. Land was kept in sight almost the entire voyage, since the primary objective of the exploration was to ascertain if the continents were connected.

Bering stopped for fresh water at a bay he named Transfiguration. Twenty-two barrels of water were brought on board. Huts were seen but no people. The next morning eight Chukchi native men in a small boat approached the *St. Gabriel,* now out to sea. One of the natives was finally persuaded to go aboard. He told Bering through an interpreter "that there was an island in the sea on which live some of our people, but I know of no other islands or lands." Several days later the *St. Gabriel* came upon the large island which Bering named St. Lawrence. Huts were seen here, too, but again no people, at least none who allowed themselves to be seen.

Bering reached latitude sixty-five degrees, thirty minutes, passed the narrow strait named for him, and called his officers for a decision. The question was whether to proceed farther north or to return, satisfied that the *St. Gabriel* "had reached and passed the most easterly point of Chukchi land."

Spanberg, the second officer on this expedition, suggested that "after we have gone on the course we are on until the sixteenth of this month, and if by that time we are not able to reach sixty-six degrees, we should then in God's name, turn about and betimes seek shelter and harbor on the Kamchatka River whence we came, in order to save men and boat."

Lieutenant Alexsei Chirikov was more daring and suggested,

As we have no positive information as to the degree north latitude Europeans have ever reached in the Arctic Ocean on the Asiatic side, we cannot know with certainty whether America is really separated from Asia unless we touch at the mouth of the Koluima, or at least the ice, because it is well known that there is always drift ice in the Arctic Ocean. Therefore, it seems to me that according to your instructions we ought to sail without questioning—unless we are hindered by ice, or the coast turns to the west—But should the land continue still farther to the north, it would be necessary on the twenty-fifth of this month to look for winter quarters in this neighborhood.

Finding the American Coast

Bering listened to Spanberg. On the sixteenth of August the order was given to turn back. The *St. Gabriel* had reached . . . [a location] well beyond the point by which he could determine that Asia was not connected with America, if visibility had been clearer. On the following morning, Bering discovered and named the Diomede Islands and would then have been the first to see mainland America only a short distance away. But the weather was foggy. The day of this discovery would come four years later, in 1732, when assistant navigator I. Fedorov and geodesist M. Gvozdez took the *St. Gabriel* north and discovered the American coast opposite Cape Chukotsk. The Russians did not land, and thus did not gain full credit for determining that North America lay just across the Bering Strait from Siberia.

In 1729 Bering voyaged into the Bering Sea once more but made no notable discoveries. In July he set out across Siberia for St. Petersburg, arriving in the Russian capital on March 1, 1730. He gave Empress Catherine the following report:

On the fifteenth of August we came to latitude sixty-seven degrees, eighteen minutes, and I concluded that according to all indications the instruction of the emperor of glorious and immortal memory had been carried out. I based my conclusion on the fact that there was no more land to the north, nor did any land join the Chukchi or East Capes, and so I turned back. Had I gone farther and met with head winds it would have been impossible to return that summer; and to winter in these regions was out of the question, because there are no forests, and the people are not under Russian jurisdiction but do as they please.

Bering was criticized for not conducting his first expedition in a more scientific way. Some argued that he should have listened to Chirikov's advice instead of Spanberg's, because by the sixteenth of August he did not really demonstrate that the two continents were separated. He still had at least forty more days of ice-free navigation in those northern waters. He should have sailed onward until sighting ice before turning back. He was at fault for not venturing to the full limits of continued safe exploration. This criticism was not unreasonable; yet Bering's achievements were considerable when one bears in mind the difficulties involved. Launching a discovery ship in distant Siberia and opening the region to development were not mean accomplishments. Bering had then successfully navigated an unknown sea, passed into the Bering Strait, discovered the Diomedes and St. Lawrence Island, ascertained the southern tip of Kamchatka Peninsula, and charted portions of the Bering Sea for the first time.

Launching the Great Northern Expedition

In St. Petersburg Bering submitted several recommendations to the senate. He called for a voyage of investigation to America and for the opening of trade between the two continents. He thought that it would be advantageous for the empire to establish a sea route from Kamchatka to Japan and thereby open another trade route. He suggested, too, a charting of the northern regions of Siberia from the Ob to the Yenisei Rivers and from there to the Lena River. Bering's suggestions were enthusiastically received. Thanks to the growing prominence of the Academy of Science, Bering would carry scientists with him. The first scientific investigations of eastern Siberia and northwestern America would be the result of Bering's second expedition, officially known as the Great Northern Expedition.

The three-part exploratory program commissioned by the Russian Senate began in early 1733. Several unsatisfactory attempts under the command of various lieutenants were made to survey and map the Arctic coast of Siberia as the first part of the project. Spanberg, who was second in command under Bering on the first Kamchatka expedition, commanded the second part responsible for charting the Kurile Islands. Spanberg made three voyages to the Kuriles, in the course of which he surveyed these stepping-stone islands to the rich kingdom of Japan. During all this time, Bering, as commander-in-chief of the entire program of five hundred and forty-six men, received increasing criticism from the senate because his progress was considered slow. Bering offered many excuses but was castigated for alleged neglect. At one point, to prod him a bit, his supplementary pay was stopped.

Disasters Strike

Under clouds of distrust and the questioning of his competence, Bering set sail on the Okhotsk Sea in 1741 for his second expedition in search of land east of Kamchatka—the third part of the senate commission. Bering commanded the *St. Peter* while Chirikov captained the *St. Paul*. Two other smaller cargo ships collided and sank before they could reach the eastern side of the Kamchatka Peninsula. The cargoes were lost—the first ominous disaster of the voyage. Two years' supply of food and materials were reduced to five months' rations.

The second disaster was one of an ill decision. At Avacha Bay on the southeast side of Kamchatka, the officers plotted their course in relation to Joseph Delisle's map, specially drawn for Bering's expedition, ignoring the 1732 sighting of the American land mass on Bering Strait by Fedorov and Gvozdez. The fateful decision was made to steer, not due east from the peninsula, but southeast in search of Gama Land, a mythical land mass which many map makers had placed in the North Pacific. In sailing southeast in search of the mythical Gama Land, the ships moved well south of the Aleutian chain and the Alaskan Peninsula before they changed course for the northeast. Precious days of the short northern summer were wasted. . . .

On May 4, 1741, it was decided to sail southeast by east to latitude forty-six degrees north, unless land was found before. Both ships sailed over the waters where Gama Land was supposed to be, then altered their courses when it became obvious that they had been duped by fantastic [and inaccurate] cartography. Soon fog made it impossible for the two ships to remain in contact. Valuable time was wasted as the two captains groped for each other before each abandoned the effort and sailed alone to the east.

Chirikov was the first to see signs of land in the air and on the water. Seals, sea gulls, and driftwood appeared and on the 15th of July he sighted land in latitude fifty-five, approximately at the lower tip of the Alexander Archipelago, near the present panhandle or southeastern region of Alaska. Rain, fog, and rocky shores prevented Chirikov from sending out a successful landing party. Finally, two days after sighting the coast, the young mate, Abram Dementief, led ten armed sailors in a longboat into a bay in search of fresh water. They did not return that night. A search party was sent in great anxiety. The following morning when two boats approached the *St. Paul*, Chirikov ordered the crew to prepare to get underway. Only when the boats came closer did he realize the men were natives and that Dementief and the others had been seized and probably murdered.

He cruised about the area, reluctant to leave but knowing the choice was inevitable. No trace of the lost sailors was seen. A council of officers agreed that resources and weather conditions made it impossible to spend further time in search of the crew members and that the *St. Paul* should continue its voyage back to Kamchatka. The *St. Paul* sailed southwest through the foggy days of August. Land at the top of the Kenai Peninsula was sighted on the first day of the month, then left behind as the ship coursed southward down into the middle of the Gulf of Alaska to about the fifty-third parallel. After a month of Pacific squalls and foggy skies, Chirikov spotted Unalaska of the Fox Islands. Later, toward the middle of September, the fog made navigation difficult. After anchoring one night in the fog, Chirikov found the next morning that he was in a huge bay of a good-sized island, probably Atka Island far out in the Aleutians. The terrain was volcanic, mountainous, apparently uninhabitable. But while waiting for the right wind, the Russians were approached by seven natives in seven kayaks and given fresh water in seal bladders. But the natives would not go aboard ship. Chirikov described them as muscular men resembling the Tartars [Mongolian people] in features, wearing no beards, but sporting multicolored hats of thin boards and feathers of birds, some with bone carvings attached to their headdress.

Fog, Disease, and Death

Chirikov continued a zigzag course setting north and south to test the existence of land. The incessant fog prevented accurate position taking. The captain inferred that since he came to land when he sailed north, and only water when he turned south, that the land to the north must be the coastline of America. It was, in actuality, the chain of the Aleutian Islands.

The last land Chirikov saw of the new world was the island of Attu, the last segment of the Aleutian chain. During all this time the strength of the crew was fast diminishing. They could not repair the ragged sails that flapped above them. Constant exposure to harsh wind, rain, and snow tore the canvas to pieces. Excessive moisture, cold, thirst, and hunger depleted the physical resources of every man aboard.

But even more serious was the dreaded disease of scurvy which now ravaged the sailors. It weakened the capillaries with resultant hemorrhages into the tissues, caused the bleeding of gums, and loosened the teeth. Anemia and gradual general debility often followed.

On the 21st of September, Chirikov was restricted to his berth as a result of scurvy. One by one the men died. First a sailor, then a lieutenant, the ship's constable, a midshipman. Finally, the astronomer of the mission, Croyère, died on October 8, the very day the *St. Paul* reached Avacha Bay, Kamchatka. Of the nearly eighty men who were aboard the *St. Paul* when it left Avacha Bay five months earlier, twenty-one were lost. . . .

First Confrontations with the Natives

On September 4, while the *St. Peter* was attempting to continue its western course against a persistent wind, the Russians encountered their first Americans. Two natives in kayaks paddled toward the ship, shouting as they came. No one on board the *St. Peter* could understand what the natives were saying, but the Americans gestured toward the land, pointed to their mouths and scooped up sea water with their hands to indicate an offering of refreshment to the Russians. The Russians tied two Chinese tobacco pipes and some glass beads to a piece of board and launched it toward the closest kayak. In turn, one of the Aleuts tied a dead falcon to a stick and passed it to a Koriak aboard the *St. Peter.* Apparently the Aleut wanted the Russians to place other gifts between the bird's claws and return the falcon on the stick, but instead, the Koriak tried to pull the Aleut closer and, in alarm, the Americans released the stick.

A boat was lowered from the *St. Peter* for a shore party. Steller, Waxell, the Koriak interpreter, and several seamen rowed to the beach. A landing on the rocky shore was impossible; so three of the boat party undressed and waded ashore to be greeted by friendly Aleuts—natives of the Aleutian Islands—who presented a piece of whale blubber. One Aleut was bold enough to paddle out to the *St. Peter* and was given a cup of brandy which he downed, then hurriedly spat out. Brandy not being well received, the Russians offered their second most prized delicacy, a lighted pipe. This, too, was rejected.

On the beach the Aleuts were quite taken with the Koriak interpreter, presumably because his features resembled their own. As the Russians prepared to return to the *St. Peter* some of the Americans held on to the Koriak, and others tried to haul the boat ashore. This confrontation between Americans and Russians was a classic case of mutual distrust and misunderstanding and was resolved by the classic method—a show of superior force. Three of the boat crew fired their muskets over the heads of the Aleuts, who swiftly released Koriak and boat and threw themselves on the ground. The Russians dashed to the boat. The first test of strength was concluded. All the elements of the future subjection of the Americans by their eastern neighbors had passed in review. Tobacco and liquor had made their initial appearance. The first echoes of the firearms soon to enslave a free people resounded from the hills. Both peoples were disappointed and frustrated by the events: the Russians because "we had not been able to observe what we had intended but on the other hand had met what we had not expected"; the Aleuts because, apparently, their intentions had been misunderstood. The Russians laughed at the Aleuts' consternation as they picked themselves up "and waved their hands to us to be off quickly as they did not want us any longer." These laughs of derision and the futile waving of the Aleuts were significant characterizations of the respective assertions of the two peoples. History was to demonstrate that the Aleuts were no match for the aggressive Russians. Yet waving the Russians away would not banish them. This first contact was a prelude and a brief but prophetic introduction to the subsequent bloody incidents that were to occur in the conquest of the Bering Sea.

1751–1763

PREFACE

World events in the middle decades of the eighteenth century were dominated by the world war known as the Seven Years' War. The war began on August 29, 1756, when Prussian king Frederick II (the Great), fearing an attack from Austria, launched a surprise attack on the Austrian ally of Saxony. Other countries used this attack as an excuse to join one side or the other and to settle old scores that had been aggravated in the previous War of the Austrian Succession (1740–1748). The Russians marched into East Prussia, Austria occupied the Prussian capital of Berlin for several days, and Britain placed an army in northwestern Germany to prevent a French attack.

The great empires of England and France engaged in battles over central Europe, but their main financial interests were in the Great Lakes region and the Northwest Territories. France was widely known for its fashionable clothing styles. French fur trappers, with their Native American allies, had been trading North American beaver, fox, bobcat, and other furs for decades.

As the population of the English colonies expanded, and settlers started pushing west of the Appalachian Mountains; the French built a string of forts to protect their interests in the region. The Native American tribes trusted the French, who were mainly interested in the fur trade, and who generally respected native traditions. The English, on the other hand, wanted vast tracts of land to farm, land where Native Americans had been thriving for millennia. As England and France fought in Europe in the Seven Years' War, their armies also clashed in the French and Indian War in North America.

The war between France and England was also fought in India, where British trading companies sought to drive the French out of the territory of Pondicherry. When the Seven Years' War, fought on three continents, drew to a close, little had changed in Europe. England had expelled France from Canada and the Northwest Territories, however, ending a French presence in Canada and the Great Lakes region that had begun in 1667 when French explorer La Salle had first traveled in the region.

First Days of the Seven Years' War

Russell F. Weigley

Much like the War of the Spanish Succession (1701–1714) the Seven Years' War involved almost all of the countries of Europe. Fought between 1756 and 1763, the Seven Years' War pitted Britain and Prussia against France, Austria, Russia, Sweden, and Spain. The war raged in all regions governed by the European monarchs, including Canada and America, where it was known as the French and Indian War. Before it was over nearly 800,000 soldiers would die.

The war began in late August 1756 when hostilities increased between Prussia and Austria over control of the Silesia region in present-day Poland. Prussian king Frederick the Great, fearful of an Austrian or Russian invasion, ordered his army into Silesia, where he was met by an inferior fighting force of Austrians. The Prussians realized early successes on the battlefield and Frederick hoped the war would soon end. Instead, counterattacks by the Russians and Swedes left Prussia struggling for survival. Meanwhile, Britain sided with Prussia and France sided with Austria. Eventually the Russians tired of the war and Prussia was able to gain control of Silesia in 1763. When it was over France had lost Canada and India to the English. This excerpt describes the discipline and skill of Prussian soldiers as they fought in the first battles of the Seven Years' War.

Russell F. Weigley is a preeminent historian of American military history and professor of history at Temple University. He has written numerous books on military affairs.

Excerpted from *The Age of Battles,* by Russell F. Weigley. Copyright © 1991 by Russell F. Weigley. Reprinted with permission from Indiana University Press.

Historians of warfare have often presented the period from about the third to the ninth decades of the eighteenth century as an era of limited war, limited in aims and means alike and gentlemanly in conduct. It is true that after the wars of religion ended [in the previous century], Europe was able to draw back from the precipice at the bottom of which lay barbarism. The warring states for the most part offered renewed obeisance to the historical limitations of the international war convention upon the violence of war, particularly the principle of noncombatant immunity. Similarly, the subsiding of [French king] Louis XIV's and [Swedish king] Charles XII's grandiose ambitions early in the eighteenth century permitted a yet further withdrawal from unrestrained violence. . . .

But the histories of the eighteenth century's limited wars were not written by the peasants who dwelt along the paths of marauding armies; if they had been, the prevalent impression about the extent of noncombatant immunity in the mid–eighteenth century might be less complacent. Nor was war much limited in frequency; the European states and particularly the great powers remained about as frequently at war as when the state system had been agitated by the designs of the French and Swedish monarchs. Perhaps most important, the checking of certain French and Swedish ambitions did not herald a universal reining-in of the aims of war—and the limitations of aims is almost certainly the critical element in making possible the limitation of means. Instead, the continuing rise of Prussia to military and diplomatic power disproportionate to its population and resources provoked an effort by the rival states of France, Austria, and Russia to eliminate it from the ranks of the great powers—no very limited aim. The most important war of the mid-century, the Seven Years War aimed at the humbling of Prussia, was therefore by no means a paradigm of limited conflict.

For all that, the eighteenth century from the Peace of Utrecht [which ended the War of Spanish Succession in 1714] to the outbreak of the wars of the French Revolution [in 1789] nevertheless constituted an era of limited war by comparison with almost any other era. Apart from dealing with upstart Prussia, the objectives for which the European states waged war were severely confined to limited territorial acquisitions. . . .

Machinelike Precision

The impression is vivid among us that eighteenth-century war resembled a prolonged parade. This impression is not the least of the reasons why we readily grow nostalgic when we contrast the comparatively civilized warfare of the eighteenth century with the barbarities of our own time. Battles were tournaments between serried ranks of colorfully uniformed toy soldiers come to life, advancing toward each other to the beating of the drums. Once the opposing armies began firing, their casualties indeed became severe, because they fired against close-ordered lines at short range. But while we must compel ourselves to remember that the battlefield was a more dangerous place then than now (short of tactical nuclear war), the notion of battlefields as paradegrounds is not altogether deceptive. That international quarrels were resolved in such arenas confirms as well as symbolizes the considerable degree of truthfulness in conventional descriptions of an age of limited war.

The same sort of confirmation and symbolism are implicit in the fact that it was Frederick (Friedrich) the Great of Prussia who became the foremost soldier of the age. This was largely on the strength of the superior training of his army, which enabled it to execute the linear battle tactics of the day with machinelike precision, and also because of a relatively slight modification Frederick introduced into paradeground-style battle tactics, the oblique order of battle, which took form gradually and continued to evolve during his reign.

To an even greater extent the various facets of Prussian military excellence inherited by Frederick appear at first glance to have been simply matters of detail, but they were critical matters nevertheless at a time when no European army possessed a superior weapons system over its enemies. The Prussian Army unlike most European armies before 1740 had a system of drill that was uniform throughout the army. This system, continually practiced, devoted much attention to marching in step even under combat conditions, to retain a coherent line while advancing against the enemy. In most armies, the theory of marching in well-dressed lines during the attack broke down in practice; it would sometimes do so in Frederick's army also, but to a considerably lesser extent.

The Prussians intensively rehearsed loading and firing until a Prussian infantry battalion could get off five rounds per minute, which in most other armies was an achievement only of elite units or of occasional individual soldiers. Under battle procedures, firing in unified volleys—each Prussian battalion had eight platoons each of which was a firing unit—also tended to break down in practice, but again practice diverged from theory a good deal less in the Prussian Army than elsewhere. To maintain a high rate of fire, the Prussians adopted an iron ramrod; the traditional wooden ones frequently broke during reloading.

The Prussians had also modified their march formations so that the files forming columns of march could more readily transform themselves into lines of battle, thus hastening the cumbersome task of deployment on which the outcome of a battle might well depend.

Frederick Becomes King

Frederick William I bequeathed to his son Frederick II in 1740 an army that he had increased from 40,000 to 83,000 men, the fourth largest in Europe. The old King had distrusted his heir as too Frenchified, even effete, in manners and habits, and young Frederick in fact had sought in 1730, when he was eighteen, to run away from his austerely military father and to look for refuge at the English court; foiled, he had been imprisoned for his pains. By the late 1730s the Prince began to show a measure of soldierly interests and promise, but his friends remained too intellectual and otherwise too diverse for his father ever to feel comfortable about his prospects. Yet he was to prove in significant ways more tough-minded than Frederick William I. The father was almost sentimentally loyal to the [Holy Roman] Empire, so that he sent a contingent of troops to fight in the Rhineland for the Empire against France in 1734 although he would risk his precious army in active campaigning almost nowhere else; the son was dedicated to no loyalties except to his own royal house and his Prussian state. The father preferred to use the army as a makeweight in diplomacy; the son believed that for the army to be worth its cost, it must fight.

On becoming King, the son promptly eliminated the one ornamental extravagance that his frugal father had permitted himself; he did away with Frederick William's Guard of Giants, a corps of some 3,000 extraordinarily tall men. Almost as promptly, the son also displayed the most important difference between his and his father's conceptions of statecraft.

Prussia was still a collection of scattered, disparate territories exceedingly difficult to defend. If the kingdom could not be consolidated geographically, Frederick II believed, then its diligently cultivated new weight in the international scales could hardly be expected to endure. And an opportunity to begin the geographic consolidation of Prussia presented itself at the very time when Frederick became King.

Causes of the Seven Years War

The Habsburg Emperor Charles (Karl) VI had labored for a number of years to avert the prospect of a War of the Austrian Succession on the model of the War of the Spanish Succession. The danger arose because he had no direct male heir. He cajoled and bribed the monarchs of Europe, including Frederick William I of Prussia, to accept a Pragmatic Sanction guaranteeing the inheritance of the Habsburg lands intact by his daughter Maria Theresa as Archduchess (Erzherzogin) of Austria and Queen (Königin) of Hungary and Bohemia, with her husband, Francis of Lorraine, Grand Duke of Tuscany, to become Emperor. Maria Theresa would then be Empress (Kaiserin) in terms of practical power. Frederick II of Prussia, however, cast covetous eyes toward the rich Austrian province of Silesia, whose prosperity probably exceeded that of any single part of his domains and whose acquisition would help round out his kingdom into a more defensible entity. The Elector Joachim II of Brandenburg had arranged a treaty in 1537 whereby three Silesian duchies—Liegnitz, Brieg, and Wohland—were to be united with Brandenburg upon the death of the last of the then-current dynasty in the duchies, the Piasts. This line had actually died out in 1675, but the Habsburgs had then taken possession of the duchies. Frederick discerned in these circumstances a sufficient pretext to grasp all of Silesia.

Frederick negotiated with both France and Great Britain, seeking the support of either by offering Prussian military aid [to Britain]. . . . Charles VI died on October 9, 1740, while the negotiations were still in process, and Frederick decided he could not wait for them to be concluded. The Russian Tsarina Anna had also just died, so Russia would be unlikely to intervene in any action he might take. Two days after the Emperor's death, Frederick informed his principal military commanders of his determination to invade Silesia. He hastened preparations in secret, but the justification he was ready to offer once his armies struck was that the Pragmatic Sanction could apply only to lands rightfully belonging to the house of Habsburg, and that in any event the Habsburgs had failed to carry out various undertakings to his father that had accompanied Prussia's accession to the Pragmatic Sanction. Frederick was also willing to profess a concern for the liberties of the Silesians, on the ground that the Austrians were not strong enough to protect them—as indeed they were not.

The First Battles

Without a declaration of war, Frederick sent his army across the Silesian frontier on December 5, 1740. The Prussian standing army was virtually at war strength; the Austrians, in contrast, had to call up reserves. Consequently the Austrian commanders believed they could do no more in Silesia than hold garrisons in a few fortresses, while the bulk of their troops fell back to the Sudeten Mountains along the borders of Bohemia. The retreat of the Silesian forces was ably conducted, however, by *Feldmarschall* Leutnant [Fieldmarshal Lieutenant] Maximilian Ulysses Reichsgraf (Imperial Count) von Browne, the scion of a transplanted Irish family that had fled the Protestant ascendancy. Browne's resourcefulness provided time for the Austrians to mobilize their armies promptly enough to limit their losses to what Frederick's audacity had made inevitable. Under the circumstances, nothing could have prevented the Prussians from soon going into winter quarters with the fortresses of Glogau, Brieg, and Neisse invested, and Silesia otherwise overrun. Glogau fell on February 28. Only by that time did the Austrians have an army in the field sufficient to challenge Frederick.

Displaying like Browne no little operational skill, the principal Austrian commander, *Feldmarschall* Adam Albert Reichsgraf Neipperg, contrived to overcome snow-covered ground as well as the larger adversities engendered by tardy preparation to relieve Neisse and . . . to put his troops astride the Prussians' line of communications. This maneuvering compelled Frederick to give battle to Neipperg at Mollwitz on March 30/April 10. While Frederick had eschewed his father's custom of using his army mainly as a showpiece, he differed from most commanders of this age of battles in professing to regard a battle as a desperate resort, claiming to believe the jeopardy into which combat losses were bound to throw the fragile Prussian edifice of army and state to be only rarely tolerable. So by forcing battle upon him, the Austrians under Browne and Neipperg had achieved a considerable recovery.

In its beginning, furthermore, Frederick's first battle seemed about to confirm the opinion of those who still held the Prussian Army in low esteem because it had garnered so little combat experience during the past generation. Frederick and his father were both essentially infantry commanders. Neither had bestowed on the cavalry anything approaching the tactical thought and training they gave the infantry, yet it proved to be the cavalry on the Prussian right that had to bear the first major shock of action, because against it the Austrians struck first. They routed it, and *Feldmarschall* Karl Graf von Schwerin persuaded the King that he must flee the scene.

Schwerin, left in command with the Prussian infantry apparently about to break next, responded by grasping the colors of the First Battalion of the *Garde* and under that standard rallying the foot-soldiers and leading them in a counterattack. So thoroughly had they been drilled that they indeed advanced almost as if on parade. Prussian discipline prevailed. Infantry volleys mowed down the repeated efforts of the Austrian horse to duplicate their initial triumph, and eventually the Austrian army gave way as well. Neipperg withdrew to Neisse, leaving Schwerin in possession of the field and with Prussian communications restored. Mollwitz was the first demonstration of what the Prussian Army could achieve through a simple superiority in the conditioning of its troops in cohesion and in precise maneuver.

Prussian Victory

The Prussian victory revitalized Frederick's efforts to find an ally. King Louis XV of France sent Charles Louis Auguste Fouquet, comte de Belle-Isle, *maréchal de France,* to negotiate with Frederick as part of a French scheme to win the election of the Elector Charles Albert (Karl Albert) of Bavaria as Holy Roman Emperor and further to reorganize the Empire in ways beneficial to France. The Prussian King and Belle-Isle came to terms, whereupon the Silesian War was transformed into the more general War of the Austrian Succession. The French, however, refrained from open belligerency except by joining in Spain's colonial war against Great Britain. On the

Continent, the French fought through proxies, with French officers wearing Bavarian cockades [ribbons worn as badges].

Although Mollwitz thus led to a French alliance, it had also freed Frederick from any urgent need for allies. He cared for nothing but Prussia's security, and for the present he desired only to assure his hold upon Silesia. Therefore he was willing to conclude with Neipperg on September 28, 1741, the agreement of Klein Schnellendorf, whereby Neisse surrendered after the performance of the rituals but without the substance of a further siege at that place, and the Austrians agreed to leave Frederick unmolested in return for his freeing Neipperg's army to face the Empire's other opponents, mainly the Bavarians, the Spanish, and the Neapolitans.

Unfortunately for Frederick, the Austrians succeeded so well against these foes that Maria Theresa decided to divulge the terms of Klein Schnellendorf in order to drive a wedge between her other enemies and Prussia. The war thereupon resumed in full vigor. But Frederick had put the interval to good military use by reorganizing and strengthening his cavalry. His heavy cavalry, the cuirassiers, had been retrained to use lighter horses so that their tactics could become swifter and more flexible; while the light cavalry, hussars with sabers and dragoons trained to fight with either blade or firearms, were expanded in numbers.

Against the musketry and bayonets of well-drilled eighteenth-century infantry, cavalry lacked the power it had displayed in Gustavus Adolphus's day. But for the cavalry flank guards to be so vulnerable to attacking infantry as Frederick's had proven at Mollwitz was of course a recipe for disaster, and on the attack the mobility and the shock effect of cavalry might still be put to good effect under appropriate circumstances. Frederick may have been slow to recognize the necessity to combine a strong mobile arm with his excellent infantry to secure decisive tactical results (though by emphasizing hard marching, he showed from the outset an appreciation of the value of mobility in the infantry). Driven by Mollwitz to acknowledge the need for a strong mounted arm if only for flank defense, he would soon display a growing perception of the offensive values of mobility and shock.

At the battle of Chotusitz or Czaslau on May 6, 1742, Frederick's mounted troops contributed as impressively as the infantry to a Prussian victory. They achieved a feat much praised in military textbooks but rare in fact, a vigorous pursuit. Partly for that reason, the success was decisive enough that on May 31/June 11 Austria and Prussia concluded the separate Peace of Breslau, Maria Theresa ceding Silesia to Frederick. . . .

Enlightened Warfare

Although the wars of Frederick the Great had grown for a time grandiose rather than limited in aim, with the intent of at least some of Frederick's enemies to destroy Prussia as a great power, the means of waging war had remained more restrained and more in harmony with the conception of the just war than they had been through much of the era of Louis XIV [1643–1715]. The contest between Frederick and those who sought the downfall of Prussia remained a contest whose principal means consisted of careerist armies, with little resort to other instruments and little violation of the critical limiting principle of noncombatant immunity by the contending armies.

That culture of the French Age of the Enlightenment . . . saw the universe as a structure of balance and harmony, wherein rational humankind ought to bring its institutions into consistency with the rational functionings of a world governed by natural law. The . . . armies of the middle eighteenth century and their method of warfare attained a remarkable congruence with the other institutions and values of an age trying to guide itself by the light of reason. If disputes between states became sufficiently intractable that they had to be submitted to the arbitrament of war, still the arbitration did not entail any all-consuming destructiveness; it was conducted rather by men who had more or less volunteered (less rather than more among the rank-and-file soldiers) to take upon themselves the risks of arbitration by violence. And these risk-takers confined their violent attentions mainly to each other. In the Age of Reason, the irrationalities of war were at least strenuously and strictly confined.

More specifically, this Age of Reason saw little resort to economic warfare, to blockades and restraint of trade. European business went on remarkably little affected by the military rivalries. Restraint of cultural interchange was even more minimal; Frederick's court remained a center of admiration for and patronage of French Enlightenment thought throughout, with French continuing as the language of the court. The opposing armies maintained rules against unnecessary endangerment of noncombatant lives and property, especially against plundering civilians, and they sought with fair success to enforce the rules. The limitations of supply using wagons over primitive roads from depots laboriously constructed in the rear necessitated frequent subsisting of armies from the foodstuffs of the territories through which they campaigned, or at least supplementing depot supply in that manner, but vigorous efforts were made to feed men and animals through orderly purchases and not by plunder. . . . Europeans of the eighteenth century were expected to wage war with moderation and within civilized limits.

The French and Indian War

Samuel Eliot Morison

In the early eighteenth century the two great empires of Europe—France and England—were locked in constant battles over who would control Europe and who would exploit their vast holdings in the New World. The French occupied Canada and forts along the Great Lakes while England ruled the colonies along the Atlantic coast to Florida. The area west of the Appalachian Mountains, already occupied by tens of thousands of Native Americans, was open to competition and war between the European powers.

By the 1750s, the population of the English colonies was expanding rapidly. At the same time, the French were building a series of forts in the western Pennsylvania wilderness and making deals with the Native Americans to side with them against the English. Although hostilities began in 1754, the French and Indian War did not officially commence until 1756. In the following excerpt Samuel Eliot Morison, author and expert on American history, details the importance of the French and Indian War.

The vital stake in all [European] wars and diplomatic maneuverings since 1700 was the American West. Who was to rule the West—England, France, or Spain? Or, as nobody could then foresee, an American republic? Yet, until well after mid-century, the West was the last thing that politicians, whether English, French, or American, thought about. From the European point of view the principal objectives were the sugar islands in the Caribbean; that is why the

Excerpted from *The Oxford History of the American People,* by Samuel Eliot Morison. Copyright © 1965 by Samuel Eliot Morison. Reprinted with permission from Oxford University Press.

major naval efforts of England and France were applied in that region. New England and New York were chiefly interested in the destruction of French power on their northern and eastern boundaries. For South Carolina and Georgia, the Spaniard in Florida and his Indian allies were the greater menace. But it was in the West that a new war began, even before the previous war ended.

In 1747 Thomas Lee, president of the Virginia Council, organized the Ohio Company, with the object of acquiring half a million acres on each side of the Ohio river. Other prominent Virginians, such as Thomas Jefferson's father, organized additional land companies and employed veteran Indian traders to push trade with the Indians in the Ohio country and to extinguish their prior claims to the land. This was a threat to French communications between Montreal and New Orleans that could not be ignored. In 1749 the governor of Canada sent a fleet of batteaux [boats] and canoes, commanded by Celeron de Bienville, to take possession of the Ohio valley.

A cold war for winning the West was on, and gradually it warmed up. In 1753 [Canadian] Governor [Ange] Duquesne built a chain of log-walled forts on the Allegheny and the upper Ohio to defend French claims. Virginia could not ignore this challenge. The French pretention to reserve the entire West north of the Ohio ran counter to her charter boundaries, and to the claims of the new land companies. [Virginia] Governor Robert Dinwiddie sent young George Washington to the forks of the Ohio to protest. Protest being unavailing, Dinwiddie commissioned George (aged twenty-two) lieutenant colonel of Virginia militia and in 1754 sent him with 150 men to forestall the French. But the Canadians got there first, built Fort Duquesne on the site of Pittsburgh, and at Great Meadows in western Pennsylvania confronted the Virginia militia. Washington fired first, but lost the fight and had to surrender. This being nominally a time of peace, the prisoners were released and a somewhat crestfallen George was allowed to go home.

That shot in the Western wilderness sparked off a series of world-shaking events which reached their culmination thirty years later [in the American Revolution]. In 1783 Major General George Washington, Commander in Chief of the United States Army, resigned his commission after winning independence for a republic not even dreamed of in 1753.

Virginia and New England were ready for hot war in 1754, but England and France were not. The Duke of Newcastle, the prime minister [of England], fancied that he could maintain England's western claims by a local war. In the fall of 1754 he sent [Major] General [Edward] Braddock to America with parts of two regiments to do the job.

In the meantime eight of the thirteen colonies had made an attempt to agree on a plan of union for common defense. The Board of Trade instructed the royal governors to meet representatives of the Six Nations [of Iroquois] at Albany and take measures "to secure their wavering friendship"; the Iroquois, impressed by the Great Meadows affair, were wondering which side to take. Leading Americans, however, wished the congress to undertake a more ambitious task. Before it met, Governor Shirley thus addressed the assembly of Massachusetts: "For forming this general union, gentlemen, there is no time to be lost: the French seem to have advanced further toward making themselves masters of this Continent within the past five or six years than they have done ever since the first beginning of that settlement."

The Albany Congress, meeting in June 1754, spent most of its time debating that question. The Plan of Union that it adopted was the work of Benjamin Franklin and Thomas Hutchinson. There was to be a president general appointed by the crown, and a "grand council" appointed by the colonial assemblies, in proportion to their contributions to the common war chest—a typical bit of Ben Franklin foxiness, to ensure that taxes would really be paid. The president, with the advice of the grand council, would have sole power to negotiate treaties, declare war, and make peace with the Indians; to regulate the Indian trade, to have sole jurisdiction over land purchases outside particular colonies, and to make grants of land to settlers and govern the Western territory until the crown formed it into new colonial governments. The Union would have power to build forts, raise armies and equip fleets, and levy taxes for the same, to be paid into a general treasury with branches in each colony.

This plan showed far-sighted statesmanship, but looked too far ahead, recommending a closer federal union than the thirteen colonies were willing to conclude during the War of Independence. Whether the British government would have consented is doubtful; but they never had a chance to express their views. Not one colonial assembly ratified the Plan. Every one refused to give up any part of its exclusive taxing power, even to a representative body. So the war which then began was carried through under the old system. No British commander had authority to raise troops or money from a colony without the consent of its assembly. The assemblies of provinces that were not directly menaced, and some of those that were, like Pennsylvania, refused to make any substantial contribution to the common cause. Even Virginia would not allow draftees to serve outside her borders until 1758.

A Bad Thrashing

English and Americans always seem to begin a war that they eventually win, with a bad thrashing. This time it was Braddock's defeat on the Monongahela, a bloody battle in that part of the Western wilderness which is now a suburb of Pittsburgh. The English ministry's strategic plan was sound: to capture four forts which the French had built on debatable territory and secure them before the hot war started. These forts, from east to west, were Beauséjour at the head of the Bay of Fundy, Crown Point on Lake Champlain, Fort Niagara at the falls, and Fort Duquesne. This last, the key to the West, was the objective of . . . Braddock, forty-five of whose sixty years had been spent in the British army in Europe. He was given two of the worst regiments in that army, at half strength, which he was expected to fill with American recruits to a total of 700 officers and men each. The colonies were expected to provide additional troops, food, wagons, and Indian auxiliaries for a march from Alexandria, Virginia, across the Blue Ridge [mountains] and the Alleghenies, and through a yet unbroken wilderness, to take Fort Duquesne.

Governors Dinwiddie of Virginia, [Horatio] Sharpe of Maryland, and Shirley of Massachusetts, enthusiasts for expelling the French from North America, met Braddock at Alexandria to make plans. Young George Washington became one of the General's aides-de-camp. So many things in this campaign went wrong that it is impossible to pin the blame on any one person; but Braddock made the most mistakes. Although a brave and energetic soldier, he knew nothing of wilderness marches or battles, and refused to learn from the Virginians. Instead of depending on pack animals for supply, he insisted on a great wagon train; and the only colony which provided its quota of wagons was Pennsylvania. Ben Franklin's diplomacy was responsible. He dropped the hint that if the farmers did not hire out their teams voluntarily, British "hussars" would come and take them; hussars were the storm troopers of that era. He procured some 150 Conestoga wagons, which Braddock said was "almost the only instance of ability and honesty" that he had "known in these provinces."

It took Braddock's army 32 days to cover the 110 miles from Fort Cumberland to Fort Duquesne through a trackless hardwood forest. A pioneer battalion of 300 axemen had to cut a crude road. By 7 July [1754] the van [forefront] was only 10 or 12 miles from its destination. Braddock formed a "flying column" of his best troops, including both regulars and provincials, and pressed on ahead. To avoid a narrow defile [single-file march], he twice forded the Monongahela river. George Washington, late in life, said that it was the most beautiful spectacle he had ever seen. Scarlet-coated regulars and blue-coated Virginians in columns of four, mounted officers and light cavalry; horse-drawn artillery and wagons, and dozens of packhorses, splashed through the rippling shallows under a brilliant summer sun into the green-clothed forest. Spirits were high and victory seemed certain; if the French did not attack at the fords, they surely never would. Rush the fort, and hurrah for old England!

But hark! What is that firing ahead, just as the last of the rear guard crosses the river?

It was a sortie from Fort Duquesne in head-on collision with Braddock's van, an engagement that neither side planned or wanted. The small French garrison at the fort had been strengthened by almost 1000 Indian warriors, who had flocked in from every part of the Old West. With the choosiness common to Indians they had refused to move the day before to ambush Braddock at the ford; but now, when the British column was safely across, they consented to go. No fewer than 637 braves, with about 150 French Canadian militia, led by 72 French officers and regulars, sortied in the early afternoon of 9 July.

Braddock had flankers [men who protected the main column of soldiers] out; he was not ambushed, only surprised. The head of his column saw a young French officer stop, turn, and wave his hat; immediately the English heard the Indians' war whoop, as the [Indians] deployed to right and left, took cover in the ravines that paralleled the road, and poured hot lead [gunshot] into the close ranks of scarlet and blue coats—the best targets they had ever encountered. The British troops could not see their deadly foes, but they could hear them plenty; and, never having fought Indians, were unnerved by the horrible war whoops. General Braddock, losing one horse after another, rushed about trying to rally his men; it was no use. His senior colonel and many other officers were killed, and he himself was shot in the lungs. Toward sundown, after the largely unseen Indians had mowed down scores of the huddled and almost leaderless redcoats, panic set in. The soldiers "broke and ran as sheep pursued by dogs" (so Washington recorded), abandoning wagons, artillery, and even muskets. Fortunately, the Indians were too busy scalping, looting, and torturing prisoners to pursue, or the entire flying column would have been massacred; as it was, of the 1459 officers and men engaged, 977 were killed or wounded.

Braddock died of his wounds after turning over the command to Colonel [Thomas] Dunbar, who made bad matters worse by abandoning Fort Cumberland and going into winter quarters at Philadelphia when the summer was but half over, leaving the Pennsylvania-Maryland-Virginia frontier completely defenseless.

An 18th-Century World War

Braddock's defeat was [a disaster]. It brought over all Indians of the Northwest to the French side, caused the Six Nations to waver in their allegiance, threw back the effective English frontier hundreds of miles, and exposed new settlements to a series of devastating In-

dian attacks. Thousands of men, women, and children who had settled the Shenandoah valley in the last forty years lost all they had,
and were lucky to escape with their lives.

British operations of 1755 were inept though not disastrous. Governor Shirley failed to take Fort Niagara. General William Johnson
"of the Mohawks," an able Irishman who acted as liaison between
the English and the Iroquois, defeated the French at Lake George on
8 September and was made a baronet [English title below Baron];
but he was unable to capture Crown Point on Lake Champlain, and
the French built Fort Ticonderoga south of it. Fort Beauséjour at the
head of the Bay of Fundy surrendered to Colonel John Winslow of
Massachusetts after two shells from the escorting British fleet had
blown up an ammunition dump, and this secured the eastern flank.

In 1756 this "Old French and Indian War," as the Americans
called it, merged into the Seven Years' War in Europe, where it was
France, Austria, Sweden, and a few small German states against
Britain and Prussia. England supported Prussia with money and engaged in naval warfare against France (and later Spain) in the Atlantic, the Mediterranean, the Caribbean, and the Indian Ocean.
There was warfare on the continent of India between French . . . and
English . . . and their respective native allies; hostilities even reached
the Philippines, where an English fleet captured Manila. This should
really have been called the First World War; hostilities were waged
over as large a portion of the globe as in [World War I] 1914–18.

The next two years were disastrous for England. The Earl of
Loudoun, who succeeded Shirley as British commander in chief in
America, was well described by his predecessor as "a pen and ink
man whose greatest energies were put forth in getting ready to begin." Virginian militia under Colonel Washington with great difficulty held the Shenandoah valley against the Indians. Canada, rein-
forced by 3000 French regulars, took the offensive and the Marquis
de Montcalm captured Fort Oswego on Lake Ontario and Fort
William Henry on Lake George. In India, [the British] lost Calcutta.
On the continent of Europe, England's ally Frederick the Great was
defeated by the French and Austrians; and the British commander in
chief, the Duke of Cumberland, surrendered an army to the French.

How things looked to a colonial philosopher, the Reverend Jonathan
Edwards, may be seen in a letter that he wrote in the fall of 1756 to a
friend who was chaplain to a Massachusetts regiment on Lake George:

> God indeed is remarkably frowning upon us every where; our enemies
> get up above us very high, and we are brought down very low: They are
> the Head, and we are the Tail. God is making us, with all our superior-
> ity in numbers, to become the Object of our Enemies almost continual
> Triumphs and Insults. . . . And in Europe things don't go much better,
> . . . Minorca was surrendered to the French on the 29 Day of last June

[1755]; . . . This with the taking of Oswego . . . will tend mightily to animate and encourage the French Nation . . . and weaken and dishearten the English, and make 'em contemptible in the Eyes of the Nations of Europe. . . . What will become of us God only knows.

Change of Fortunes

Yet the entire aspect of the war changed in 1758 after William Pitt became secretary of state and prime minister. [Pitt] had a flair for grand strategy and a genius for choosing able men. While most Englishmen regarded the American war as secondary, Pitt saw that the principal object for England should be the conquest of Canada and the American West, thus carving out a new field for Anglo-American expansion. His strategy was simple and direct. He would send no more English troops to the continent of Europe, but subsidized Frederick to fight the French there. To the British navy he gave a triple task: to contain the French fleet in its home bases, escort convoys over the transatlantic route, and cooperate with the army in amphibious operations. And he concentrated the military might of Britain and her colonies in the American theater, under young and energetic commanders. The naval part was crucial. Canada, with a population under 60,000, could not hold out against the English colonies with a population of one million, unless the French could get reinforcements across the Atlantic.

At the Battle of Dettingen, 1743, four young English officers— Jeffrey Amherst, George Townshend, Robert Moncton, and James Wolfe had received their baptism of fire. Now the eldest was only forty-one years old and the youngest, Wolfe, was thirty-one. He was a lanky, narrow-shouldered young man with vivid red hair, the most earnest student of the art of war in the British army. In ambition, genius, and audacity, and in his fierce concentration on making himself master of his profession, Wolfe was the most Napoleonic soldier in English history. "An offensive, daring kind of war," he wrote, "will awe the Indians and ruin the French. Block-houses and a trembling defensive encourage the meanest scoundrels to attack us."

Such was his advice to Jeffrey Amherst, whom Pitt selected as commander in chief in America. Stolid and unemotional, Amherst had the right character to neutralize the impetuosity of Wolfe, his No. 1 brigadier general. These two, making a perfect team with Admiral Boscawen, in July 1758 recaptured Louisbourg, far better fortified than in 1745 and more skillfully defended. The same year, Colonel John Bradstreet, with a force of New Englanders, captured Fort Frontenac, where the St. Lawrence flows out of Lake Ontario; and Brigadier John Forbes, with George Washington on his staff, marched across Pennsylvania and captured Fort Duquesne, renaming it Pittsburgh after the great war minister.

Then came 1759, England's "wonderful year," so charged with British glory that it was said the very bells of London were worn thin pealing for victories, and British throats went hoarse bawling out [the patriotic song] "Heart of Oak." Guadeloupe in the West Indies fell to a well-conducted amphibious operation. The French power in India was destroyed, and the French fleet intended to reinforce Canada was smashed . . . at Quiberon Bay. Sir William Johnson and his Iroquois braves helped the British to capture Fort Niagara, key to the Great Lakes. And the campaign of Quebec surpassed all.

British Take Quebec

The British army under Wolfe was transported by a fleet of over 200 sail, commanded by Vice Admiral Charles Saunders. Entering the St. Lawrence on 6 June, Saunders appointed Captain James Cook (of later Pacific fame) to sail ahead. . . . [Cook] then performed the amazing feat of sailing his entire fleet up to Quebec in three weeks, without a single grounding or other casualty.

General Amherst, marching overland from New York, was supposed to cooperate. He recaptured Crown Point and Ticonderoga but was too slow and methodical to get within striking distance of Quebec. . . . But Wolfe was not discouraged. His total force, exclusive of sailors and marines, amounted to only 4000 officers and men, but included some of the crack units of the British army. Owing to Amherst's delay, the Marquis de Montcalm was able to concentrate some 14,000 French troops and militia in and around Quebec. His position appeared to be impregnable. The guns of the citadel commanded the river, and the land approach from the east was barred by two smaller rivers.

Admiral Saunders first landed a force on 27 June on the Île d'Orléans, four miles below Quebec. Montcalm's army was deployed along the north shore of the river, between the St. Charles and the Montmorency, with a detachment under [Admiral L.A. de] Bougainville west of the city; but he neglected to secure the south bank. . . .

At sunset 12 September, Saunders put on a simulated landing at the Montmorency front, which pulled a large part of Montcalm's force off base. Late that evening, 1700 English embarked in boats from the transports up-river, and at 2:00 A.M. on the 13th, with a fresh breeze astern and an ebb tide under their keels, they began floating downstream, unobserved by Bougainville. . . .

The boats reached the bottom of the defile. Twenty-four rugged volunteers climbed up the cliff, put the French picket guard to the sword, gave the prearranged signal, and the troops jumped ashore and swarmed up the steep path, muskets slung on their backs. As fast as the boats emptied they returned to the ships or to the south shore for reinforcements. Thus, by break of day, 13 September 1759, some

4500 British were deployed on the Plains of Abraham, a grassy field forming part of the Quebec plateau, close to the walls of the citadel.

Wolfe's object was to challenge Montcalm to an open-field battle, the only kind he knew how to fight; and the French accepted. Presently white-uniformed veterans of famous regiments—La Sarre, Guyenne, Languedoc, Royal-Roussillon, Béarn—were coming on the double from the Montmorency front, rushing through the narrow streets of Quebec and deploying on the other side to face the English. At 10:00 A.M. some 4000 of them, who had formed outside the walls, advanced to the attack, flying regimental colors and cheering "Vive le Roi [Long Live the King]! " For fifteen or twenty minutes they marched, and not a shot rang out; Wolfe had learned the value of precise, accurate, and concentrated fire power. Three-quarters of his 4500 troops were deployed in one line, which waited silently until the enemy was only 40 yards away. Then the command "Fire!" rang out and the muskets crashed in a rolling roar. A second volley followed and no more were needed; the ground was already covered with French dead and wounded. Then the English soldiers charged the dazed survivors with fixed bayonets, and kilted [Scottish] Highlanders, shouting wildly, attacked with claymores [double-edged swords] and broadswords, completing the rout of the French. Wolfe, personally leading a picked force of grenadiers, was shot down, and only had time to order the enemy's retreat to be cut off before dying on the field of glory. Montcalm, mortally wounded in the retreat, died next day. Each side suffered about equal losses, 640 killed and wounded. Quebec promptly surrendered to the British. Never did so short and sharp a fight have so important a result.

Soon Canada was sealed off from Europe by ice, but in the spring of 1760 a reorganized French and Canadian army under the Chevalier de Lévis moved against Quebec. Brigadier Murray, commanding a small, half-starved British garrison in the city, managed to hold them off. On 9 May a warship appeared down river, unannounced. Anxious eyes on both sides sought to make out her flag. Lévis, knowing nothing of the destruction of the French fleet at Quiberon Bay the previous November, was confident that he saw the white ensign of royal France, heralding a relief expedition. And when his aide made out a red cross of St. George on the ensign—for this ship was the van of a British fleet—the Chevalier's heart was broken. He abandoned the siege and fell back on Montreal. On 8 September 1760 . . . Governor the Marquis de Vaudreuil, deserted by many French regulars and the Canadian militia, surrendered the whole of Canada to Great Britain.

In North America the war was over, except for the Pontiac conspiracy, a last flare-up by the Indians of the Ohio country who refused to accept the consequences of French defeat. . . .

This Peace of Paris in 1763 marked the end of France as a North American power. Of the great empire won by [17th-century explorer

Samuel de] Champlain, [fur trader Rene Robert Cavelier de] La Salle, and hundreds of explorers, warriors, traders, and priests, France retained only the two little islands of St. Pierre and Miquelon off Newfoundland. In the West Indies, besides a few smaller islands, she kept Saint-Domingue, Martinique, and Guadeloupe. Spain ceded to Great Britain East and West Florida, which became the sixteenth and seventeenth English continental colonies. France, in order to compensate Spain for the loss of the Floridas and Minorca, ceded to her the vast province of Louisiana, including all French claims to territory west of the Mississippi. Thus the Mississippi became a boundary between the English and Spanish empires.

Britain was now supreme on the seas, in the subcontinent of India, and in North America.

The Iroquois Clash with British Settlers

David Horowitz

In the middle years of the eighteenth century, the great powers of France and England were engaged in bloody battles that raged across Europe. One of the prizes these empires fought for was control over the vast territories of North America. While the French befriended the Native Americans and established trading posts along the Great Lakes, England attempted to push the French out of its western territories in Ohio, western Pennsylvania, and western New York. Unfortunately tens of thousands of Native Americans in the region were caught in the middle.

The Native Americans who occupied most of present-day New York were known as the Six Nations of the Iroquois. The Six Nations were composed of the Seneca, Cayuga, Onondaga, Oneida, Mohawk, and Tuscarora tribes. This confederacy was formed in the 1500s by a chief named Deganawidah, who convinced the original Five Nations (the Tuscarora joined later) to give up intertribal warfare. By the mid–eighteenth century, the tribes were alternately clashing with and making deals with French and British governors.

In 1754, representatives from the New England colonies met with leaders of the Six Nations to persuade them to join the colonists in a war against the French. The tribes of the Six Nations did their best to protect their lands from white invasion—efforts that soon proved futile. After the French were beaten by the British, the natives were quickly pushed to the west. Meanwhile, one of the representatives,

Ben Franklin, proposed the Albany Plan of Union under which the colonies would become a self-governing federation, independent of the British. Although this plan was not accepted, it was later used as a model for the Constitution.

In the following excerpt, David Horowitz, author of several histories, details the clash between the white governors and the tribes of the Six Nations.

[In June 1754] delegates from all the colonies north of the Potomac were gathering in Albany for a crucial military conference with the Six Nations [of the Iroquois tribes].

The conference had been called because of growing concern over the allegiance of the native allies. . . . [In 1753] colonial relations with the Iroquois had reached an impasse. An illicit commerce in arms and furs between [the English in] Albany and [the French in] Montreal undercut the Iroquois trade and made the Six Nations suspicious that the English and French might combine against them. Even more threatening was the colonial appetite for land, which had been whetted by the new immigration. "This hunger after Land," observed Peter Wraxall, the Secretary of Indian Affairs for New York, "is become now a kind of Epidemical Madness, every Body being eager to accumulate vast Tracts without having an intention or taking measures to settle or improve it. . . ."

No Lands Left

On June 12, 1753, seventeen Mohawks appeared at Fort George in New York for a conference with . . . Governor [Danvers Osborn]. The Mohawk spokesman was an aging sachem whom the Dutch called Hendrick. "We are come to remind you of the ancient alliance agreed on between our respective Forefathers," he said. "We were united together by a Covenant Chain and it seems now likely to be broken not from our Faults but yours." The Mohawks, he said, had been faithful allies in the last war with the French [in the 1740s] and as a result stood in imminent danger from the new French advance. Yet the colonists had failed to fortify the frontiers or make other military preparations.

Another grievance concerned land: "When our Brethren the English first came among us we gave and sold them Lands, and have continued to do so ever since, but it seems now as if we had no Lands left for ourselves." In many instances of land sales the colonists claimed more land than had actually been sold to them. Hendrick cited several cases. When the meeting reconvened four days later, the Governor's reply was vague and unpromising. Some of the Mohawk land grievances, he said, were unjustified; the rest involved transactions before his tenure of office. These he intended to refer to the Commissioners of Indian Affairs in Albany.

The Mohawks were outraged by the Governor's response; none of their grievances had been answered. Nor could they expect any better from Albany: "Brother you tell us that we shall be redressed at Albany, but we know them so well, we will not trust to them, for they are no people but Devils, so we rather desire that you'll say, Nothing shall be done for us."

Hendrick concluded with a warning that the Mohawks would now send word to the other five nations that "the Covenant Chain is broken between you and us."

In London, the implications of the rupture were quickly grasped, and a letter was sent to New York: "When we consider of how great a consequence the friendship and alliance of the six Nations is to all His Majesties Colonies and Plantations in America, we cannot but be greatly concerned and surprised, that the Province of New York should have . . . given occasion to the complaints made by the Indians." Worse, the colonists had exacerbated the situation by "the dissatisfactory answer given to the Indians, [and] their being suffered to depart (tho' the Assembly was then sitting) without any measures taken to bring them to Temper or to redress their complaints."

The Albany Conference

To rectify matters, London advised that a conference with the Iroquois be convened and that New York immediately convey its interest in renewing the Covenant Chain, offering to satisfy the Indians by reasonable purchases "for such lands as have been unwarrantably taken from them." Since the uncertainty of the Iroquois alliance affected the other colonies as well, they were also advised to join in making the overture and in concluding "one general treaty in His Majesty's name" with the natives.

The proposed conference took place at Albany in June 1754. One hundred and fifty Indians gathered to meet the colonial delegates and were presented with thirty wagonloads of gifts. Hendrick and several other sachems addressed the delegates and voiced the Indian grievances.

They consisted largely of the complaints rehearsed by the Mohawks at Fort George. The frontier was undefended against the French, and the Indians—exposed to attack—were unclear as to the colonies' intentions. Their land was being taken by unscrupulous means. "We understand that there are writings for all our lands, so that we shall have none left but the very spot we live upon and hardly that," they told the Albany delegates. "We find we are very poor, we [thought we] had yet land round about us, but it is said there are writings for it all."

An additional grievance concerned the sale of liquor, the primary currency of the Indian trade: "There is an affair about which our hearts tremble and our minds are deeply concerned; this is the selling of Rum in our Castles. It destroys many both, of our old and young people. We request of all the Governments here present, that it may be forbidden to carry any of it amongst the [Six] Nations."

The Toll of Alcohol

Unknown to the natives before its introduction by Europeans, alcohol quickly became a principal item in the exchange between the two cultures. "Although Drunkennesse be justly termed a vice, which the Savages are ignorant of," wrote Thomas Morton in *The New English Canaan,* "yet the benefit is very great that comes to the planters by the sale of strong liquor to the Salvages, who are much taken with the delight of it, for they will pawne their wits, to purchase the acquaintance of it." Already rum was "the life of the trade" in the northern fur regions, Morton reported; one could have no trade at all in those parts, unless he provided the Indians with "lusty liquors."

Over the years, the rum assiduously supplied to the Indians by English and Dutch traders (the French coin was a less desired brandy) took its toll among the tribes of the coastal regions. The effects of alcohol on the natives seemed without parallel among whites. Communal drinking bouts frequently resulted in burnings, stabbings and other violent outbursts. Many tribal conflicts could be traced directly to its source. Under the influence of alcohol, native traders frequently undervalued their goods in the marketplace, and bartered their furs for spirits rather than for the necessities they had come for. Widespread drunkenness accompanied and hastened the demoralization and disintegration of tribes that had suffered displacement and defeat. "The too frequent use of [rum] with the permission or Neglect of our Colony Governments," summarized one official report, "hath destroyed more Indians than all their wars put together have done."

At the conclusion of the Albany Conference, the delegates acknowledged the justice of many of the Indians' charges: that the disunity of the colonies had prevented them from taking measures of defense; that the Iroquois alliance had been neglected; that their relations had generally suffered by being subordinated to "private gain" rather than "the public interest"; and that the Indians had been supplied with rum by traders "in vast and almost incredible quantities" and then "abused in their Trade" while under its influence. They also conceded that the granting of large tracts to private persons and companies for speculative purposes had weakened the frontiers and that it was "absolutely necessary that speedy and effectual measures be taken to secure the Colonies from the slavery they are threatened with."

Uniting the Colonies

To defend the colonial frontier against the French, the delegates recommended a plan with far-reaching implications: the uniting of the colonies under "one General Government . . . in America." A President General and Grand Council would manage the affairs of the United Colonies relating to matters of defense and commerce with the Indians, including the purchase of frontier lands.

The author of the plan, Benjamin Franklin, had long been convinced of the importance of uniting the colonial interest, and of securing "Room enough" on the far side of the mountains for the colonies to expand. "It would be a very strange thing," Franklin had written three years earlier, "if *Six Nations* of ignorant savages should be capable of forming a scheme for such a union [which] . . . has subsisted for ages and appears indissoluble," and yet a similar union should be impractical for a dozen English colonies "to whom it is more necessary and . . . advantageous," and who "cannot be supposed to want an equal understanding of their interests."

Yet the goal of union proved premature. Although Franklin promoted it under the dramatic slogan "Join or Die," the colonial assemblies could not overcome their parochial rivalries to ratify it. "Everyone cries a union is necessary," Franklin wrote to the Governor of Massachusetts, "but when they come to the manner and form of the union their weak noodles are perfectly distracted."

About the time that the Albany Conference was getting under way, the fort which Washington had erected in Great Meadows was attacked and destroyed by the French. A third of its defenders were killed or wounded and Washington was forced to surrender. After signing a statement of capitulation and agreeing to quit the territory belonging to France, he was allowed to return to Virginia. During the retreat, his troops, who had come with the expectation of valley land, deserted him, making any further engagements of the enemy impossible.

The French Threat

Washington's defeat and the withdrawal of the Virginians east of the mountains convinced London of the gravity of the French threat. Since the colonies were incapable of defending their ground in the west, it was decided to commit English regulars [soldiers] to the frontier struggle. The Forty-fourth and Forty-eighth regiments of foot soldiers under the command of General Edward Braddock were dispatched to the colonies. Braddock was to recruit additional troops in America and organize campaigns against the French forts at Niagara, Lake Champlain and Louisburg, as well as the forks of the Ohio. He himself was to lead the assault on Fort Duquesne.

Arriving in America, Braddock found little support in his efforts to supply or supplement his army. The assemblies of Virginia and

New York voted him perfunctory funds. Wagons and horses were secured only with great difficulty and after long delays. In Pennsylvania, the general apathy was compounded by a Quaker Assembly guided by pacifist principles. "I am, Sir, almost ashamed to tell You," the Governor wrote Braddock, "that We have in this Province upward of Three Hundred Thousand Inhabitants, and besides our own Consumption raise Provisions enough to supply an Army of One Hundred Thousand Men, which is yearly exported from this City ... And yet when their *All* is invaded they refuse to contribute to the necessary Defence of their Country, either by establishing a Militia or furnishing Men, Money, or Provisions."

After considerable delays, Braddock's army was equipped and he was able to set out with Washington and the Virginians across the Blue Ridge. For a month they marched through dense uninhabited wilderness, cutting a road over the mountains. But when they came to within ten miles of Fort Duquesne, they were ambushed by a force of three hundred French and six hundred Indians. These were Ottawas of the Great Lakes region, Chippewas, and other northern tribes. The attackers split into two streams, flanking Braddock's army and seizing the high ground on either side. Caught in the cross-fire, the troops that Braddock had taken across the Blue Ridge were cut to pieces. "The dead, the dying, the groans, lamentations and cries along the road of the wounded for help," Washington recalled years later, "were enough to pierce a heart of adamant."

Nearly a thousand men were slain or wounded, including Braddock himself, who was mortally hit and died shortly after the battle. Seven years later, the Moravian missionary John Heckewelder rode past the site and found the scattered bones and skulls of Braddock's men. "The sound of our horses' hoofs continually striking against them," he wrote, "made dismal music, as, with the Monongahela full in view, we rode over this memorable battleground."

Native Americans Attack English

The defeat of Braddock's army at the forks of the Ohio was the signal for a wholesale defection of the valley Indians from the English cause. Braddock had been presented to them as "a great General" sent from "your Father, the King of Great Britain, to defeat the designs of the French in taking your lands without your consent." On his march to the Ohio, Braddock had met with a Delaware sachem named Shingas, and five other chiefs of the Shawnee, Mingo and Delaware nations, to secure their help in expelling the French. But when they asked what he intended to do with the land if he should drive out the French and their Indians, Braddock replied that the English would inhabit and inherit it; and when Shingas asked him if the Indians who were friends to the English might still have a hunting ground in the valley sufficient to support themselves and their families, Braddock reiterated, "no Savage Shoud Inherit the Land." The following morning Shingas and the other chiefs came and told Braddock that "if they might not have Liberty to Live on the Land they would not Fight for it."

Three months after Braddock's defeat, a party of Shingas' warriors appeared at a home on Penns Creek in the Susquehanna Valley and told the inhabitants, "We are Allegheny Indians, and your enemies. You must all die." The attackers then shot the owner of the farm, tomahawked his son and took his two daughters prisoner. During the next three days, seventeen settlers were killed, others taken captive, and farmhouses burned throughout the area. Later, Shingas sent a message to those Delawares who had remained in the Susquehanna Valley: "We, the Delawares of Ohio, do proclaim War against the English. We have been their Friends many years, but now have taken up the Hatchet against them, and we will never make it up with them whilst there is an English man alive."

The Penns Creek massacre began a reign of terror against the Pennsylvania frontier settlements by Delaware, Shawnee and Mingo warriors, and the bloodiest warfare in the history of the colonies. Farms were set afire, settlers and their families massacred and livestock slaughtered. "You cannot conceive what a vast Tract of Country has been depopulated by these merciless Savages," the Governor reported in mid-November; and the Indian trader George Croghan sent word that "almost all the women and children over Sasquehannah have left their habitations and the roads are full of starved, naked, indigent multitudes."

Reclaiming Native Lands

The Indian terror was not confined to the Pennsylvania highlands but followed the line of settlement to the Appalachian frontiers of Maryland and the valley of Virginia. When the waves of Scotch-Irish immigrants had entered the valley twenty years earlier, they had found it a grassland prairie, suitable for grazing and open for settlement. The prairie had been created by the Indians, although only two small villages of Tuscaroras and Shawnees inhabited it. Before the settlers came, the valley was their hunting ground. Every year they came over the mountain trails from their villages on the Ohio to hunt the buffalo that came to graze in its pastures. At the end of each season, the Indians set fire to the open ground to preserve it as a grassland. Now the Shawnees and other Indians of the Alleghenies returned to reclaim it.

Two weeks before Shingas' warriors appeared at Penns Creek, an outpost on the Shenandoah River reported attacks by a band of 150 natives:

> They go about and commit their outrages at all hours of the day, and nothing is to be seen or heard of, but desolation and murder heightened with

all barbarous circumstances, and unheard of instances of cruelty. They spare the lives of the young women, and carry them away to gratify the brutal passions of lawless savages. The smoke of the burning plantations darkens the day and hides the neighboring mountains from our sight.

While the Delawares, Shawnees and Mingos razed the back-country settlements, the defeats of Washington and Braddock in the Ohio Valley had thrown the Iroquois Confederacy into a state of confusion. For them, the conflict in the Ohio Valley was a source of bitter irony. "We don't know what you Christians French and English together intend," an Indian spokesman remarked. "We are so hemm'd in by both, that we have hardly a Hunting place left, in a little while, if we find a Bear in a Tree, there will immediately Appear an owner for the Land to Challenge the Property."

This Land Belongs to Us

At the Albany Conference, the Mohawk sachem Hendrick summed up Iroquois concern: "Brethren.—The Governor of Virginia, and the Governor of Canada are both quarrelling about lands which belong to us, and such a quarrel as this may end in our destruction; they fight who shall have the land."

In terms of settlement, the Iroquois had more to fear from the English farmers than from the French traders. By the middle of the eighteenth century, the population of French Canada was only 55,000, compared to the 1,200,000 inhabitants of the thirteen British colonies. Yet the Iroquois had grown to greatness with the expansion of the English domain. Their sway over the tribes in the territory extending from New England to the valleys beyond the Allegheny was premised on English control of the fur trade and English supremacy in arms. Both were shaken by the defeats on the Ohio. Delawares, Shawnees and Mingos no longer heeded their "uncles" on the Onondaga Council. Even some Senecas and Cayugas now defected to the French, despite the League's formal declaration of neutrality.

In the east, however, the Mohawks joined the English defense of Albany. At Lake George, Hendrick, then approaching his eightieth year, led a band of two hundred warriors in the assault on Fort Edward. Before the battle, which was to be his last, the aged sachem warned the English that the troops available were not sufficient for the task. "If they are to fight, they are too few," he said; "if they are to die, they are too many."

A Swedish Visitor Describes American Slavery

Peter Kalm

Slavery was a fact of life in eighteenth-century America. In the following excerpt, a Swedish traveler named Peter Kalm describes American slavery in the 1750s.

The servants which are made use of in the English American colonies are either free persons or slaves; . . . Formerly the Negroes were brought over from Africa, and bought by almost everyone who could afford it. The Quakers alone scrupled to have slaves, but they are no longer so nice, and they have as many slaves as other people. However, many people cannot conquer the idea of its being contrary to the laws of Christianity to keep slaves. There are likewise several free Negroes in town [Philadelphia], who have been lucky enough to get a very zealous Quaker for their master, who have them their liberty, after they had faithfully served him for some time.

At present they seldom bring over any Negroes to the English colonies, for those which were formerly brought thither have multiplied considerably. In regard to their marriage they proceed as follows: In case you have not only male but likewise female Negroes, they must intermarry, and then the children are all your slaves. But

Excerpted from "A Swedish Visitor Describes American Slaves," by Peter Kalm in *The Annals of America* (Chicago: Encyclopaedia Britannica, 1968) edited by Mortimer J. Adler.

if you possess a male Negro only, and he has an inclination to marry a female belonging to a different master, you did not hinder your Negro in so delicate a point; but it is no advantage to you, for the children belong to the master of the female. It is therefore advantageous to have Negro women.

. . . The Negroes in the North American colonies are treated more mildly and fed better than those in the West Indies. They have as good food as the rest of the [white] servants, and they possess equal advantages in all things, except their being obliged to serve their whole lifetime, and get no other wages than what their master's goodness allows them. They are likewise clad at their master's expense. On the contrary, in the West Indies, and especially in the Spanish Islands they are treated very cruelly; therefore no threats make more impression upon a Negro here than that of sending him over to the West Indies, in case he would not reform. . . .

In the year 1620 some Negroes were brought to North America by a Dutch ship, and in Virginia they bought twenty of them. These are said to have been the first that came hither. When the Indians, who were then more numerous in the country than at present, saw these black people for the first time, they thought they were a true breed of devils, and therefore they called them "Manitto" for a great while; this word in their language signified not only God, but likewise the devil. Some time before that, when they saw the first European ship on their coasts, they were perfectly persuaded that God himself was in the ship. This account I got from some Indians, who preserved it among them as a tradition which they received from their ancestors; therefore the arrival of the Negroes seemed to them to have confused everything. But since that time, they have entertained less disagreeable notions of the Negroes, for at present many live among them, and they even sometimes intermarry, as I myself have seen.

Catherine the Great Reforms Russia

Vincent Cronin

Catherine II, or Catherine the Great, was empress of Russia from 1762 to 1796. Catherine continued the work of Peter the Great, who in the early years of the eighteenth century worked to transform Russia into a modern nation.

Catherine was born Sophie Fredericke Augusta on May 2, 1729, in the city of Stettin, in present-day Poland. The daughter of a German prince, Catherine married Peter, the nephew of the Russian empress Elizabeth, at the age of fifteen. When Elizabeth died in 1761, Peter became Peter III, emperor of Russia. Peter, however, was extremely unpopular with Russian army officers, one of whom was Catherine's lover. The officers staged a coup in 1762, murdered Peter, and installed the thirty-three-year-old Catherine as the absolute ruler of Russia.

Catherine never learned to speak Russian properly and rumors of her many love affairs dominated her reign. In spite of this, the empress was extremely intelligent and conscious of the many cultural and scientific trends of the age. Using Western Europe as a model, Catherine built towns, opened schools, and reformed Russia's economy, advancing the nation's standing as a world power.

Vincent Cronin is an Oxford- and Harvard-educated author who has written extensively about European history and civilization including biographies of Napoléon and Louis XV.

In order to begin to rule [Catherine II] the new Empress required to know certain basic facts. So she went to the Senate. 'How many towns are there in Russia? Catherine asked this body of thirty distinguished men, which included the Heads of the Colleges or Ministries. No one knew. Catherine suggested looking at the map. There was no map. Catherine then took five roubles from her purse and sent a clerk across the Neva to the Academy of Sciences to buy a copy of the latest map of Russia. When the clerk returned, Catherine presented the map to the Senate and the towns were counted.

With that gesture and at that moment Catherine left the sheltered world of a civilized Court and stepped into Russia as it was: ignorant, superstitious, disorganized, unruly, sometimes hungry, often diseased, always [believed by a] European [to be] appallingly backward. [Catherine] wanted to begin straight away bettering things, and for that she needed money. Again she turned to the Senate. What was the condition of the finances? This the Senate knew, roughly. As a result of the Seven Years' War, they said, Russia was heavily in debt and her credit so low that Holland had refused a two million rouble loan which Empress Elizabeth had tried to float. In the current year revenue of 28 million roubles would fall short of expenditure by the staggering sum of 7 million.

Catherine was shocked by the deficit and disturbed too when the senators, having imparted the figures, left everything for a complicated lawsuit about one meadow near the small town of Mosalsk, spending six whole weeks just listening to the records of the case.

Increase Wealth and Knowledge

Catherine decided that her first and overriding task would be to increase Russia's wealth. Everything else depended on that. And since Russia was primarily agricultural she began with the land. She sent experts to outlying regions to study soil and propose suitable crops; she made grants to landowners to learn the improved techniques being devised in England, whereby turnips, clover and rye grass were alternated with grain crops, and to buy the agricultural machines that were beginning to be invented there. She arranged for silkworms to be cultivated, and encouraged the rearing of honey-bees; she extended the Ukraine tobacco plantations and offered bounties for high yields; she commissioned a descriptive catalogue of Russian plants; she encouraged the introduction of modern methods of breeding sheep and cattle; she promoted scientific horse-breeding, and Alexis Orlov, one of the pioneers in this sphere, crossed Arabs and Friesians with notable success.

Catherine saw the need for creating a pool of practical knowledge. As a foreigner [growing up in Poland and Germany], she knew of societies and publications in other countries. With these in mind she founded the Free Economic Society where landowners could meet to exchange information and discuss problems. Technical essays were published in the Society's journal, which Catherine paid for, and in the Academy of Science's bulletins. According to a British visitor, Archdeacon Coxe, 'No country can boast, within the space of so many years, such a number of excellent publications on its internal state.'

To work the underpopulated land Catherine saw that more labour was needed. She set Gregory Orlov at the head of a board to encourage immigration. It placed advertisements in foreign, mainly German, newspapers, inviting settlers and offering attractive terms: six months' free lodging; seed, livestock and ploughs; exemption from taxes for five, ten or thirty years, according to a man's skills. The response was excellent; furniture piled into covered wagons, thousands took the road Catherine and her mother had taken twenty years before, to work the rich black soil of southern Russia. These settlers played an important part in feeding a population that was to grow steadily through the next three decades.

Tapping Russia's Mineral Riches

Catherine paid special attention to wealth under the earth. She sent geologists to collect and assess ores from Russia's seemingly desert lands, among them Samuel Bentham, the inventive engineer brother of impractical Jeremy, who collected in Siberia half a ton of assorted minerals, mainly copper and iron ore, including loadstones, and wrote a report for Catherine, suggesting that the ores be extracted not by gunpowder but by pulverizing machinery.

Once new deposits were found, Catherine allowed merchants to own and work the mines, not just the gentry, as in previous reigns. To provide technicians she founded in St Petersburg Russia's first School of Mines, including a simulated underground mine, with shafts and tunnels, where trainees could learn under realistic conditions.

Catherine took a special interest in silver, because by law that metal belonged to the crown and because when she came to the throne she found a grave shortage of silver roubles—only four per head of the population. Here she was fortunate to strike it rich. In 1768 her prospectors found important silver deposits on the frontier of Mongolia, and by 1773 supplies from these mines, 3000 miles away, were swelling her budget. From all varieties of metal Catherine was to increase mining revenue by 30 per cent during her reign to an annual 13 million roubles.

Furs had long been an important item in Russia's natural wealth. As early as 1245 the King of England's tailor went to Lynn in Norfolk and bought from Edmund of Gothland [millions of dollars worth] of 'grey-work', the fur of the Arctic squirrels taken in winter by Russian trappers and marketed in Novgorod. Catherine encouraged the existing fur trade, mainly in Siberia, and promoted hunting expeditions to the recently-discovered Aleutian Islands: that of Dmitri Bragin, lasting five years, brought back 200,000 roubles' worth of furs, mainly sea-otter.

Opening Factories

When she turned from Russia's natural wealth to manufacturing, Catherine found that under the dilatory [previous empress] Elizabeth, senators, notably Peter Shuvalov, had taken matters into their own hands and established a tight system of monopolies and controls. Catherine had an aversion to theories, particularly economic theories. She preferred to work from common sense and her observations of human nature, and these inclined her to what would be called free trade. One of her first actions on coming to the throne was to end these monopolies and controls. As early as October 1762 she decreed that except in Moscow, which was overcrowded, and in St Petersburg, which was a show city with its own needs, anyone could start a manufactory. Later she decreed that anyone could set up a loom and weave for profit. Soon enterprising State peasants were running quite large textile businesses, and there came into being a whole range of cottage industries: linen, pottery, leather goods and furniture.

For more sophisticated enterprises Catherine called on expert help from abroad, and partly because she wanted to play down her German connection she turned most often to England. She brought over Admiral Knowles to build warships and dockyards, paying him three times as much as a Russian admiral, and she sent workmen from the important Tula steelworks to England to study latest methods of making barometers, thermometers, mathematical instruments and spectacles. Sensitive to cold, Catherine made a point of placing a thermometer not only in certain rooms of her palaces, but in all the rooms, as well as outside all the windows. The incidence of breakage by servants was high, so Catherine arranged to buy up all the thermometers produced by the Tula works.

Catherine developed manufactories for textiles, especially in the Moscow region, for linen in the Yaroslav region, and for leather, tallow and candles along the central Volga. Altogether during her reign Catherine was to increase the number of manufactories from 984 to 3161.

Catherine brought in German, Austrian and French craftsmen to improve the imperial porcelain works; she also enlarged and improved the output of the imperial tapestry works. Tapestries were still an essential furnishing for well-to-do houses and handy as gifts to important friends. Catherine gave the second Earl of Buckinghamshire, the envoy who admired her horsemanship, a very fine tapestry depicting Peter the Great on horseback winning the battle of Poltava, which may be admired to this day in Blickling Hall, Norfolk.

Expanding Foreign Trade

In the sphere of foreign trade Catherine achieved remarkable results by the simple expedient of abolishing export duties. Russia's main exports were timber for masts, hemp, flax, their seeds and oils, fats, raw leather, furs, linen cloth and iron, 'Old Fox', the brand name of Urals iron, being particularly sought after. . . .

One aspect of Catherine's foreign trade is of great interest. When she came to the throne, China had just seized a district on the River Amur believed to contain silver which Russia claimed was hers. Catherine strengthened her army in Siberia to eleven regiments, then sent a special envoy to settle the dispute and to reopen trade. The Treaty of Kyakhta, signed in October 1768, soon had camel caravans passing to and from Manchuria. China exported cottons, silks, tobacco, porcelain, lacquerware, preserved and jellied fruits, silver and tea—superior, Russians claimed, to the tea drunk in Europe, which lost some of its flavour in the salt air of a long voyage. Russia sent China furs, leather, linens, foreign-made cloth, Bengal and Turkish opium. During the early part of her reign Catherine corresponded with [French philosopher] Voltaire, then running his Ferney estate on sound business lines. Between fulsome compliments Voltaire asked Catherine if she would be kind enough to market some of the watches made at Ferney; Catherine agreed and the bales of one of her camel caravans carried Voltaire's Swiss watches to be sold to the mandarins of Peking. Russia's exports to China rose from nil at the beginning of the reign to 1,806,000 roubles in 1781, bringing Catherine customs and excise revenue of 600,000 roubles.

These measures, combined with tight cost control and an end to tax-farming, produced remarkably quick results. As early as 1765 Catherine had repaid three-quarters of the debt from Elizabeth's reign, and turned a budget deficit of seven million roubles into a surplus of 5.5 million, while State revenue was increasing by three per cent annually. She was now in a position to undertake major reforms.

Rule in an Enlightened Manner

Catherine found Russia divided into eleven *gubernii,* or governments, each administered by a governor-general, usually a soldier, who received no salary and had a tiny staff. The governor-general's task was to keep order with knout [whip] and bayonet; usually he also amassed enough in bribes to be able to retire at the end of three years in comfort.

Some of the *gubernii* were unmanageably large, and Catherine began by dividing the largest, making fifteen in all. . . . She brought to trial the Governor of Smolensk and his staff for taking bribes, and the Governor of Belgorod and his staff for running an illegal vodka distillery, replacing them with honest men, and paying all governors an adequate salary.

In April 1764 Catherine issued instructions to the governor-generals. They were to rule in an enlightened and rational manner; they were to take an accurate census, map their provinces, and report on the people, their customs, agriculture and trade. They were no longer just to keep order: they were to build and repair roads and bridges, fight fires, and ensure that orphanages and prisons were properly run. For this they would need staff. Catherine doubled the number of provincial civil servants and by 1767 was spending nearly one quarter of her budget on provincial government and services. . . .

Designing Towns

Catherine had good memories of her girlhood in Zerbst, the sturdy walled town with its craftsmen, its brewery, its strong community feeling. And near Zerbst were other thriving towns, such as Köthen, where the people made gold and silver lace, and where Bach had been Kappelmeister. She wanted to create such towns in Russia, where towns were so few that the Senate should certainly have known their number.

In 1763 the centre of Tver burned down. Instead of allowing it to be rebuilt in the old fire-trap style, pine or spruce houses set higgledy-piggledy in enclosures surrounded by animal pens and storage sheds, Catherine referred the matter to a Commission on Building, under Prince Ivan Betskoy, a former diplomat, fifty-nine years old, who had spent much of his life in Europe and had been a close friend of her mother.

On Catherine's instructions, Betskoy's Commission drew up a plan for Tver, which would also serve for all future towns. A main street joined two big squares, one for administrative buildings, the other for shops and stalls. From this radiated side streets, on the grid-iron pattern of classical Roman times; in order to reduce the risk of fire they averaged 75 feet wide. The whole town was four versts (2.6 miles) in diameter.

With a gift of 100,000 roubles from Catherine and a 200,000-rouble Government loan, Tver was rebuilt on this plan. In the first eight years of the reign sixteen other towns burned down and were rebuilt on the same neat model.

In 1775, with the second stage of her modernization programme, Catherine began creating new towns as administrative centres for the new districts brought into being by her provincial reorganization. She gave merchants priority in buying lots in the centre of each town, where two-storey brick or stone houses were to be built, arranged interest-free loans to cover the cost and exempted owners from taxes for five years. The zone contiguous to the centre consisted of widely spaced one-storey stuccoed wooden houses on stone foundations; in the outer zone wooden houses were built in straight streets. Manufactories were restricted to the suburbs, those such as tanneries that polluted the water had to be sited downstream from the residential zones.

Not all Catherine's new towns were built from scratch. Sometimes a village got a few administrative buildings and a grand name: Black Muck for instance became Imperial City. On the other hand, a typical new town, Ostrakhov, possessed by the end of the reign 293 new houses, 73 of stone or brick, 132 shops, and a quota of those public welfare buildings which will be discussed presently. Catherine, who rarely boasted, took pride in the fact that between 1775 and 1785 in a land with no civic traditions outside the capitals, and little stone suitable for houses, she created 216 new towns. . . .

Educating Girls

More than most people in the eighteenth century [Catherine] believed in the power of education to improve a people, while in Russia she found a land almost without education. It lacked schools altogether other than a few Church schools—mainly seminaries—and Peter the Great's technical colleges for future army and navy officers. On all sides Catherine found that appalling ignorance coupled with complacency which Peter the Great's engineer, John Perry, had called 'the check and discouragement to ingenuity'.

At the beginning of her reign, in collaboration with Prince Betskoy, Catherine wrote 'A General Statute for the Education of the Youth of Both Sexes', publishing it in March 1764. It is just a short essay, but it states certain important principles on which Catherine intended to act: education is the responsibility of the State; it must begin early, at five or six; it must consist not only of book-learning but of character-training; and—this was a startling innovation—it must provide for girls as well as boys.

Catherine began with girls. She converted a St Petersburg convent built by Elizabeth into a boarding-school. . . . Girls entered the Smolny Institute, as it was called, at five or six and remained till eighteen. They were divided into two 'streams'. Daughters of gentry learned religion, Russian, foreign languages, arithmetic, geography, history, heraldry, the elements of law, drawing, music, knitting and sewing, dancing and society manners. The other stream, burghers' daughters, took many of the same subjects, but foreign languages were replaced by more domestic skills. Catherine laid down that from time to time a hundred poor women should dine in the school, so that girls could learn their responsibilities towards the unfortunate, and make them gifts of alms or linen. She often visited the school herself and watched performances of plays there; in 1773 she was seen by [French philosopher Denis] Diderot surrounded by all the girls—440 of them—'embracing her, jumping up to her arms, her head, her neck'. Diderot, who liked a good cry, gave the scene his accolade: 'It was a sight touching to the point of tears.'. . .

Schools for the People

On 5th December 1786 Catherine issued her important Statute for Schools, the first educational act covering the whole of Russia. A 'minor school' with two teachers was to be established in every district town, and a 'major school' with six teachers in every provincial town. Major schools taught mathematics, physics, science, geography, history, and religion, which Catherine specified should be expounded by laymen; in the higher classes pupils going on to gymnasia and university would learn Latin and foreign languages.

The schools were free but attendance was not compulsory. As a newspaper advertisement explained, the new system was intended for all and 'the new schools are called "people's" schools because in them every one of Her Majesty's subjects can receive education suitable to his station.'

Catherine immediately opened 25 major schools in 25 provinces, and by 1792 every province save the Caucasus had a major school. Whereas in 1781, apart from the Smolny Institute, Russia had only six State schools with 27 teachers for 474 boys and 12 girls, by 1796 Russia had 316 schools, in which 744 teachers taught 16,220 boys and 1121 girls. Figures for a slightly later date show that 22 per cent of the pupils were middle class and 30 per cent State peasants.

Had she wished to dazzle Europe, Catherine would have opened more universities. But she knew that Russia lacked the teachers to staff such prestige institutions. She confined herself to drawing up projects for universities that she hoped would one day come into being and concentrated her resources on basic education, which was what Russia needed. She did, however, considerably increase the number of grants for study abroad. Law students she sent to Leipzig, budding prelates to Oxford and Cambridge, in order that they might there widen their learning 'for the use of the State'.

Improving Public Health

When, at the beginning of her reign, she looked at public health, Catherine found here the same dark void as in education. 'If you go to a village and ask a peasant how many children he has he will say ten, twelve, and sometimes even twenty. How many of them are alive? He will say one, two, three, rarely four. This mortality should be fought against.'. . .

In 1763 Catherine founded Russia's first College of Medicine, comprising a director, a president and eight members. It had an annual revenue of 470,000 roubles, plus one per cent of the salaries of military and civil service personnel, who in return received free medical treatment. The object of the College was to train sufficient Russian doctors, surgeons and apothecaries to serve all the provinces, and to further medical knowledge. In 1778 the College published the first *Pharmacopoeia Russica;* in 1789 rules for apothecaries and for midwives, and a scale of charges for medical treatment. In 1795 it was provided with its own printing press.

Peter the Great had founded good military hospitals; it was Catherine who founded hospitals for civilians. In 1763, when the document establishing the College of Medicine was presented for her signature, Catherine added in her own hand: 'The College must not forget to submit plans to me for hospitals in the provinces.' In 1775, when she reorganized the provinces, Catherine decreed that each provincial capital must have a hospital, each county—comprising between twenty and thirty thousand inhabitants—a doctor, a surgeon, an assistant surgeon and a student doctor. Salaries were higher in the remote provinces, and State doctors were allowed also to treat paying patients. Until there should be sufficient indigenous doctors, Catherine attracted many Germans with the offer of an 800-rouble retirement pension.

Catherine founded, in the name of her son Paul, a small model hospital in Moscow which the prison reformer John Howard, who visited Russia, said would do honour to any country. Another visitor, Francesco de Miranda, the future liberator of Venezuela, was struck by the Russian habit of transferring patients to summer hospitals, so that the winter ones could be cleaned and disinfected before the cold weather set in. He also noticed that the majority of patients had scurvy or V.D. In this connection Catherine founded, in 1783, a hospital in St Petersburg exclusively for venereal diseases. Of its sixty beds half were for men, half for women. It was not permitted to ask the name of any person who applied for admission: he or she was given a night-dress and a cap inscribed with the word Secrecy.

Catherine's example prompted efforts by her gentry. Baron von Keichen, for example, founded a 300-bed St Petersburg hospital overlooking the Fontanka canal, a brick building, to which in 1790 the College of Medicine added wooden annexes with 250 more beds.

Catherine gave special attention to orphans, foundlings and unwanted infants. She built a five-storey Foundling Home in Moscow, superior to anything in Europe, which included a lying-in hospital, a church and a dairy farm of eighty cows. Mothers wishing their children to be accepted had only to ring the doorbell; a basket was lowered, the mother placed her baby inside, stating its name and whether it had been baptized, and the basket was drawn up again. Each child had its own bed, the sheets of which were changed weekly, and the gifted children could continue their schooling, free, to gymnasium level. The Moscow Foundling Home took in 2000 infants annually and became the model for similar smaller homes in St Petersburg, Tula, Kaluga, Yaroslav and Kazan.

Storch in 1796 gives the following figures for infant mortality: London 32 per cent; Berlin 27.6 per cent; St Petersburg 18.4 per cent. St Petersburg of course enjoyed much better facilities than Russia as a whole, but Storch's figures speak well for Catherine's work in the field of child care.

So much for the visible results of Catherine's domestic reforms. There would be more reforms later in the reign, and achievements in many other fields. But the ones considered amount to civilizing in a fundamental sense: increasing the yield of the land, fostering trade, replacing military by civilian rule, founding towns and creating in each provincial centre, school, law courts and hospital.

James Watt's Steam Engine

Henry Thomas and Dana Lee Thomas

James Watt was born into poverty in Scotland, but had a natural talent for mechanics and engineering. By utilizing the thermodynamic properties of steam in a condenser, Watt improved the primitive steam engines of the eighteenth century. Watt's steam engines transformed mining and manufacturing processes, which led to the English Industrial Revolution.

Henry Thomas has had a long, distinguished career as an educator and writer. His son, Dana Lee Thomas, is a Harvard graduate and prolific biographer.

James Watt was the son of a shipbuilder who had fallen on hard times. But despite its poverty, the family managed to maintain its respectability. A young niece who visited their home reported to her friends, "Mrs. Watt is a braw [fine], braw woman—and very ladylike. Do you know she had two candles lighted on the table?" This was the sign of a generous hostess in the little Scottish village of Greenock in the middle of the eighteenth century.

Jamie Watt was too sickly to be sent to school for a formal education. Two of his brothers had died before he was born and his mother became overly protective with him. She taught him to read and write at home. She gave him an educational background that was everything but scientific, and Watt as a child was backward in scientific pursuits. He was especially poor in arithmetic. However, from somewhere along the ancestral line he had inherited exceedingly clever fingers. He loved to break his toys, pick up the pieces and re-build them into new toys. And he spent his hours of illness, which were frequent, making clever gadgets in his bed. "Jamie," said one discerning uncle, "will build a fortune someday with his fingers.". . .

His propensity for dreaming irked his practical family. One day while having tea with his aunt, he provoked her into an indignant outburst. "Jamie, I've never seen such a queer boy as you. For the last hour, you haven't spoken a word—just taken the lid off that ket-tle, putting it on again, holding a spoon over the steam, watching it rise from the spout and catching it as it gathers into drops of water. Aren't you ashamed to be spending your time on that silly stuff? Why don't you run off and play like other boys?"

As he entered his teens, he was sent to school and he became fas-cinated with geometry. And he suddenly developed an interest in chemistry and physics. At fifteen he read and re-read . . . *Elements of Philosophy*—the basic primer for natural science for that day—and he built various mechanical machines that indicated highly orig-inal thinking.

A Jack-of-All-Trades

His formal schooling was brief. Long before he could graduate, his mother died. His older brother John had run away to sea. His father's ship business had reached a new low financially and Jamie was com-pelled to go to work. His mechanical skill found suitable employ-ment. He became apprenticed to an optician who was a Jack-of-all-trades. He not only ground lenses, but manufactured fishing rods, repaired fiddles, tuned spinets, and upholstered furniture. James gradually mastered a variety of trades and his dexterity continued to amaze his boss.

But the job did not entirely satisfy him. He desired to do even more specialized mechanical work. He wanted to become an expert in the fashioning of mathematical instruments—a craft that required superior skill and which found very few pupils equal to its exacting demands.

At the suggestion of a relative of his mother's, a professor of sci-ence at Glasgow University, Watt left for London where he was ad-vised, "You can get much better mechanical instruction than is pos-sible here in Scotland."

He apprenticed himself to an instrument maker in London. But he was heartsick because he had to ask his struggling father to support him during this period of training. It wasn't much, only two dollars a week, but it strained his father's resources to the utmost. "I look forward to the day when I can take care of myself and repay you for all you have done," James wrote to his father.

At the end of the year, Watt applied for membership in the Glasgow Guild of Hammermen. But his application was turned down. A seven years' apprenticeship was required as a qualification for membership. Watt had learned his trade in one year, but such amazing precocity was incomprehensible to the Guild. They simply didn't believe it. He asked the Guild for permission to rent a shop, "not for business but for scientific experiments," but this request was also turned down.

At this point his friends at Glasgow University came to his aid. According to the university charter, the faculty had the right to assign work within the campus. And Watt was offered a workroom in one of the college buildings. He was free, without the Guild's authorization, to make and sell his instruments and to conduct his experiments.

A Brilliant Scholar

To make his business pay, he followed the plan of his former employer, the optician. He manufactured all sorts of things—fishing tackle, guitars, lenses, fiddles, flutes, quadrants, sectors, compasses—and just to show his versatility—an occasional organ. A thorough researcher in everything, before he made his musical instruments, he studied the laws of harmony, and by the time he had completed his first organ, "there were few men in Britain," in the opinion of one scholar, "who knew more of the science of music than James Watt."

The workshop of this formally uneducated craftsman was frequented by the leading professors in the university. They marveled at his skill and knowledge. In many instances, he amazed the scholars by giving them information in their own specialty that was new to them. "I had the vanity," wrote Professor Robinson, some years afterward, "to think myself pretty proficient in my favorite study—mathematic philosophy. I was therefore quite mortified to find this youngster better acquainted with some facts in the field than I myself."

It was amazing how thorough a scholar this untutored Scotsman actually became. When he heard about a German book that dealt with the machinery of mining in the Hartz Mountains, he set out to learn the German language so that he could study the subject in the original. He learned French and Italian for the same reasons. And not only did he learn these languages for his scientific researches, he became a student of the literature of each language so that he could become acquainted with the culture and thinking of the people who spoke it.

The Steam Engine

It was Professor Robinson who first interested Watt in steam engines. The university at that time owned a Newcomen engine—a contraption that had been purchased for experiments in natural philosophy. It was a thoroughly crude device bristling with pipes, boilers, and pistons that unleashed a mountain of noise to bring forth a mouse of power.

The imperfections of this machine challenged Watt's curiosity. He began to read up on the subject and to experiment with various models erected on the principles of this device. He used druggist's vials for boilers and hollowed canes for pipes, But he couldn't get the models to work properly. Every time he started a piston, there would be a few sputtering strokes and then the power would fizzle out.

But Watt continued to persevere in his researches. "He won't give up," prophesied Professor Robinson, "until he has either made something workable out of it, or has discovered its worthlessness."

And then suddenly Watt stumbled upon the secret of unleashing the hidden power. In the course of his experiments, he discovered the principle of latent heat. He found that a tremendous amount of heat lies hidden in nature ready to be mechanically freed. For instance, *one pound* of steam inserted into freezing water will bring *five pounds* of water to the boiling point. In other words, a quantity of water transformed into steam will release enough hidden energy to convert five times its own weight of water into steam heat.

James Watt

And now that he had discovered the generating power of heat, it was just a question of time, Watt believed, before he would learn how to enlist this in the service of man. He would build an engine to capture all this latent energy and then direct it to the pushing of a piston, the turning of a wheel, the pumping of a mine.

Transforming Industrial History

However, there was a formidable obstacle in Watt's path. It wouldn't be enough for him merely to harness the steam in the engine. He had to find a way to regulate and control its power once it was unleashed. And this unleashing of the steam in the models he now erected suffered the loss of four fifths of its energy. This loss was the result of the cooling of the cylinder during the action of the engine; and the cooling of the cylinder was caused by the fact that the piston, after its upward stroke, could not be sent to the bottom for another upward stroke, without the injection of a stream of cold water. It was to be years before Watt solved this tremendous problem of *preserving* the latent heat in the cylinder after he had succeeded in harnessing it. The solution came to him while he was taking a walk one Sunday afternoon in 1765. "I knew that in order to make a perfect steam engine it was necessary that the cylinder should always be as hot as the steam that entered it. . . . Suddenly the idea came into my mind that as steam was an elastic body it would rush into a vacuum, and if a communication were made between the cylinder and an exhausted vessel, it would rush into it and might be condensed without cooling the cylinder."

This startlingly simple idea—a separate condenser—was destined to transform the industrial history of mankind. The most revolutionary ideas are usually the most obvious. And yet it requires the minds of genius to receive and interpret them.

The principle of the modern steam engine, was theoretically worked out by the indomitable little Scotsman on that historic Sunday in 1765. The condenser would carry the steam into a separate vessel, leaving the cylinder uniformly hot. A circular piston would keep pumping the steam through this cylinder, maintaining the cylinder at the same high temperature as the steam that entered it. In this process there would be very little loss of the latent heat of the steam as it was converted into an energy that would transform the social and economic structure of the world.

An Unresponsive Public

Watt's personal life was a series of disappointments, tragedies interlarded by persistent hard work. He married, and his wife met an untimely death. The public was at first unresponsive to his invention and he went through years of financial struggle. He suffered long periods of ill health. He formed a partnership to manufacture his first engines, but he was a frightfully poor businessman. "I would sooner face a loaded cannon than settle a disputed account or make a bargain." One steam engine after another, though built according to the theoretical specifications, failed in performance. Sometimes it was the fault of the workmen; sometimes his own miscalculations; sometimes it was a misfit cylinder or piston that resulted in the breakdown of the entire engine. . . . And always, Watt remained humble with regard to his work. Whenever a customer complained about an engine, the inventor would reply, "My work is poor enough, I know; but I am trying to make it better."

Sensitive to a degree, it hurt him deeply when his failures caused inconvenience to other people. "You cannot conceive," he remarked to a friend concerning one of his imperfect machines, "how mortified I am with this disappointment. . . . I cannot bear the thought of other people becoming losers by my schemes."

And it wasn't only his failures that provoked criticism, but his successes as well. After completing one of his successful machines, he invited a group of scientists and mining experts to inspect it. At first the tremendous noise of the machine occasioned general satisfaction. But when Watt trimmed the engine to end the stroke more gracefully and cut down on the noise, the audience expressed its disappointment at the "reduced efficiency" of the machine. "The noise," Watt observed philosophically, "seems to convey great ideas of power to the ignorant, who seem no more taken with modest merit in an engine than in a man."

A New Age of Steam Power

Eventually, however, the engine and the man were recognized for their worth. Watt entered into a second partnership with a man whose uncanny business sense supplemented his own scientific ability, and the inventor for the first time tasted the sweets of financial security. As a matter of fact, Watt and his partner Matthew Boulton took to each other as a duck takes to water. They became fast friends. Boulton, a manufacturer [from the city of] Birmingham [England], was one of the originators of the idea of low prices through mass production. And he was an idealist as well as a manufacturer. He recruited for his apprentices orphans, parish wards, and foundlings. And he maintained a home where his apprentices were properly sheltered, fed, and educated.

The firm of Boulton and Watt literally compelled the world to awaken to a new age—the Age of Steam Power, the Industrial Revolution. During the growing pains of the business, they had to fight rival manufacturers from all over Europe who sent spies to infiltrate their plant and find out the secret of the new engine "that threatened to revolutionize the world." One of the firm's best engines was deliberately sabotaged by an engineer who had been bribed with money by a rival company. On one occasion, Watt himself was offered a large sum of money to leave his partner and enter the service of the Russian emperor. When Boulton heard of the offer, he wrote to Watt, "Your going to Russia staggers me. . . . I wish to advise you for the best without regard to self; but I find I love myself so well that I should be sorry to have you go."

Watt turned down the offer. He remained loyal to his partner and together they achieved final financial success in their enterprise. Business orders for the Watt machines poured in, and Watt attended personally to the installation of every model. He was on the go every waking hour.

Fame at Last

In addition to constantly improving his steam engine, Watt worked on numerous other inventions. He developed a copying press for manuscripts, a surveying quadrant, a machine for drying clothes, a micrometer for the measuring of fine angles, a drawing machine, a sculpture reproducer, an instrument for the computation of distances between planets and stars, a method for determining the specific gravity of liquids, a reading lamp that "made the night almost as brilliant as the day."

In addition, James Watt was the scientist who discovered the chemical composition of water. "We are authorized to conclude," he wrote in April 1783, "that water is a compound of two gases—oxygen and hydrogen."

And despite his numerous occupational activities, he found time to play. He joined the Lunar Society, a club of scientists and writers devoted to an exchange of stimulating ideas. The friendship of this group was broken only by death. And the last surviving member of this organization was James Watt.

His middle and advanced years were happy ones. He took trips to Paris where his admirers got him "drunk on Burgundy and flattery." He accepted tragedy with the same dignity as good fortune, remained calm and courageous at the death of his wife and one of his sons. While not conventionally religious, he was convinced that the universe was created according to a plan. "The mechanism of the universe seems to be running without a hitch." Toward the end of his life, he surrendered his interest in the Boulton and Watt partnership to his surviving son who was a shrewd businessman but a more inferior inventor than his father. The old man bought a home in Wales, cultivated a garden, planted trees. And he continued to the end to putter around with his inventions—"my improvements" as he modestly referred to them. As his friends began to drop one by one from the tree of life, he declared sadly, "I seem destined to stand alone among strangers." But, he added philosophically, "Perhaps it is a wise dispensation of Providence so to diminish our enjoyments in this world that when our turn comes we may leave with a lessening of regret."

1764–1783

PREFACE

Revolution against English rule took place between 1775 and 1783. After the French and Indian War ended, the British treasury was nearly bankrupt. In an effort to pay for the war that had won vast regions of North America east of the Mississippi River for the colonies, the British government needed to raise taxes. Since the British subjects in the thirteen colonies benefited most from the war, Parliament enacted a series of duties and taxes on various products such as newspapers, playing cards, sugar, and tea.

People in the colonies, however, were incensed that the government in far-off London taxed them while they had no representatives in Parliament to protect their interests. This taxation without representation was the basis for America's drive for independence.

To enforce the tax laws—and to quell rebellion—the British shipped thousands of soldiers to Boston, the heart of the revolutionary movement. The inevitable clashes with patriots led to war by 1775.

The British fought the war with many disadvantages. They were forced to send troops three thousand miles from home to fight a well-armed patriotic populace from Maine to Georgia. The land was wild with forests, swamps, rivers, and hills, unlike the smooth, flat battlefields the British soldiers were accustomed to in Europe. Although the British army performed well, and won many battles, in the end, its troops could not triumph over tens of thousands of patriots who were willing to fight and die for their homeland.

Revolution Against Britain

Howard Zinn

In modern times, the American Revolution is seen as a struggle between commoner American patriots and the British monarchy, who unfairly taxed the colonies without representation. Most of the men who led the Revolution, however, were extremely wealthy by the standards of the day. In fact Benjamin Franklin, Patrick Henry, Thomas Jefferson, John Hancock, George Washington, and others were some of the richest men in America.

While these well-to-do merchants and farmers resisted paying taxes to the British, average people of the colonies were engaged in innumerable smaller struggles. The poor rioted against wealthy landlords, expensive food, and high rents, and blacks rebelled against slavery and discrimination. In this atmosphere, the rich and privileged men who wrote the Declaration of Independence needed the support of poor and working-class people for the cause of democracy and freedom.

In this excerpt, best-selling author Howard Zinn discusses the strong resistance to British authority and how the revolutionary leaders mobilized rich and poor alike to fight for independence.

Zinn is an author whose books focus on the influence of historical events on average people. Zinn's *A People's History of the United States* is a standard school text in American history in many countries.

A round 1776, certain important people in the English colonies made a discovery that would prove enormously useful for the next two hundred years. They found that by creating a nation, a symbol, a legal unity called the United States, they could take over land, profits, and political power from . . . the British Empire. In the process, they could hold back a number of potential rebellions and create a consensus of popular support for the rule of a new, privileged leadership.

When we look at the American Revolution this way, it was a work of genius, and the Founding Fathers deserve the awed tribute they have received over the centuries. They created the most effective system of national control devised in modern times, and showed future generations of leaders the advantages of combining paternalism [governing in a fatherly manner] with command.

Starting with Bacon's Rebellion [in which a few colonists tried to overthrow the royal governor] in Virginia, by 1760, there had been eighteen uprisings aimed at overthrowing colonial governments. There had also been six black rebellions, from South Carolina to New York, and forty riots of various origins.

By this time also, there emerged, according to [author] Jack Greene, "stable, coherent, effective and acknowledged local political and social elites." And by the 1760s, this local leadership saw the possibility of directing much of the rebellious energy against England and her local officials. It was not a conscious conspiracy, but an accumulation of tactical responses.

After 1763, with England victorious over France in the Seven Years' War (known in America as the French and Indian War), expelling them from North America, ambitious colonial leaders were no longer threatened by the French. They now had only two rivals left: the English and the Indians. The British, wooing the Indians, had declared Indian lands beyond the Appalachians out of bounds to whites (the Proclamation of 1763). Perhaps once the British were out of the way, the Indians could be dealt with. Again, no conscious forethought strategy by the colonial elite, but a growing awareness as events developed.

With the French defeated, the British government could turn its attention to tightening control over the colonies. It needed revenues to pay for the war, and looked to the colonies for that. Also, the colonial trade had become more and more important to the British economy, and more profitable: it had amounted to about 500,000 pounds [$62 million] in 1700 but by 1770 was worth 2,800,000 pounds [$350 million].

So, the American leadership was less in need of English rule, the English more in need of the colonists' wealth. The elements were there for conflict.

Shaping Public Opinion

The war had brought glory for the generals, death to the privates, wealth for the merchants, unemployment for the poor. There were

25,000 people living in New York (there had been 7,000 in 1720) when the French and Indian War ended [in 1763]. A newspaper editor wrote about the growing "Number of Beggers and wandering Poor" in the streets of the city. Letters in the papers questioned the distribution of wealth: "How often have our Streets been covered with Thousands of Barrels of Flour for trade, while our near Neighbors can hardly procure enough to make a Dumplin to satisfy hunger?"

[Author] Gary Nash's study of city tax lists shows that by the early 1770s, the top 5 percent of Boston's taxpayers controlled 49% of the city's taxable assets. In Philadelphia and New York too, wealth was more and more concentrated. . . .

In Boston, the lower classes began to use the town meeting to vent their grievances. The governor of Massachusetts had written that in these town meetings "the meanest Inhabitants . . . by their constant Attendance there generally are the majority and outvote the Gentlemen, Merchants, Substantial Traders and all the better part of the Inhabitants."

What seems to have happened in Boston is that certain lawyers, editors, and merchants of the upper classes, but excluded from the ruling circles close to England—men like James Otis and Samuel Adams—organized a "Boston Caucus" and through their oratory and their writing "molded laboring-class opinion, called the 'mob' into action, and shaped its behaviour." This is Gary Nash's description of Otis, who, he says, "keenly aware of the declining fortunes and the resentment of ordinary townspeople, was mirroring as well as molding popular opinion."

We have here a forecast of the long history of American politics, the mobilization of lower-class energy by upper-class politicians, for their own purposes. This was not purely deception; it involved, in part, a genuine recognition of lower-class grievances, which helps to account for its effectiveness as a tactic over the centuries. As Nash puts it:

> James Otis, Samuel Adams, Royall Tyler, Oxenbridge Thacher, and a host of other Bostonians, linked to the artisans and laborers through a network of neighborhood taverns, fire companies, and the Caucus, espoused a vision of politics that gave credence to laboring-class views and regarded as entirely legitimate the participation of artisans and even laborers in the political process.

In 1762, Otis, speaking against the conservative rulers of the Massachusetts colony represented by [Royal Governor] Thomas Hutchinson, gave an example of the kind of rhetoric that a lawyer could use in mobilizing city mechanics and artisans:

> I am forced to get my living by the labour of my hand; and the sweat of my brow, as most of you are and obliged to go thro' good report and evil report, for bitter bread, earned under the frowns of some who have no natural or divine right to be above me, and entirely owe their grandeur

and honor to grinding the faces of the poor. . . .

Boston seems to have been full of class anger in those days. In 1763, in the Boston *Gazette,* someone wrote that "a few persons in power" were promoting political projects "for keeping the people poor in order to make them humble."

Attack on Wealth

This accumulated sense of grievance against the rich in Boston may account for the explosiveness of mob action after the Stamp Act of 1765. Through this Act, the British were taxing the colonial population to pay for the French war, in which colonists had suffered to expand the British Empire. That summer, a shoemaker named Ebenezer MacIntosh led a mob in destroying the house of a rich Boston merchant named Andrew Oliver. Two weeks later, the crowd turned to the home of Thomas Hutchinson, symbol of the rich elite who ruled the colonies in the name of England. They smashed up his house with axes, drank the wine in his wine cellar, and looted the house of its furniture and other objects. A report by colony officials to England said that this was part of a larger scheme in which the houses of fifteen rich people were to be destroyed, as part of "a War of Plunder, of general levelling and taking away the Distinction of rich and poor."

It was one of those moments in which fury against the rich went further than leaders like Otis wanted. Could class hatred be focused against the pro-British elite, and deflected from the nationalist elite? In New York, that same year of the Boston house attacks, someone wrote to the New York *Gazette,* "Is it equitable that 99, rather 999, should suffer for the Extravagance or Grandeur of one, especially when it is considered that men frequently owe their Wealth to the impoverishment of their Neighbors?" The leaders of the Revolution would worry about keeping such sentiments within limits.

Mechanics were demanding political democracy in the colonial cities: open meetings of representative assemblies, public galleries in the legislative halls, and the publishing of roll-call votes, so that constituents could check on representatives. They wanted open-air meetings where the population could participate in making policy, more equitable taxes, price controls, and the election of mechanics and other ordinary people to government posts.

Especially in Philadelphia, according to Nash, the consciousness of the lower middle classes grew to the point where it must have caused some hard thinking, not just among the conservative Loyalists sympathetic to England, but even among leaders of the Revolution. "By mid-1776, laborers, artisans, and small tradesmen, employing extralegal measures when electoral politics failed, were in clear command in Philadelphia." Helped by some middle-class

The famed Boston Tea Party was the colonists' way of rebelling against the high taxes imposed on them by the English monarchy.

leaders (Thomas Paine, Thomas Young, and others), they "launched a full-scale attack on wealth and even on the right to acquire unlimited private property."

During elections for the 1776 convention to frame a constitution for Pennsylvania, a Privates Committee urged voters to oppose "great and overgrown rich men . . . they will be too apt to be framing distinctions in society." The Privates Committee drew up a bill of rights for the convention, including the statement that "an enormous proportion of property vested in a few individuals is dangerous to the rights, and destructive of the common happiness, of mankind; and therefore every free state hath a right by its laws to discourage the possession of such property."

In the countryside, where most people lived, there was a similar conflict of poor against rich, one which political leaders would use to mobilize the population against England, granting some benefits for the rebellious poor, and many more for themselves in the process. The tenant riots in New Jersey in the 1740s, the New York tenant uprisings of the 1750s and 1760s in the Hudson Valley, and the rebellion in northeastern New York that led to the carving of Vermont out of New York State were all more than sporadic rioting. They were long-lasting social movements, highly organized, involving the creation of countergovernments. They were aimed at a handful of rich landlords, but with the landlords far away, they often had to direct their anger against farmers who had leased the disputed land from the owners.

Just as the Jersey rebels had broken into jails to free their friends, rioters in the Hudson Valley rescued prisoners from the sheriff and one time took the sheriff himself as prisoner. The tenants were seen as "chiefly the dregs of the People," and the posse that the sheriff of Albany County led to Bennington in 1771 included the privileged top of the local power structure.

The land rioters saw their battle as poor against rich. A witness at a rebel leader's trial in New York in 1766 said that the farmers evicted by the landlords "had an equitable Title but could not be defended in a Course of Law because they were poor and . . . poor men were always oppressed by the rich." Ethan Allen's Green Mountain rebels in Vermont described themselves as "a poor people . . . fatigued in settling a wilderness country," and their opponents as "a number of Attorneys and other gentlemen, with all their tackle of ornaments, and compliments, and French finesse."

Land-hungry farmers in the Hudson Valley turned to the British for support against the American landlords; the Green Mountain rebels did the same. But as the conflict with Britain intensified, the colonial leaders of the movement for independence, aware of the tendency of poor tenants to side with the British in their anger against the rich, adopted policies to win over people in the countryside. . . .

Stamp Act Riots

The key battles [of the Revolutionary movement] were being fought in the North, and here, in the cities, the colonial leaders had a divided white population; they could win over the mechanics, who were a kind of middle class, who had a stake in the fight against England, who faced competition from English manufacturers. The biggest problem was to keep the propertyless people, who were unemployed and hungry in the crisis following the French war, under control.

In Boston, the economic grievances of the lowest classes mingled with anger against the British and exploded in mob violence. The leaders of the Independence movement wanted to use that mob energy against England, but also to contain it so that it would not demand too much from them.

When riots against the Stamp Act swept Boston in 1767, they were analyzed by the commander of the British forces in North America, General Thomas Gage, as follows:

> The Boston Mob, raised first by the Instigation of Many of the Principal Inhabitants, Allured by Plunder, rose shortly after of their own Accord, attacked, robbed, and destroyed several Houses, and amongst others, that of the Lieutenant Governor. . . . People then began to be terrified

at the Spirit they had raised, to perceive that popular Fury was not to be guided, and each individual feared he might be the next Victim to their Rapacity. The same Fears spread thro' the other Provinces, and there has been as much Pains taken since, to prevent Insurrections, of the People, as before to excite them.

Gage's comment suggests that leaders of the movement against the Stamp Act had instigated crowd action, but then became frightened by the thought that it might be directed against their wealth, too. At this time, the top 10 percent of Boston's taxpayers held about 66 percent of Boston's taxable wealth, while the lowest 30 percent of the taxpaying population had no taxable property at all. The propertyless could not vote and so (like blacks, women, Indians) could not participate in town meetings. This included sailors, journeymen, apprentices, servants.

Dirk Hoerder, a student of Boston mob actions in the Revolutionary period, calls the Revolutionary leadership "the Sons of Liberty type drawn from the middling interest and well-to-do merchants . . . a hesitant leadership," wanting to spur action against Great Britain, yet worrying about maintaining control over the crowds at home.

It took the Stamp Act crisis to make this leadership aware of its dilemma. A political group in Boston called the Loyal Nine—merchants, distillers, shipowners, and master craftsmen who opposed the Stamp Act—organized a procession in August 1765 to protest it. They put fifty master craftsmen at the head, but needed to mobilize shipworkers from the North End and mechanics and apprentices from the South End. Two or three thousand were in the procession (Negroes were excluded). They marched to the home of the stampmaster and burned his effigy. But after the "gentlemen" who organized the demonstration left, the crowd went further and destroyed some of the stampmaster's property. These were, as one of the Loyal Nine said, "amazingly inflamed people." The Loyal Nine seemed taken aback by the direct assault on the wealthy furnishings of the stampmaster.

The rich set up armed patrols. Now a town meeting was called and the same leaders who had planned the demonstration denounced the violence and disavowed the actions of the crowd. As more demonstrations were planned for November 1, 1765, when the Stamp Act was to go into effect, and for Pope's Day, November 5, steps were taken to keep things under control; a dinner was given for certain leaders of the rioters to win them over. And when the Stamp Act was repealed, due to overwhelming resistance, the conservative leaders severed their connections with the rioters. They held annual celebrations of the first anti–Stamp Act demonstration, to which they invited, according to Hoerder, not the rioters but "mainly upper and middle-class Bostonians, who traveled in coaches and carriages to Roxbury or Dorchester for opulent feasts."

The Boston Massacre

When the British Parliament turned to its next attempt to tax the colonies, this time by a set of taxes which it hoped would not excite as much opposition, the colonial leaders organized boycotts. But, they stressed, "No Mobs or Tumults, let the Persons and Properties of your most inveterate Enemies be safe." Samuel Adams advised: "No Mobs—No Confusions—No Tumult." And James Otis said that "no possible circumstances, though ever so oppressive, could be supposed sufficient to justify private tumults and disorders. . . ."

Impressment [forced military conscription] and the quartering of troops by the British were directly hurtful to the sailors and other working people. After 1768, two thousand soldiers were quartered in Boston, and friction grew between the crowds and the soldiers. The soldiers began to take the jobs of working people when jobs were scarce. Mechanics and shopkeepers lost work or business because of the colonists' boycott of British goods. In 1769, Boston set up a committee "to Consider of some Suitable Methods of employing the Poor of the Town, whose Numbers and distresses are dayly increasing by the loss of its Trade and Commerce."

On March 5, 1770, grievances of ropemakers against British soldiers taking their jobs led to a fight. A crowd gathered in front of the custom-house and began provoking the soldiers, who fired and killed first Crispus Attucks, a mulatto worker, then others. This became known as the Boston Massacre. Feelings against the British mounted quickly. There was anger at the acquittal of six of the British soldiers (two were punished by having their thumbs branded and were discharged from the army). The crowd at the Massacre was described by John Adams, defense attorney for the British soldiers, as "a motley rabble of saucy boys, negroes, and molattoes, Irish teagues and outlandish jack tarrs [pirates or sailors]." Perhaps ten thousand people marched in the funeral procession for the victims of the Massacre, out of a total Boston population of sixteen thousand. This led England to remove the troops from Boston and try to quiet the situation.

Impressment was the background of the Massacre. There had been impressment riots through the 1760s in New York and in Newport, Rhode Island, where five hundred seamen, boys, and Negroes rioted after five weeks of impressment by the British. Six weeks before the Boston Massacre, there was a battle in New York of seamen against British soldiers taking their jobs, and one seaman was killed. . . .

A Bond Against the British

In Virginia, it seemed clear to the educated gentry that something needed to be done to persuade the lower orders to join the Revolutionary cause, to deflect their anger against England. One Virginian wrote in his diary in the spring of 1774: "The lower Class of People here are in tumult on account of Reports from Boston, many of them expect to be press'd & compell'd to go and fight the Britains!" Around the time of the Stamp Act, a Virginia orator addressed the poor. "Are not the gentlemen made of the same materials as the lowest and poorest among you? . . . Listen to no doctrines which may tend to divide us, but let us go hand in hand, as brothers. . . ."

It was a problem for which the rhetorical talents of Patrick Henry were superbly fitted. He was, as [author] Rhys Isaac puts it, "firmly attached to the world of the gentry," but he spoke in words that the poorer whites of Virginia could understand. Henry's fellow Virginian Edmund Randolph recalled his style as "simplicity and even carelessness. . . . His pauses, which for their length might sometimes be feared to dispell the attention, rivited it the more by raising the expectation."

Patrick Henry's oratory in Virginia pointed a way to relieve class tension between upper and lower classes and form a bond against the British. This was to find language inspiring to all classes, specific enough in its listing of grievances to charge people with anger against the British, vague enough to avoid class conflict among the rebels, and stirring enough to build patriotic feeling for the resistance movement.

Tom Paine's *Common Sense,* which appeared in early 1776 and became the most popular pamphlet in the American colonies, did this. It made the first bold argument for independence, in words that any fairly literate person could understand: "Society in every state is a blessing, but Government even in its best state is but a necessary evil. . . ."

Paine disposed of the idea of the divine right of kings by a pungent history of the British monarchy. . . .

Paine dealt with the practical advantages of sticking to England or being separated; he knew the importance of economics:

> I challenge the warmest advocate for reconciliation to show a single advantage that this continent can reap by being connected with Great Britain. I repeat the challenge; not a single advantage is derived. Our corn will fetch its price in any market in Europe, and our imported goods must be paid for by them where we will. . . .

As for the bad effects of the connection with England, Paine appealed to the colonists' memory of all the wars in which England had involved them, wars costly in lives and money:

> But the injuries and disadvantages which we sustain by that connection are without number. . . . any submission to, or dependence on, Great Britain, tends directly to involve this Continent in European wars and quarrels, and set us at variance with nations who would otherwise seek our friendship. . . .

He built slowly to an emotional pitch:

Everything that is right or reasonable pleads for separation. The blood of the slain, the weeping voice of nature cries, 'TIS TIME TO PART.

Common Sense went through twenty-five editions in 1776 and sold hundreds of thousands of copies. It is probable that almost every literate colonist either read it or knew about its contents. Pamphleteering had become by this time the chief theater of debate about relations with England. From 1750 to 1776 four hundred pamphlets had appeared arguing one or another side of the Stamp Act or the Boston Massacre or the Tea Party or the general questions of disobedience to law, loyalty to government, rights and obligations. . . .

On Behalf of a United People

Later, during the controversy over adopting the Constitution, Paine would once again represent urban artisans, who favored a strong central government. He seemed to believe that such a government could represent some great common interest. In this sense, he lent himself perfectly to the myth of the Revolution—that it was on behalf of a united people.

The Declaration of Independence brought that myth to its peak of eloquence. Each harsher measure of British control—the Proclamation of 1763 not allowing colonists to settle beyond the Appalachians, the Stamp Tax, the Townshend taxes, including the one on tea, the stationing of troops and the Boston Massacre, the closing of the port of Boston and the dissolution of the Massachusetts legislature—escalated colonial rebellion to the point of revolution. The colonists had responded with the Stamp Act Congress, the Sons of Liberty, the Committees of Correspondence, the Boston Tea Party, and finally, in 1774, the setting up of a Continental Congress—an illegal body, forerunner of a future independent government. It was after the military clash at Lexington and Concord in April 1775, between colonial Minutemen and British troops, that the Continental Congress decided on separation. They organized a small committee to draw up the Declaration of Independence, which Thomas Jefferson wrote. It was adopted by the Congress on July 2, and officially proclaimed July 4, 1776.

Declaring Independence

By this time there was already a powerful sentiment for independence. Resolutions adopted in North Carolina in May of 1776, and sent to the Continental Congress, declared independence of England, asserted that all British law was null and void, and urged military preparations. About the same time, the town of Malden, Massachusetts, responding to a request from the Massachusetts House of Representatives that all towns in the state declare their views on independence, had met in town meeting and unanimously called for independence: ". . . we therefore renounce with disdain our connexion with a kingdom of slaves; we bid a final adieu to Britain."

"When in the Course of human events, it becomes necessary for one people to dissolve the political bands . . . they should declare the causes. . . ." This was the opening of the Declaration of Independence. Then, in its second paragraph, came the powerful philosophical statement:

> We hold these truths to be self-evident, that all men are created equal, that they are endowed by their Creator with certain unalienable Rights, that among these are Life, Liberty and the pursuit of Happiness. That to secure these rights, Governments are instituted among Men, deriving their just powers from the consent of the governed, that whenever any Form of Government becomes destructive of these ends, it is the Right of the People to alter or to abolish it, and to institute new Government. . . .

It then went on to list grievances against the king, "a history of repeated injuries and usurpations, all having in direct object the establishment of an absolute Tyranny over these States." The list accused the king of dissolving colonial governments, controlling judges, sending "swarms of Officers to harass our people," sending in armies of occupation, cutting off colonial trade with other parts of the world, taxing the colonists without their consent, and waging war against them, "transporting large Armies of foreign Mercenaries to compleat the works of death, desolation and tyranny."

All this, the language of popular control over governments, the right of rebellion and revolution, indignation at political tyranny, economic burdens, and military attacks, was language well suited to unite large numbers of colonists, and persuade even those who had grievances against one another to turn against England.

Left Out of the Declaration

Some Americans were clearly omitted from this circle of united interest drawn by the Declaration of Independence: Indians, black slaves, women. Indeed, one paragraph of the Declaration charged the King with inciting slave rebellions and Indian attacks:

> He has excited domestic insurrections amongst us, and has endeavoured to bring on the inhabitants of our frontiers, the merciless Indian Savages, whose known rule of warfare is an undistinguished destruction of all ages, sexes and conditions.

Twenty years before the Declaration, a proclamation of the legislature of Massachusetts of November 3, 1755, declared the Penobscot Indians "rebels, enemies and traitors" and provided a bounty: "For every scalp of a male Indian brought in . . . forty pounds. For every scalp of such female Indian or male Indian under the age of twelve years that shall be killed . . . twenty pounds. . . ."

Thomas Jefferson had written a paragraph of the Declaration accusing the King of transporting slaves from Africa to the colonies and "suppressing every legislative attempt to prohibit or to restrain this execrable commerce." This seemed to express moral indignation against slavery and the slave trade (Jefferson's personal distaste for slavery must be put alongside the fact that he owned hundreds of slaves to the day he died). Behind it was the growing fear among Virginians and some other southerners about the growing number of black slaves in the colonies (20 percent of the total population) and the threat of slave revolts as the number of slaves increased. Jefferson's paragraph was removed by the Continental Congress, because slaveholders themselves disagreed about the desirability of ending the slave trade. So even that gesture toward the black slave was omitted in the great manifesto of freedom of the American Revolution.

The use of the phrase "all men are created equal" was probably not a deliberate attempt to make a statement about women. It was just that women were beyond consideration as worthy of inclusion. They were politically invisible. Though practical needs gave women a certain authority in the home, on the farm, or in occupations like midwifery, they were simply overlooked in any consideration of political rights, any notions of civic equality.

To say that the Declaration of Independence, even by its own language, was limited to life, liberty, and happiness for white males is not to denounce the makers and signers of the Declaration for holding the ideas expected of privileged males of the eighteenth century. Reformers and radicals, looking discontentedly at history, are often accused of expecting too much from a past political epoch—and sometimes they do. But the point of noting those outside the arc of human rights in the Declaration is not, centuries late and pointlessly, to lay impossible moral burdens on that time. It is to try to understand the way in which the Declaration functioned to mobilize certain groups of Americans, ignoring others. Surely, inspirational language to create a secure consensus is still used, in our time, to cover up serious conflicts of interest in that consensus, and to cover up, also, the omission of large parts of the human race.

The Boston Massacre

James Bowdoin, Joseph Warren, and Samuel Pemberton

British troops first arrived in Boston, Massachusetts, in 1767 to keep order and protect tax collectors. The troops were quartered in various private buildings and Bostonians resented their presence. Fights between soldiers and civilians were common, and on March 5, 1770, after being pelted with snowballs, the soldiers fired into a crowd gathered in front of the Customs House, killing five people.

After the event, which became known as the Boston Massacre, James Bowdoin, Joseph Warren, and Samuel Pemberton appointed a committee to ascertain who was responsible for the "murders and massacres." The excerpt below was based on those findings and published in a pamphlet that was eventually sold in thirteen colonies. This pamphlet helped rally public support for the American Revolution throughout the colonies.

It may be a proper introduction to this narrative, briefly to represent the state of things for some time previous to the [Boston] Massacre; and this seems necessary in order to the forming a just idea of the causes of it.

At the end of the late [French and Indian] War, in which this province bore so distinguished a part, a happy union subsisted between Great Britain and the colonies. This was unfortunately interrupted [in 1765] by the Stamp Act; but it was in some measure restored by the repeal of it [in 1766]. It was again interrupted by other acts of parliament for taxing America. . . .

Excerpted from *History of the Boston Massacre,* by James Bowdoin, Joseph Warren, and Samuel Pemberton, edited by Frederic Kidder (Albany, 1870).

The residence of the commissioners here [to collect the duty on tea] has been detrimental, not only to the commerce, but to the political interests of the town and province; and not only so, but we can trace from it the causes of the late horrid massacre. Soon after their arrival here in November, 1767, instead of confining themselves to the proper business of their office, they became partisans of Governor [Francis] Bernard in his political schemes. . . .

Unfortunately for us, they have been too successful in their said representations, which, in conjunction with Governor Bernard's, have occasioned his majesty's faithful subjects of this town [Boston] and province [Massachusetts] to be treated as enemies and rebels, by an invasion of the town by sea and land; to which the approaches were made with all the circumspection usual where a vigorous opposition is expected. While the town was surrounded by a considerable number of his majesty's ships of war, two regiments landed and took possession of it; and to support these, two other regiments arrived some time after from Ireland; one of which landed at Castle Island, and the other in the town.

Forced to Quarter Troops

Thus were we, in aggravation of our other embarrassments, embarrassed with troops, forced upon us contrary to our inclination—contrary to the spirit of [the 13th-century Charter of Liberties the] Magna Charta—contrary to the very letter of the [English] Bill of Rights [written in 1689], in which it is declared, that the raising or keeping a standing army within the kingdom in time of peace, unless it be with the consent of parliament, is against law, and without the desire of the civil magistrates, to aid whom was the pretence for sending the troops hither; who were quartered in the town in direct violation of an act of parliament for quartering troops in America; and all this in consequence of the representations of the said commissioners and the said governor, as appears by their memorials and letters lately published.

As they were the procuring cause of troops being sent hither, they must therefore be the remote and a blameable cause of all the disturbances and bloodshed that have taken place in consequence of that measure. . . .

We shall next attend to the conduct of the troops, and to some circumstances relative to them. Governor Bernard without consulting the council, having given up the State-house to the troops at their landing, they took possession of the chambers, where the representatives of the province and the courts of law held their meetings; and (except the council-chamber) of all other parts of that house; in which they continued a considerable time, to the great annoyance of those courts while they sat, and of the merchants and gentlemen of the town, who had always made the lower floor of it their exchange. They had a right so to do, as the property of it was in the town; but they were deprived of that right by mere power. The said governor soon after, by every stratagem and by every method but a forcible entry, endeavored to get possession of the Manufactory house, to make a barrack of it for the troops; and for that purpose caused it to be besieged by the troops, and the people in it to be used very cruelly; which extraordinary proceedings created universal uneasiness, arising from the apprehension that the troops under the influence of such a man would be employed to effect the most dangerous purposes; but failing of that, other houses were procured, in which, contrary to act of parliament, he caused the troops to be quartered. After their quarters were settled, the main guard was posted at one of the said houses, directly opposite to, and not twelve yards from, the State-house (where the general court, and all the law courts for the county were held), with two field pieces pointed to the State-house. This situation of the main guard and field pieces seemed to indicate an attack upon the constitution, and a defiance of law; and to be intended to affront the legislative and executive authority of the province.

The general court, at the first session after the arrival of the troops, viewed it in this light, and applied to Governor Bernard to cause such a nuisance to be removed; but to no purpose. Disgusted at such an indignity, and at the appearance of being under duress, they refused to do business in such circumstances; and in consequence thereof were adjourned to Cambridge, to the great inconvenience of the members.

Besides this, the challenging the inhabitants by sentinels posted in all parts of the town before the lodgings of officers, which (for about six months, while it lasted), occasioned many quarrels and uneasiness.

Outrage and Massacre

Capt. [James] Wilson, of the 59th, exciting the negroes of the town to take away their masters' lives and property, and repair to the army for protection, which was fully proved against him—the attack of a party of soldiers on some of the magistrates of the town—the repeated rescues of soldiers from peace officers—the firing of a loaded musket in a public street, to the endangering a great number of peaceable inhabitants—the frequent wounding of persons by their bayonets and cutlasses, and the numerous instances of bad behavior in the soldiery, made us early sensible that the troops were not sent here for any benefit to the town or province, and that we had no good to expect from such conservators of the peace.

It was not expected, however, that such an outrage and massacre, as happened here on the evening of the fifth instant, would have been perpetrated. There were then killed and wounded, by a discharge of musketry, eleven of his majesty's subjects, viz:

Mr. Samuel Gray, killed on the spot by a ball [bullet] entering his head.

Crispus Attucks, a mulatto, killed on the spot, two balls entering his breast.

Mr. James Caldwell, killed on the spot, by two balls entering his back.

Mr. Samuel Maverick, a youth of seventeen years of age, mortally wounded; he died the next morning.

Mr. Patrick Carr mortally wounded; he died the 14th instant.

Christopher Monk and John Clark, youths about seventeen years of age, dangerously wounded. It is apprehended they will die.

Mr. Edward Payne, merchant, standing at his door; wounded.

Messrs. John Green, Robert Patterson, and David Parker; all dangerously wounded.

The actors in this dreadful tragedy were a party of soldiers commanded by Capt. [Thomas] Preston of the 29th regiment. This party, including the captain, consisted of eight, who are all committed to jail. . . .

Eyewitness Accounts

Robert Polley declares, that on Monday evening, the 5th instant, as he was going home, he observed about ten persons standing near Mr. Taylor's door; after standing there a small space of time, he went with them towards Boylston's alley, opposite to Murray's barracks; we met in the alley about eight or nine armed soldiers; they assaulted us, and gave us a great deal of abusive language; we then drove them back to the barracks with sticks only; we looked for stones or bricks, but could find none, the ground being covered with snow. Some of the lads dispersed, and he, the said Polley, with a few others, were returning peaceably home, when we met about nine or ten other soldiers armed: one of them said, "Where are the sons of bitches?" They struck at several persons in the street, and went towards the head of the alley. Two officers came and endeavored to get them into their barracks; one of the lads proposed to ring the bell; the soldiers went through the alley, and the boys huzzaed, and said they were gone through Royal Exchange lane into King street.

Samuel Drowne declares that, about nine o'clock of the evening of the fifth of March current, standing at his own door in Cornhill, he saw about fourteen or fifteen soldiers of the 29th regiment, who came from Murray's barracks, armed with naked cutlasses, swords, &c., and came upon the inhabitants of the town, then standing or walking in Cornhill, and abused some, and violently assaulted others as they met them; most of whom were without so much as a stick in their hand to defend themselves, as he very clearly could discern, it being moonlight, and himself being one of the assaulted persons. All or most of the said soldiers he saw go into King street (some of them through Royal Exchange lane), and there followed them, and soon discovered them to be quarrelling and fighting with the people whom they saw there, which he thinks were not more than a dozen, when the soldiers came there first, armed as aforesaid. Of those dozen people, the most of them were gentlemen, standing together a little below the Town-house, upon the Exchange. At the appearance of those soldiers so armed, the most of the twelve persons went off, some of them being first assaulted.

The violent proceedings of this party, and their going into King street, "quarrelling and fighting with the people whom they saw there" (mentioned in Mr. Drowne's deposition), was immediately introductory to the grand catastrophe.

Throwing Snowballs

These assailants, who issued from Murray's barracks (so called), after attacking and wounding divers persons in Cornhill, as above mentioned, being armed, proceeded (most of them) up the Royal Exchange lane into King street; where, making a short stop, and after assaulting and driving away the few they met there, they brandished their arms and cried out, "Where are the boogers! where are the cowards!" At this time there were very few persons in the street beside themselves. This party in proceeding from Exchange lane into King street, must pass the sentry posted at the westerly corner of the Custom-house, which butts on that lane and fronts on that street. This is needful to be mentioned, as near that spot and in that street the bloody tragedy was acted, and the street actors in it were stationed: their station being but a few feet from the front side of the said Custom-house. The outrageous behavior and the threats of the said party occasioned the ringing of the meeting-house bell near the head of King street, which bell ringing quick, as for fire, it presently brought out a number of the inhabitants, who being soon sensible of the occasion of it, were naturally led to King street, where the said party had made a stop but a little while before, and where their stopping had drawn together a number of boys, round the sentry at the Custom-house. Whether the boys mistook the sentry for one of the said party, and thence took occasion to differ with him, or whether he first affronted them, which is affirmed in several depositions; however that may be, there was much foul language between them, and some of them, in consequence of his pushing at them with his bayonet, threw snowballs at him, which occasioned him to knock hastily at the door of the Custom-house. From hence two persons thereupon proceeded immediately to the main guard, which was posted (opposite to the State-house) at a small distance, near the head of the said street. The officer on guard was Capt. Preston, who with seven or eight soldiers, with fire-arms and charged bayonets, issued from the guard house, and in great haste posted himself and his soldiers in the front of the Custom-house, near the corner aforesaid. In passing to this station the soldiers pushed several persons with their bayonets, driving through the people in so rough a manner that it appeared they intended to create a disturbance. This occasioned some snowballs to be thrown at them, which seems to have been the only provocation that was given. Mr. Knox . . . declares, that while he was talking with Capt. Preston, the soldiers of his detachment had attacked the people with their bayonets; and that there was not the least provocation given to Capt. Preston or his party; the backs of the people being toward them when the people were attacked. He also declares that Capt. Preston seemed to be in great haste and much agitated, and that, according to his opinion, there were not then present in King street above seventy or eighty persons at the extent.

The said party was formed into a half circle; and within a short time after they had been posted at the Custom-house, began to fire upon the people.

Captain Preston is said to have ordered them to fire, and to have repeated that order. One gun was fired first; then others in succession, and with deliberation, till ten or a dozen guns were fired; or till that number of discharges were made from the guns that were fired. By which means eleven persons were killed and wounded, as above represented. . . .

Restrained from Firing Again

Soon after the firing, a drum with a party from the main guard went to Murray's and the other barracks, beating an alarm as they went, which, with the firing, had the effect of a signal for action. Whereupon all the soldiers of the 29th regiment, or the main body of them, appeared in King street under arms, and seemed bent on a further massacre of the inhabitants, which was with great difficulty prevented. They were drawn up between the State-house and main guard, their lines extending across the street and facing down King street, where the town-people were assembled. The first line kneeled, and the whole of the first platoon presented their guns ready to fire, as soon as the word should be given. They continued in that posture a considerable time; but by the good providence of God they were restrained from firing. . . .

After the firing, and when the slaughter was known, which occasioned the ringing of all the bells of the town, a large body of the inhabitants soon assembled in King street, and continued there the whole time the 29th regiment was there under arms, and would not retire till that regiment, and all the soldiers that appeared, were ordered, and actually went, to their barracks: after which, having been assured by the Lieutenant-Governor, and a number of the civil magistrates present, that every legal step should be taken to bring the criminals to justice, they gradually dispersed. For some time the appearance of things was dismal. The soldiers outrageous on the one hand, and the inhabitants justly incensed against them on the other; both parties seeming disposed to come to action. In this case the consequences would have been terrible. But by the interposition of his honor, some of his majesty's council, a number of civil magistrates, and other gentlemen of weight and influence, who all endeavored to calm and pacify the people, and by the two principal officers interposing their authority with regard to the soldiers, there was happily no further bloodshed ensued; and by two o'clock the town was restored to a tolerable state of quiet. About that time, Capt. Preston, and a few hours after, the party that had fired, were committed to safe custody.

One happy effect has arisen from this melancholy affair, and it is the general voice of the town and province it may be a lasting one—all the troops are removed from the town. They are quartered for the present in the barracks at Castle Island; from whence it is hoped they will have a speedy order to remove entirely out of the province, together with those persons who were the occasion of their coming hither.

The Declaration of Independence

The Declaration of Independence announces that the American colonies are free of rule by Great Britain. Written by Thomas Jefferson and approved by the Continental Congress on July 4, 1776, the document today remains the foundation for America's freedom.

Jefferson's writings were influenced by the words and ideas of English philosopher John Locke and French philosophers Montesquieu and Rousseau.

Statesman Thomas Jefferson was governor of Virginia, U.S. minister to France, and president of the United States from 1801 to 1809. He was also an architect, naturalist, and linguist.

When in the Course of human events, it becomes necessary for one people to dissolve the political bands which have connected them with another, and to assume among the Powers of the earth, the separate and equal station to which the Laws of Nature and of Nature's God entitle them, a decent respect to the opinions of mankind requires that they should declare the causes which impel them to the separation.

We hold these truths to be self-evident, that all men are created equal, that they are endowed by their Creator with certain unalienable Rights, that among these are Life, Liberty, and the pursuit of Happiness. That to secure these rights, Governments are instituted among Men, deriving their just powers from the consent of the governed, That whenever any Form of Government becomes destructive of these ends, it is the Right of the People to alter or to abolish

Excerpted from *The Declaration of Independence,* by Thomas Jefferson, 1776.

it, and to institute new Government, laying its foundation on such principles and organizing its powers in such form, as to them shall seem most likely to effect their Safety and Happiness. Prudence, indeed, will dictate that Governments long established should not be changed for light and transient causes; and accordingly all experience hath shown, that mankind are more disposed to suffer, while evils are sufferable, than to right themselves by abolishing the forms to which they are accustomed. But when a long train of abuses and usurpations, pursuing invariably the same Object evinces a design to reduce them under absolute Despotism, it is their right, it is their duty, to throw off such Government, and to provide new Guards for their future security.—Such has been the patient sufferance of these Colonies; and such is now the necessity which constrains them to alter their former Systems of Government. The history of the present King of Great Britain is a history of repeated injuries and usurpations, all having in direct object the establishment of an absolute Tyranny over these States. To prove this, let Facts be submitted to a candid world.

Complaints Against King George III

He has refused his Assent to Laws, the most wholesome and necessary for the public good.

He has forbidden his Governors to pass Laws of immediate and pressing importance, unless suspended in their operation till his Assent should be obtained; and when so suspended, he has utterly neglected to attend to them.

He has refused to pass other Laws for the accommodation of large districts of people, unless those people would relinquish the right of Representation in the Legislature, a right inestimable to them and formidable to tyrants only.

He has called together legislative bodies at places unusual, uncomfortable, and distant from the depository of their Public Records, for the sole purpose of fatiguing them into compliance with his measures.

He has dissolved Representative Houses repeatedly, for opposing with manly firmness his invasions on the rights of the people.

He has refused for a long time, after such dissolutions, to cause others to be elected; whereby the Legislative Powers, incapable of Annihilation, have returned to the People at large for their exercise; the State remaining in the mean time exposed to all the dangers of invasion from without, and convulsions within.

He has endeavoured to prevent the population of these States; for that purpose obstructing the Laws of Naturalization of Foreigners; refusing to pass others to encourage their migration hither, and raising the conditions of new Appropriations of Lands.

He has obstructed the Administration of Justice, by refusing his Assent to Laws for establishing Judiciary Powers.

He has made Judges dependent on his Will alone, for the tenure of their offices, and the amount and payment of their salaries.

He has erected a multitude of New Offices, and sent hither swarms of Officers to harrass our People, and eat out their substance.

He has kept among us, in times of peace, Standing Armies without the Consent of our legislature.

He has affected to render the Military independent of and superior to the Civil Power.

He has combined with others to subject us to a jurisdiction foreign to our constitution, and unacknowledged by our laws; giving his Assent to their acts of pretended legislation:

Benjamin Franklin, Thomas Jefferson, John Adams, Robert Livingston, and Roger Sherman are shown drafting the Declaration of Independence.

For quartering large bodies of armed troops among us:

For protecting them, by a mock Trial, from Punishment for any Murders which they should commit on the Inhabitants of these States:

For cutting off our Trade with all parts of the world:

For imposing taxes on us without our Consent:

For depriving us in many cases, of the benefits of Trial by Jury:

For transporting us beyond Seas to be tried for pretended offences:

For abolishing the free System of English Laws in a neighbouring Province, establishing therein an Arbitrary government, and enlarging its Boundaries so as to render it at once an example and fit instrument for introducing the same absolute rule into these Colonies:

For taking away our Charters, abolishing our most valuable Laws, and altering fundamentally the Forms of our Governments:

For suspending our own Legislature, and declaring themselves invested with Power to legislate for us in all cases whatsoever.

Waging War Against Us

He has abdicated Government here, by declaring us out of his Protection and waging War against us.

He has plundered our seas, ravaged our Coasts, burnt our towns, and destroyed the lives of our people.

He is at this time transporting large armies of foreign mercenaries to compleat the works of death, desolation and tyranny, already begun with circumstances of Cruelty & perfidy scarcely paralleled in the most barbarous ages, and totally unworthy the Head of a civilized nation.

He has constrained our fellow Citizens taken Captive on the high Seas to bear Arms against their Country, to become the executioners of their friends and Brethren, or to fall themselves by their Hands.

He has excited domestic insurrections amongst us, and has endeavoured to bring on the inhabitants of our frontiers, the merciless Indian Savages, whose known rule of warfare, is an undistinguished destruction of all ages, sexes and conditions.

In every stage of these Oppressions We have Petitioned for Redress in the most humble terms: Our repeated Petitions have been answered only by repeated injury. A Prince, whose character is thus marked by every act which may define a Tyrant, is unfit to be the ruler of a free People.

Nor have We been wanting in attention to our British brethren. We have warned them from time to time of attempts by their legislature to extend an unwarrantable jurisdiction over us. We have reminded them of the circumstances of our emigration and settlement here. We have appealed to their native justice and magnanimity, and we have conjured them by the ties of our common kindred to disavow these usurpations, which, would inevitably interrupt our connections and correspondence. They too have been deaf to the voice of justice and of consanguinity. We must, therefore, acquiesce in the necessity, which denounces our Separation, and hold them, as we hold the rest of mankind, Enemies in War, in Peace Friends.

We, therefore, the Representatives of the United States of America, in General Congress, Assembled, appealing to the Supreme Judge of the world for the rectitude of our intentions, do, in the Name, and by Authority of the good People of these Colonies, solemnly publish and declare, That these United Colonies are, and of Right ought to be Free and Independent States; that they are Absolved from all Allegiance to the British Crown, and that all political connection between them and the State of Great Britain, is and ought to be totally dissolved; and that as Free and Independent States, they have full Power to levy War, conclude Peace, contract Alliances, establish Commerce, and to do all other Acts and Things which Independent States may of right do. And for the support of this Declaration, with a firm reliance on the Protection of Divine Providence, we mutually pledge to each other our Lives, our Fortunes and our sacred Honor.

JOHN HANCOCK

New Hampshire

JOSIAH BARTLETT
WM. WHIPPLE

MATTHEW THORNTON

Massachusetts Bay

SAML. ADAMS
JOHN ADAMS

ELBRIDGE GERRY
ROBT. TREAT PAINE

Rhode Island

STEP. HOPKINS

WILLIAM ELLERY

Connecticut

ROGER SHERMAN
SAM'EL HUNTINGTON

WM. WILLIAMS
OLIVER WOLCOTT

New York

WM. FLOYD
PHIL. LIVINGSTON

FRANS. LEWIS
LEWIS MORRIS

New Jersey

RICHD. STOCKTON
JNO. WITHERSPOON
FRAS. HOPKINSON

JOHN HART
ABRA. CLARK

Pennsylvania

ROBT. MORRIS

BENJAMIN RUSH

BENJA. FRANKLIN

JOHN MORTON

GEO. CLYMER

JAS. SMITH

GEO. TAYLOR

JAMES WILSON

GEO. ROSS

Delaware

CAESAR RODNEY

GEO. READ

THO. M'KEAN

Maryland

SAMUEL CHASE

WM. PACA

THOS. STONE

CHARLES CARROLL of Carrollton

Virginia

GEORGE WYTHE

RICHARD HENRY LEE

TH. JEFFERSON

BENJA. HARRISON

THOS. NELSON, jr.

FRANCIS LIGHTFOOT LEE

CARTER BRAXTON

North Carolina

WM. HOOPER

JOSEPH HEWES

JOHN PENN

South Carolina

EDWARD RUTLEDGE

THOS. HEYWARD, junr

ARTHUR MIDDLETON

THOMAS LYNCH, junr

Georgia

BUTTON GWINNETT

LYMAN HALL

GEO. WALTON

A White Travels Among the Native American Indians

Jonathan Carver

After Britain defeated France in the French and Indian War, Captain Jonathan Carver was hired by the king of England to explore the vast North American wilderness that was now British spoils of war. Carver spent three years walking and canoeing through the Upper Great Lakes and Mississippi River region looking for the fabled Northwest Passage said to connect America and India. Along the way, Carver befriended Native Americans and kept detailed journals describing their religions, hunting practices, dress, and lifestyles.

In the following excerpt, Carver describes the appearance and dress of the Dakota tribe (whom he refers to as Naudowessies) who lived around St. Anthony Falls in present-day Minneapolis, Minnesota.

The Indian nations do not appear to me to differ so widely in their make, colour, or constitution from each other as represented by some [other] writers. They are in general slight made, rather tall and strait, and you seldom see any among them deformed. Their skin is of a reddish or copper colour, their eyes are large and black, and their hair of the same hue, but very rarely is it curled. They have good teeth and their breath is as sweet as the air they draw in; their cheek-bones rather raised, but more so in the women than the men. The for-

Excerpted from *Jonathan Carver's Travels Through America* by Jonathan Carver, 1778.

mer are not quite so tall as the European women, however you frequently meet with good faces and agreeable persons among them, although they are more inclined to be fat than the other sex.

Many writers have asserted, that the Indians, even at the maturest period of their existence, are only furnished with hair on their heads and that, notwithstanding the profusion with which that part is covered, those parts which among the inhabitants of other climates are usually the seat of this excrescence remain entirely free from it. But from minute enquiries, and a curious inspection, I am able to declare (however respectable I may hold the authority of these historians in other points) that their assertions are erroneous and proceeding from the want of a thorough knowledge of the customs of the Indians.

After the age puberty, their bodies, in their natural state, are covered in the same manner as those of Europeans. The men, indeed, esteem a beard very unbecoming and take great pains to get rid of it, nor is there any ever to be perceived on their faces, except when they grow old and become inattentive to their appearance. . . .

Hair Styles and Clothing

The Naudowessies [Dakota Sioux] and the remote [Indian] nations pluck [hairs] out with bent pieces of hard wood, formed into a kind of nippers whilst those who have communication with Europeans procure from them wire which they twist into a screw or worm. Applying this to the part, they press the rings together and with a sudden twitch draw out all the hairs that are inclosed between them.

The men of every nation differ in their dress very little from each other, except those who trade with the Europeans. These exchange their furs for blankets, shirts and other apparel which they wear as much for ornament as necessity. The latter fasten by a girdle around their waists about half a yard of broadcloth which covers the middle parts of their bodies. Those who wear shirts never make them fast either at the wrist or collar; this would be a most insufferable confinement to them. They throw their blanket loose upon their shoulders and, holding the upper side of it by the two corners, with a knife in one hand and a tobacco pouch, pipe, &c. in the other, thus accoutred [dressed] they walk about in their villages or camps. But in their dances they seldom wear this covering.

Those among the men who wish to appear [more stylish] than the rest, pluck from their heads all the hair except a spot on the top of it, about the size of a crown-piece, where it is permitted to grow to a considerable length. On this are fastened plumes of feathers of various colours with silver or ivory quills. The manner of cutting and ornamenting this part of the head distinguishes different nations from each other.

Painting and Piercing

They paint their faces red and black, which they esteem as greatly ornamental. They also paint themselves when they go to war. But the method they make use of on this occasion differs from that wherein they use it merely as a decoration.

The young Indians, who are desirous of excelling their companions in finery, slit the outward rim of both their ears. At the same time they take care not to separate them entirely, but leave the flesh thus cut still untouched at both extremities. Around this spongy substance, from the upper to the lower part, they twist brass wire till the weight draws the amputated rim into a bow of five or six inches diameter, and drags it almost down to the shoulder. This decoration is esteemed to be excessively [stylish] and becoming.

It is also a common custom among them to bore their noses and wear in them pendants of different sorts. I observed that sea shells were much worn by those of the interior parts and reckoned very ornamental. But how they procured them I could not learn—probably by traffick with other nations nearer the sea.

They go without any covering for the thigh except that before spoken of round the middle, which reaches down half way the thighs. But they make for their legs a sort of stocking either of skins or cloth. These are sewed as near to the shape of the leg as possible, so as to admit of being drawn on and off. The edges of the stuff of which they are composed are left annexed to the seam and hang loose for about the breadth of a hand, and this part, which is placed on the outside of the leg, is generally ornamented by those who have any communication with Europeans, if of cloth, with ribands or lace, if of leather, with embroidery and porcupine quills curiously coloured. Strangers who hunt among the Indians in the parts where there is a great deal of snow find these stockings much more convenient than any others.

Their shoes are made of the skin of the deer, elk, or buffalo. These, after being sometimes dressed according to the European manner, at others with the hair remaining on them, are cut into shoes, and fashioned so as to be easy to the feet and convenient for walking. The edges round the ancle are decorated with pieces of brass or tin fixed around leather strings, about an inch long, which being placed very thick make a cheerful tinkling noise either when they walk or dance.

Women's Styles

The women wear a covering of some kind or other from the neck to the knees. Those who trade with the Europeans wear a linen garment the same as that used by the men, the flaps of which hang over the petticoat. Such as dress after their ancient manner make a kind of shift with leather which covers the body but not the arms. Their petticoats are made either of leather or cloth, and reach from the waist to the knee. On their legs they wear stockings and shoes, made and ornamented as those of the men.

They differ from each other in the mode of dressing their heads, each following the custom of the nation or band to which they belong and adhering to the form made use of by their ancestors from time immemorial. I remarked that most of the females who dwell on the east side of the Mississippi decorate their heads by inclosing their hair either in ribands, or in plates of silver. The latter is only made use of by the higher ranks, as it is a costly ornament. The silver they use on this occasion is formed into thin plates of about four inches broad, in several of which they confine their hair. That plate which is nearest the head is of considerable width, the next narrower and made so as to pass a little way under the other. In this manner they fasten into each other and, gradually tapering, descend to the waist. The hair of the Indian women being in general very long, this proves an expensive method.

But the women that live to the west of the Mississippi, viz, the Naudowessies, the Assinipoils [Assiniboin], &c. divide their hair in the middle of the head, and form it into two rolls, one against each ear. These rolls are about three inches long, and as large as their wrists. They hang in a perpendicular attitude at the front of each ear, and descend as far as the lower part of it.

The women of every nation generally place a spot of paint, about the size of a crown-piece, against each ear. Some of them put paint on their hair and sometimes a small spot in the middle of the forehead.

Huts and Teepees

The Indians, in general, pay a greater attention to their dress and to the ornaments with which they decorate their persons than to the accommodation of their huts or tents. They construct the latter in the following simple and expeditious manner.

Being provided with poles of a proper length, they fasten two of them across near their ends with bands made of bark. Having done this, they raise them up and extend the bottom of each as wide as they purpose to make the area of the tent. They then erect others of an equal height and fix them so as to support the two principal ones. On the whole they lay skins of the elk or deer, sewed together, in quantity sufficient to cover the poles, and by lapping over to form the door. A great number of skins are sometimes required for this purpose, as some of their tents are very capacious. That of the chief warrior of the Naudowessies was at least forty feet in circumference and very commodious.

They observe no regularity in fixing their tents when they encamp, but place them just as it suits their conveniency.

The huts also, which those who use not tents erect when they travel, for very few tribes have fixed abodes or regular towns or villages, are equally simple and almost as soon constructed.

They fix small pliable poles in the ground and bend them till they meet at the top and form a semi-circle, then lash them together. These they cover with mats made of rushes platted, or with birch bark which they carry with them in their canoes for this purpose.

These cabins have neither chimnies nor windows. There is only a small aperture left in the middle of the roofs through which the smoke is discharged, but as this is obliged to be stopped up when it rains or snows violently, the smoke then proves exceedingly troublesome.

Living Arrangements

They lie on skins, generally those of the bear, which are placed in rows on the ground; and if the floor is not large enough to contain beds sufficient for the accommodation of the whole family, a frame is erected about four or five feet from the ground in which the younger part of it sleep. . . .

The Naudowessies make the pots in which they boil their victuals of the black clay or stone which resists the effects of the fire nearly as well as iron. When they roast, if it is a large joint or a whole animal such as a beaver, they fix it as Europeans do on a spit made of a hard wood and placing the ends on two forked props, now and then turn it. If the piece is smaller they spit it as before, and fixing the spit in an erect but slanting position, with the meat inclining towards the fire, frequently change the sides till every part is sufficiently roasted.

They make their dishes in which they serve up their meat and their bowls and pans out of the knotty-excrescences of the maple tree or any other wood. They fashion their spoons with a tolerable degree of neatness, as these require much less trouble than larger utensils, from a wood that is termed in America Spoon Wood and which greatly resembles box wood.

Every tribe are now possessed of knives and steels to strike fire with. These being so essentially needful for the common uses of life, those who have not an immediate communication with the European traders purchase them from of such of their neighbours as are situated nearer the settlements, and generally give in exchange for them slaves.

The Music
of Mozart

William Mann

By the time Wolfgang Amadeus Mozart was three years old, he could pick out tunes on the piano. At the age of four he could learn a minuet in thirty minutes and play it perfectly. When the child prodigy was six, his father, Leopold, put aside his own musical career to devote time to Wolfgang and his accomplished sister, Nannerl. The public loved to witness the talents of child prodigies in the 1760s, so Leopold sought to improve his family's finances by taking his brilliant children on a tour of the royal courts of Europe.

Music historian William Mann details Mozart's career to the age of twenty-five, ten years before his untimely death. Mann plays several instruments, studied music at Cambridge University, and has written several books on composers such as Johann Sebastian Bach, Richard Strauss, and Mozart.

L eopold Mozart taught his son the violin and clavier, musical theory, Latin and other academic subjects. Father Mozart was a highly knowledgeable and intellectually cultivated person, a composer of merit (he wrote the *Toy Symphony,* often attributed to Haydn), though he gave up his own career as soon as Wolfgang's genius manifested itself, for the sake of his prodigious son. Wolfgang's elder sister Nannerl (Annie) was also a decent harpsichordist, so Leopold took them on tour [in 1762], first to Munich and Vienna, then to France, England, the Netherlands and Italy. The strain of so much travel on a young boy, with all the public display involved, must have adversely affected Wolfgang's physical constitution, and contributed to later bouts of illness and a premature death. Nevertheless it was through all those travels in so many countries and musical centres that Wolfgang Mozart mastered the Italian, French and German styles of music, elements of which he was to combine in his mature work, filtered through his personal creative genius.

As a little boy in London, he astonished royalty, nobility and the general public with his keyboard improvisations, not to mention playing with a cloth to cover the keys (very easy really, but apparently magical to the untutored), and reading difficult music at sight. More important was his contact with J.C. [Johann Christian] Bach, the composer who most influenced him then, and whom he revered like another father. . . . In London, while his father was ill, he wrote his first orchestral symphonies [at the age of nine] (some now lost). In Rome he heard [Gregorio] Allegri's *Miserere,* a piece forbidden performance elsewhere, and wrote it out after one hearing. He was also given the papal order of Knight of the Golden Spur and commissioned to compose his first operas.

A Prolific Composer

Returned from instructive travels, Mozart was able to enliven Salzburg's old-fashioned music. He was given a job as violinist, in which capacity he wrote five splendid violin concertos in 1775 for himself as soloist, though he wrote better solos still in the *Sinfonia concertante* of 1779 for violin and viola solo, K 364. (K refers to Baron Köchel's chronological catalogue of all Mozart's works, everybody's way of referring to them.) He composed copious orchestral serenades for festive occasions, such as Salzburg University passing-out [graduation] parties—these are symphonic at a light level, with extra dances, a march to start and finish, often a violin concerto in the middle. . . . There were symphonies, more and more striking. . . . He began to compose concertos for himself, at first as harpsichordist . . . though he soon preferred the fortepiano [precursor to the modern piano], and for the newer instrument he composed, during his Vienna years, his most marvellous and original instrumental works.

The Salzburg court had no facilities for opera, Mozart's self-acknowledged strong suit by now (he had written old-fashioned serious operas for Italy with resounding success—the best is *Lucio Silla*), though his talent had been acknowledged by semi-concert performances of several stage works. The new Salzburg Archbishop Colloredo—it was an aristocratic rather than clerical post—gave Mozart small scope to develop church music, no chance in opera, and grudging permission to travel. In 1777 Mozart journeyed to Paris, via

Mannheim, where he fell in love with the soprano Aloysia Weber. She was the second of four daughters in the family of a professional musician. . . . The family was extremely kind to Mozart: no doubt they hoped he would be able to advance their fortunes. Aloysia and her elder sister were singers and the third daughter, Constanze, was studying singing—Mozart eventually married her. He planned to travel to Italy in the company of the sixteen-year-old Aloysia and write operas there, but was dissuaded in no uncertain terms by his father in a stormy correspondence.

Wolfgang Amadeus Mozart

In Paris he wrote his *Paris* Symphony, also a *Sinfonia concertante* for four wind instruments, now extant only in a dubious transcription. One soloist was the Bohemian horn-player Punto, whose own horn concertos borrow from Mozart's four (written for a Salzburg friend and colleague), and make highly enjoyable listening. Other works from Paris include a delightful set of piano variations on a theme we know as *Twinkle, twinkle, little star,* and an impassioned, almost hysterical, piano sonata in A minor, K 310. . . .

New Musical Drama

During that Paris visit, Mozart grew up. His mother died; his fame brought him little work; he hated the French and their proud, superficial taste. He was offered a prestigious post as church organist and turned it down, but accepted a less glorious one in Salzburg. A commission from Munich prompted the heroic opera *Idomeneo* (1781). The form was out of date, but Mozart was now under the spell of Gluck's reforms: choruses, few recitatives, noble melodious airs, ballet, ensembles, orchestral set-pieces and high gripping drama. They are all in *Idomeneo,* which is as great as any later, more famous Mozart opera.

The old heroic opera of [Domonico] Scarlatti, [Johann Adolf] Hasse and [George Frederick] Handel was quite dead, except among the staunchest conservatives who included the opera's most regular customers. *Idomeneo* did not suit them: it had too much emotional recitative with excitable orchestral accompaniment, too much counterpoint in the orchestral music altogether. The arias were quite divine, but the . . . opera's old heroic image was hardly perceptible—this was a new sort of musical drama. Mozart knew how to follow it up, but he had to go elsewhere to fulfil his operatic ambitions. After the first three performances of *Idomeneo* in Munich, he was recalled to the service of the Salzburg Archbishop, just then staying in Vienna for the funeral of Maria Theresa, and the accession of her son Joseph II. The success of *Idomeneo* irked the Archbishop: he was not willing to congratulate one of his servants on a success elsewhere. In June 1781 Mozart asked for a better post; the Archbishop refused. His life there was ignominious, the accepted lot of many less talented servant-musicians, as he well knew. Writing to his father about a trip to Vienna with the Archbishop, Mozart said:

> We lunch about twelve o'clock, unfortunately somewhat too early for me. Our party consists of two valets . . . the confectioner, the two cooks and—my insignificant self. By the way, the two valets sit at the top of the table, but at least I have the honour of being placed above the cooks. Well, I almost believe myself back in Salzburg! A good deal of silly, coarse joking goes on at table, but no one cracks jokes with me, for I never say a word, or, if I have to speak, I always do so with the utmost gravity; and as soon as I have finished my lunch, I get up and go off.

Mozart soon resigned and was physically booted out of the Archbishop's service. He became a freelance musician in Vienna and, with great difficulty, survived in that way of life until his death, just ten years later.

1784–1800

PREFACE

After the Americans prevailed in the Revolutionary War, some of the finest political thinkers of the eighteenth century gathered in the American capital of Philadelphia to draft a new constitution of the United States. This document, and its amended Bill of Rights, promising individual liberty free from government intrusion, was truly revolutionary for its time. News of America's newfound freedom swept across the Atlantic and millions of people living under repressive regimes in Europe left the Old World behind and moved to the United States.

France had helped the colonists fight for their freedom, but was itself mired in the politics and inefficient government of King Louis XVI. Drawing inspiration from Enlightenment philosophers, and seeing democracy in action in the United States, the French too underwent revolution in 1789.

Suffering under extreme taxation by the nobility, with their personal lives censored and restricted by the king, the French wrote their own Declaration of Independence, called the Declaration of the Rights of Man and Citizen. This document stripped much of the power from the French king and took the powers of taxation from the nobility.

Unlike the American Revolution, however, the French Revolution was marred by dozens of factions fighting for power. Ranging from left-wing socialists to right-wing nobility eager to regain power, chaos was rampant over the course of the next decade.

After the French assembly ordered the execution of King Louis XVI and his wife, Queen Marie Antoinette, the infighting reached horrific proportions. A faction led by former lawyer Maximilien Robespierre embarked on a Reign of Terror that saw more than thirty-five thousand people beheaded by the guillotine within a two-year period.

By 1799 Napoléon Bonaparte had named himself emperor and the French Revolution had come to an end. While Americans thrived under their new system of democracy, France continued to be governed by a series of regimes until it finally became a republic in 1870.

Forming a Constitutional Government

D.W. Meinig

When the colonies won their independence from Britain, they needed a new government that could provide for the new nation's defense, regulate commerce between states, and regulate other official responsibilities. Drawing on the writings of Enlightenment philosophers, the founding fathers, including Thomas Jefferson and Benjamin Franklin, took on the task of forming a new government based on liberty and democracy.

The First Continental Congress, made up of representatives of the thirteen colonies, was formed to oppose British sanctions against the colonies and to urge the colonies to prepare for war. The Second Continental Congress convened in 1775 after the first shots of the Revolutionary War were fired in Lexington and Concord, Massachusetts. In July 1776 this Congress adopted the Declaration of Independence, and later the Articles of Confederation, which established an ad hoc constitutional government.

Unfortunately, the Congress did not have clear powers to collect taxes to pay off war debts, which brought the new nation to the verge of bankruptcy. To rectify these problems, the Constitutional Convention was held in Philadelphia on May 25, 1787; there fifty-five delegates representing twelve states produced the Constitution of the United States. It was ratified by all thirteen states on May 29, 1790.

D.W. Meinig details the problems faced by the Continental Congress and the formulation of a new government under the Constitu-

Excerpted from *The Shaping of America,* by D.W. Meinig. Copyright © 1986 by Yale University Press. Reprinted with permission from Yale University Press.

tion. Meinig is Maxwell Professor of Geography at Syracuse University and author of several books on American history and geography.

In 1765 Massachusetts called for a congress of delegates to gather in New York City to formulate a concerted response to the Stamp Act. By the time the representatives from nine colonies assembled (New Hampshire had declined, and the governors of Virginia, North Carolina, and Georgia prevented the election of delegates) a good deal of informal intercolonial consultation had taken place. Formal action at the congress resulted in no more than a number of petitions and memorials to Parliament and the king, and even these were not signed by all delegates owing to differing instructions and uncertainties as to their powers. But during the course of this crisis an organized intercolonial resistance movement had emerged all along the seaboard. It sprang up independently in a number of seaports, but the most intensive efforts began and remained centered in New York City, from where traveling agents and couriers reached out as far as Portsmouth and Albany on the north and Savannah on the south to form a loose association of local groups known as the Sons of Liberty. The degree to which the widespread and often violent resistance to the Stamp Act may be credited to this movement is uncertain, but even though the Sons of Liberty organization faded away after the repeal of the act, the intercolonial correspondence networks it had so vigorously fostered were firmly established and informally continued and expanded.

Thus when in a resurgence of crisis [against the British] in 1773 the Virginia House of Burgess called upon all the other colonial assemblies to join in establishing a Committee of Correspondence "whose business it shall be to obtain the most early and authentic intelligence of all such acts and resolutions of the British Parliament or proceedings of Administration, as may relate to or effect [sic] the British colonies in *America*" and to disseminate such intelligence quickly to all, it got a quick response, and with the creation of such a formal network designed to promote intercolonial solidarity "a revolutionary political union was in the making." It was this organization that paved the way for the call, again from Virginia, to convene a Continental Congress in Philadelphia in September 1774.

The Continental Congress

Fifty-five delegates from twelve colonies attended the first Continental Congress, but they differed considerably in just what bodies they represented. Three delegations had been sent directly by their colonial legislatures (Massachusetts, Rhode Island, Pennsylvania), six others had been elected by some sort of provincial congress or convention of county or town officials, but three (Connecticut, New York, South Carolina) carried no formal authorization, and Georgia was not represented at all. This gathering . . . created no intercolonial structure, but it was in itself a new level of association and out of such experience the convening of a Second Continental Congress in the aftermath of Lexington and Concord was almost routine. To this second Philadelphia meeting in May 1775 came sixty-nine delegates from thirteen colonies (Georgia now included); those from Rhode Island, Connecticut, New Jersey, Pennsylvania, Delaware, and South Carolina had been sent by their colonial assemblies, and all the others had been authorized by some kind of representative gathering. This body quickly created a Continental army, appointed George Washington as commander in chief, and began to define the terms of their association. . . .

Delegates in July 1776 . . . declared that "these United Colonies are, and of Right ought to be FREE AND INDEPENDENT STATES," and it was little more than a formalization of the de facto operations of the Continental Congress. It took the Congress, absorbed in the imperatives of the war, more than a year to endorse a final document, which strongly emphasized state sovereignty and the limitations of congressional power. Each state was accorded one vote and all important measures required nine votes to pass. As [author] Gordon Wood has noted, "The 'United States of America' thus possessed a literal meaning it is hard to appreciate today"; it was "a firm league of friendship" among the thirteen for "common defence, the security of their liberties, and their mutual and general welfare," with no central executive power. The terms of this limited association were then submitted to the states and were soon mired in disagreements over very basic issues. Major contentions involved proposals to substitute some sort of proportionate representation related to the great variations in population and wealth among the states (as Franklin had originally proposed . . . in 1765), and the disposition of western lands to which the several states had very unequal claims and access. Final ratification came only after the first steps were taken to resolve the latter issue by the cession of such lands to Congress for the good of the whole. Thus, not until March 1, 1781, nearly four years after they had been first presented, were the "Articles of Confederation" officially signed, defining the mode by which the thirteen members of the United States of America were formed into and agreed to conduct themselves as a "perpetual union."

Making New States

However, the Articles of Confederation only defined half of the new geopolitical creature, and the members of the union were confronted with the grave difficulty of defining the other half. By the terms of the 1783 treaty [securing American independence] the territory of the United States was more than doubled from that under effective occupation or jurisdiction of the seaboard colonies. A vast new West between the [Appalachian] mountains and the Mississippi had been appended to Atlantic America, and, although the states had agreed to cede to Congress their claims to that West, the exact terms and timings of those cessions and just how Congress would organize and manage this immense realm remained uncertain. A crucial basic principle had been established in 1780 when Congress stated that this national territory would be "settled and formed into distinct republican states, which shall become members of the federal union, and have the same rights of sovereignty, freedom and independence, as the other states." This principle had emerged from intensifying discussions since 1776 on the vexing problems of western lands, and was explicitly endorsed as an inducement to bring about such cessions.

Thus at issue thereafter was the size, number, and boundaries of such states and the procedure by which they could become members of the union. A committee assigned to prepare a plan for "the temporary government of the Western Territory" presented a report in March 1784. It recommended subdivision into fourteen new states, as illustrated in a rough sketch drawn by its chairman, Thomas Jefferson, whose influence and predilections were plainly apparent in the geometric pattern aligned on a central meridian and parallels, together with a suggested list of contrived polysyllabic names (such as Assenisipia, Cherronesus, Metropotamia, and Michigania—but also Washington). Congress amended the report, eliminating the names but modifying only slightly the basic geometry, and spelled out provisions for the formation of temporary governments that would control each district until it had a free population equal to that of the least populous of the thirteen original states, whereupon it could petition for admission to the confederation as an equal member. This Ordinance of 1784 did not become the actual tool by which the West was shaped because Congress ruled that it should apply only after all states had actually ceded their western claims. Nevertheless, it stood as a statement of principles, the basis for further debate in the formulation of more specific legislation.

The Northwest Ordinance

Pressures for actual implementation of a plan for the West rapidly intensified. The Land Ordinance of 1785, defining a system of surveys and sales of congressional lands, was a first attempt to bring some order to the frenzied scramble among a welter of avaricious interests, large and small, local, national, and international, to reap some profit out of this vast national domain. In strategic locales all over the West earlier traders and squatters were becoming outnumbered by speculators of one kind or another. National leaders saw an imperative need to impose some kind of legal government upon such populations in remote districts. Congressional attempts to prohibit intrusions and expel squatters from the homelands of the Miami and Shawnee Indians failed. As new legislation to deal with chaotic and dangerous conditions in the area between the Ohio and the Great Lakes was being debated, Congress was further impelled by the highly effective lobbying of the Ohio Company, which connived with officials to obtain a huge block of land in that area and sought government protection of its interests. A definitive response came in 1787 when Congress created "the territory northwest of the River Ohio" as a temporary jurisdiction. That act specified that not less than three nor more than five states should be formed within this area (a reduction from the eight and a half proposed in Jefferson's sketch), and defined the boundaries for three eventual states lying between the Ohio and the lower Great Lakes. This "Northwest Ordinance" also laid down a three-stage process for the transition into statehood. Initially the territory was to be served by a governor, a secretary, and judges appointed by Congress; as soon as a district had five thousand free adult male inhabitants it could choose an assembly, which body could nominate a list of candidates from which Congress would select a council, with the congressionally appointed governor retaining full veto power over all legislation; when this district had 60,000 free inhabitants it could petition for admission as a state on an equal footing with the original states. This 1787 ordinance was clearly an adaptation of that of 1784, but the differences were important. It dealt with only the northern half of the West, the only lands that had as yet been fully ceded (except for a Western Reserve of Connecticut) to Congress, it defined fewer and larger states, it significantly strengthened the hold of Congress over the territorial phase of government, and it altered the minimum population essential for statehood. If, as many historians maintain, the major change was the fact that it lodged political control of the West "in the hands of Eastern promoters instead of Western squatters," it retained the really fundamental guarantee of eventual statehood as a full partner in the union.

The Constitutional Convention

In fact it turned out to be a guarantee of partnership in a very different association than the one in being during the debate. For the Northwest Ordinance was a last act of Congress under the Articles of Confederation, completed while the Constitutional Convention was under way in Philadelphia with a radical revision in the very basis of the union. That convention came about because many influential persons and interests became convinced that the United States could not survive unless the power of the central government was greatly strengthened and the course of direction sharply altered.

Out of bitter experience with an arbitrary imperial government Americans had at first devised a union that kept power in the constituent state governments, which were considered to be closer to the people and more responsive to local interests. But once the emergency of war had passed, state governments proved to be extremely self-centered, contemptuous even of the very limited authority they had granted the Congress:

> They violated the Articles of Confederation by ignoring the nation's treaties with foreign countries, by waging war with the Indians, by building navies of their own. They sent men with less vision and less ability to represent them and at times failed to send any, so that Congress could scarcely muster a quorum to do business.

Most serious of all, the states rendered Congress impotent by failing to answer requisitions for money while at the same time taxing the commerce of one another, issuing paper money, and undermining the credit of and confidence in the parts as well as the whole. Attempts to amend the Articles to give Congress power to levy a modest tax on foreign imports were twice defeated by the negative vote of a single state. Such pervasive and progressive internal weakness left the United States helpless in a perilous world. Its credit was no good, its ships were seized, it had no leverage to pry the British out of their old posts on American soil or to pressure the Spanish from interfering with Mississippi traffic. Out of such experience came a broadening consensus that the initial terms of the union must be revised.

Fast Approaching Anarchy

The direct lineage of the Philadelphia Convention of 1787 is traceable to Mt. Vernon, where in 1785 George Washington, as president of a company formed to promote the building of a canal connecting the Potomac with the Ohio [Rivers], hosted a meeting of commissioners from Maryland and Virginia to work out a basis for cooperation on this interstate project. This led to a proposal to invite representatives from Pennsylvania and Delaware to join in creating a commercial policy for the whole Chesapeake-Delaware region, and this idea soon expanded to an invitation to all the states to gather in Annapolis in September 1786 to deal with general commercial problems and possible amendments to the Articles of Confederation. The response to that call was disappointing; only five states sent representatives, but one of these was Alexander Hamilton of New York, who took the lead in getting the Annapolis group to urge Congress to call a special convention of delegates from all the states to consider all changes necessary to create a "federal government adequate to the exigencies of the Union." Eventually, reluctantly, Congress did so, spurred on by local rebellions and rumblings throughout the country so ominous as to cause George Washington, along with many others, to express fear that "we are fast verging to anarchy and confusion."

Twelve states responded, Rhode Island alone refusing to participate, and as most of the men they sent were influential leaders convinced of the need for a much stronger central government, work on a comprehensive revision got under way rapidly. The fame of the debates and decisions of the 1787 Philadelphia Convention has been justified by the results: a constitution that has stood the test of two centuries of experience in an often-tumultuous and ever-expanding nation. We must limit our focus here to the central geopolitical issues, one of which was crucial to everything else. Put in terms of high principle, the question was how to create a strong national government that would be responsive to the people yet operate within a genuine federal system of states. Put more baldly, it was the problem of how to allocate power amongst the varied constituent parts of the union. The issue, inherent in the nature of federations, had been long recognized but never fully confronted and resolved. After festering for a dozen years it was laid bare in the opening discussions and its ominous character revealed. The Virginia delegation proposed that state representation in Congress be proportionately based on population or wealth, whereupon the delegation from

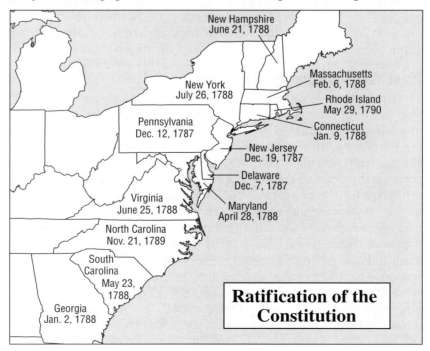

Ratification of the Constitution

Delaware threatened to withdraw from the convention and, by implication, from any union so designed. The issue thereby became immediately defined as one of the small states versus the large states, with spokesmen for each group arguing from reason and equity, the former unwilling to be at the mercy of Virginia, Massachusetts, and Pennsylvania (understood by all to be the largest in population by a considerable margin), the latter unwilling to be at the mercy of a coalition of tiny states and finding it unconscionable that the fewer than 50,000 inhabitants of Delaware should balance the more than 600,000 of Virginia. Such arguments quickly exposed the most basic question: was this political creation a *nation* or a *confederacy of sovereign states?* Were the states mere districts of people composing one political society or were they thirteen distinct political societies? Was it "We the People" or "We the States" that sought to establish a more perfect union? A deadlocked convention referred the matter to a committee for resolution.

The famous compromise finally hammered out declared that the United States of America was at once a nation and a federation, a union of people and a union of states. The creation of a bicameral national legislature in which states were given an equal voice in the upper house and representation proportionate to population in the lower, together with the specification of certain powers, terms of office, and modes of election for each house, ultimately gained the support of the convention. Such a solution required definition of how representation on the basis of population would be calculated and that exposed another division of interests, but this one, as Madison observed, "did not lie between the large and small States: it lay between the Northern & Southern" and this "principally from their having or not having slaves." The existence of slavery itself generated angry debate but no decisive action; the problem of whether slaves, being denied most of the rights of citizenship, should be counted in the population base for political representation was resolved by extension of an existing compromise formula, used in taxation, of calculating a slave as three-fifths of a person. Each state was to have at least one representative and not to exceed one for every 30,000 inhabitants (excluding Indians not taxed), based on an official census to be taken every ten years. As no reliable enumeration existed at the time, the need to reach an agreement led to an initial lower house of sixty-five representatives, allocated among the thirteen states in proportions determined in committee by drawing upon various estimates of populations and wealth. The results of the first national census, taken in 1790, necessitated major adjustments in the 1787 proportions and total.

The divergent interests of north and south shaped other important compromises built into this national framework. Northern shipping interests, shorn of British markets and maritime protections, wanted Congress to have the power to regulate commerce and create a strong national policy in their support, whereas southerners, heavily dependent upon staple trades, sought the least possible regulation in order to foster the cheapest possible rates. Furthermore, a glaring feature of American commerce was the slave trade. After it was made clear very early that any attempt to abolish slavery in all the states would immediately dissolve the convention and doom the union, the antislavery forces narrowed their focus to prohibiting further imports. There was powerful support for this not only among northerners but from influential delegates from Virginia and Maryland as well (which states had already passed such laws, in part, it was alleged, to protect the value of their own rapidly increasing slave populations). However, spokesmen from the Carolinas and Georgia flatly declared that they would never be at the dictate of Congress on the matter and that to prohibit such trade was in effect to exclude these states from the union. Out of these controversies came the compromise wherein Congress was given the power "to regulate Commerce with foreign Nations, and among the several States, and with the Indian Tribes" in return for a specific assurance that "the Migration or Importation of such Persons as any of the States now existing shall think proper to admit, shall not be prohibited by Congress prior to the Year one thousand eight hundred and eight."

Such patterns of divergent regional interests underlay many of the most intensive discussions of the Constitutional Convention, as they had throughout the life of the confederation to that point. . . .

Certainly the issues relating to the Constitution were extremely complex, and there is ample indication that they generated discussion and disagreement within every substantial community in America. Neither the creation of the document itself nor the reactions to it yield to any simple set of geographical explanations, but no assessment can get very far without taking into account the complex regional patterns imprinted upon Atlantic America over the course of nearly two centuries. The United States of America over which George Washington assumed the presidency in April 1789 was in formal terms a much more united body than its predecessor, an unprecedented federation of states based on the consent of the people. It was an immense and remarkable political experiment and its success as a federation and a nation would be determined in no small part by how well it might cope with problems deeply embedded in its historical human geography.

Immigrants in America's Wilderness

Jean de Crèvecoeur

In the following excerpt French traveler and journalist Jean de Crèvecoeur details his journey with a companion, Monsieur Herman, into the Pennsylvania wilderness in the years after the American Revolution. There Crèvecoeur encounters a Polish immigrant who had been driven from his homeland after Russia seized the province where he lived. Like scores of other European immigrants, Crèvecoeur's subject was overwhelmed by the wealth and liberty he found in his newly adopted nation.

Crèvecoeur's books about America after the Revolution were some of the most popular travel books in Europe and inspired thousands of people to move to the United States.

"To own a piece of land," I said to [my travel companion] Monsieur Herman, "to farm it, is here the universal ambition. Furthermore, since the beginning of the colonies, agriculture, although still in its infancy, has been the favorite occupation of both classes of society [rich and poor] and the foundation for the prosperity of these states. However, the colonists do not all succeed. Here, as elsewhere, success does not crown all undertakings. Here, as elsewhere, man is exposed to danger from accidents, bad weather, and the caprices of fate. The settlers do not all bring with them the necessary disposition, nor the habits, nor the intelligence that this new way of life requires. They do not all have the same amount of strength, of courage, of judgment, and they are not all equally happy. Illness, insects, negligence, and laziness often destroy their hopes. If, when the time comes that the land must be paid for, the settler is not able to supply the necessary sum of money, the law gives back the land to its original owner, after recompensing the purchaser for any improvements he has made. And even among those who owe nothing, how many times is it not found to be true that some grow lazy when they find out that with just two days of work they can live for the rest of the week! Examples like these are found much more often among the foreign born colonists than among the settlers from the northern states, whose way of life, intelligence, and industry are so often worthy of great praise."

In the meantime we were traveling on toward the salt lick farms in the district around Philippopolis and west of Mount Ararat, when on the evening of the third day after crossing the great river, as we were making our way through a large swamp—which I have since found out is the source for one of the branches of the Wyolusing [River]—we heard a clock striking. Encouraged by this sound, so unusual in such a sparsely populated country, we continued on our way more gaily and soon arrived at a field of corn, a young orchard, and a house, a newly built house, it is true, but one with four little wooden windows.

"All this," said Monsieur Herman, "gives signs of being a good place to stop. Let us rejoice and forget the fatigues of this long day's journey."

Hospitality of the Woods

We still had some little distance to go when a man with a distinguished looking form and countenance appeared and said to us, "Welcome, gentlemen; get down and come in. You have either powerful motives or a great deal of courage to dare a trip through a country still so thinly populated. Have you not strayed from your road?"

"One is not off his road," replied my companion, "when he has the good luck to meet a colonist such as you seem to be, and the good luck to be invited to spend the night under such a fine roof."

"Ah! Gentlemen, don't praise the hospitality of the woods more than it deserves. If you knew how great my pleasure is and how real the need of hearing news from informed travelers, you would realize that it is I who thank you for a good turn."

"You underrate what you want to give us."

"Well! Think of it as reciprocity, and I shall be satisfied."

"How many years have you been living here?" I asked him.

"Seven," he replied. "Tomorrow I shall let you see that I haven't wasted my time. When a person wants immediate results, it costs something; but money that is wisely spent in clearing land and drying up swamps returns more than a hundred percent. My ambition is some day to have great meadows and pasturelands on which to raise and feed many cattle and horses. I have great respect for the plow, but I take even more to the scythe, because that kind of farming requires fewer hands. Ten years ago this country was scarcely known and was frequented only by hunters; the land was hardly worth six silver sous [one sous equals about twenty-five cents] an acre. What a difference today! It is the same everywhere.". . .

A Long Journey from Poland

"Is this a healthy country?" asked Monsieur Herman.

"Except for a kind of fever that comes at certain times of the year," he replied. "But it is caused by the ignorance of the settlers rather than by the climate. After getting hot from their labor, they lie down in the shade of a tree; perspiration stops and they grow cold. I brought with me out here a simple and sure remedy, which has already been of great benefit to many of these colonists."

"You talk like a man who understands medicine."

"I practiced it a little in Europe."

"What! Are you a European?"

"Alas! yes. I am from Poland, and Poland is no more. You have heard of our confederations, of the first division of our lands—which took away five million subjects from the king of that unfortunate country—and of the general dismemberment made by the Northern Powers. [The "first division" was made by Russia, Austria, and Germany in 1772; the "general dismemberment" occurred in 1795.] Since that time the wails of my unfortunate compatriots have resounded through the world in vain. What a deplorable event! Russia having seized the province where I was born, I was forced to go as a surgeon into the hospitals and dress the wounds of those who had ravaged my land and then enslaved it. Angered by this shameful servitude, I formed the plan of breaking my bonds or perishing. Everything in this world, as you must know, depends on chance. I owe my escape to chance—to my lucky arrival at Copenhagen and to the good fortune of being of assistance to a captain of a ship ready to leave for Lisbon. He had hardly discharged his cargo there when he took on another for New York, where we arrived after forty-seven days. And in less than four months, from the village of Orsa on the Dnieper River, I found myself landed on this continent. What is it then that controls the fate and fortune of men? Some days after my arrival, because of my knowledge of the German language, I made the friendship of Doctor Ebeling, the minister of the Lutheran church at New York, who recommended me to his colleague, the Reverend

Mulhausen, at German Flats, on the Mohawk River. This worthy and respectable churchman welcomed me as if I had been one of his countrymen; and when I had finished telling him of my misfortunes, he became even more friendly and interested. After making it known in his neighborhood that I was a surgeon, he volunteered to give me advice and direct my first steps in this new land.

"Oh! when compared with the slavery I had just left, how sweet and delicious seemed this new independence and this thoughtfulness, which I was quick to enjoy! It was for me like a second birth. Of all the moments of the day, the time of waking was most filled with charms for me, because then, since my dreams often took me back to Poland, to find myself an inhabitant of North America and a citizen of this new state was a new and exquisite joy. At last, feeling for the first time a happy existence, I swore to forget the past and to concern myself only with pleasing hopes for the future.

A New Social Compact

"If my imagination was vividly struck at the sight of the beautiful rivers, the great lakes, and the mighty waterfalls of this country, how much also were my heart and mind aroused by a close examination of the bases on which these new societies were founded! The mildness and the justice of the laws; the ease with which one can acquire land; the civil importance that goes with that possession; the ample recompense assured by work and skill; the harmony and the great number of children that are found in almost every family; in short, the general happiness! At the sight of this moving spectacle, I began to conceive a better impression of human nature and to love my fellow men. After I had practiced medicine for a few years in the land of the Mohawks, the Reverend Mulhausen gave me his daughter in marriage and made me a present of the 750 acres which I own here. It is to him that I owe the greatest, as well as the most precious, of blessings, the best of wives. There she is, that angel of goodness and sweetness, to whom I owe everything—the children she has given me, the land that I am clearing, and the happiness, as well as the order, the comfort, and the neatness of my little dwelling.

"Furthermore, it is the long and interesting conversations of her revered father," he continued, "that have given me the advantage of learning the history of these states during the period of their colonial infancy, the details regarding the new social compact which has held them together since their separation from the mother country, the boundaries that separate them from the three neighboring nations, and the code of civil laws on which rest the freedom of the individual and the freedom of religion. What a contrast between the absurd and barbaric feudal customs known in Poland for so many centuries and the system, adopted by these states, which protects

both life and property! What a contrast between the religious oppression which has been the source of nearly all the ills that have in-
undated my fatherland and the constant protection that this government accords all religions equally, a protection that is not the result
of tolerance, but of justice, since it is founded not on opinion but on
natural law.

Comfort and Abundance

"One day my revered father-in-law said to me, 'For a long time I
have been at once a minister of the gospel, a physician, and a farmer.
I dare appeal to the divine inspector of hearts, as well as to my neighbors; they will judge whether or not I have done everything that is
in my power to fulfill the duties of those three positions in life. I took
charge of the clearing of four hundred acres of land that the government had donated to the church of this district at the time we were
given a map of incorporation, and since then I have been asked to set
aside two-thirds of that land for the support of a free school. I have
grown old while following the beautiful and interesting career which
you are about to enter. But the fruits of this old age are neither sad
nor bitter, unlike the experience of those who pursue goals less hon-
orable and less useful. The store of knowledge I have acquired is a
little treasure which I wish to bequeath to you as to one who is
charged with contributing to the happiness of my daughter. In this
way I shall have a part in your success. My desire is only the natural
result of the friendship and affection which I feel toward the man
whom I have esteemed enough to make my son-in-law.

"'They are deceived,' my father-in-law continued, 'who expect to
become rich at farming; it does not make people rich in these northern states. The seasons pass too quickly, the winters are too long, and
help is still too costly. But for those who work hard, it brings comfort and abundance. In order to succeed in the woods, one must have
some money to start with, so that he will not be crushed by the yearly
interest on borrowed funds; he must also have some knowledge of
this new way of life. Since the job of farming is like a bundle composed of several parts, everything that pertains to work, to supervision, and to planning must be equally the object of your daily attention. It is indispensable to know the nature and quality of soils in order to plant in them only the seeds that suit them best, and to have
some of the skill of the veterinarian, although the animals who roam
at liberty and eat enough salt are rarely sick. . . .

Justice and Liberty

"'As a son loves his parents, you must love your new country. Bend
all your efforts to propagate the system of public education that has

been practiced so long in the northern states, the most useful perhaps that modern times have discovered. The light of a good education spread through all classes of society strengthens the happiness of family life and assures the tranquillity and glory of the nation. Honor a government that reason has founded on the eternal bases of justice and liberty. During peace, consecrate your talents and your example; during war, your courage and your blood, if they are necessary. At this price only can a good citizen pay his debts to his country. Scorn those orators who, in order to curry favor with the public, blame without ceasing the form and the laws of government, as if what comes from man can be perfect. To want to go beyond the bounds of human reason ought to be looked upon as foolishness, and these fanatics, as the enemies of the public peace.

" 'Like you I saw the light of day in a country where for centuries men were bound to the soil; like you, after overcoming a thousand obstacles, I landed on the shores of this new world, towards which penury, despair, intolerance, and misfortune lead the debris of the old, as the waves of the sea carry the debris of the tempest to the nearby land. Just as a plant, blighted by the shade of trees, spreads out and grows as soon as it has been transplanted to a place where it can enjoy the dew of the sky and the rays of the sun, so the happy seeds that I had received from nature, long stifled by misery and ignorance, sprouted soon after my arrival in this country and produced fruit. I remember it well. The day after my naturalization, full of joy and hope at the sight of a country, of a city, where work, industry, and useful talents were so amply rewarded, and where there was so much space, I forgot that I was a Salzburger and thought of myself only as a member of the new family of the United States.'

"That, Gentlemen, is what this venerable man, this worthy minister of the gospel, has so often told me."

Ben Franklin's Antislavery Views

Benjamin Franklin

American statesman, inventor, printer, and diplomat Benjamin Franklin was a signer of the Declaration of Independence. Franklin held strong antislavery views and was a member of the Pennsylvania Society for Promoting the Abolition of Slavery. In the excerpt below, Franklin explains his position on slavery and his plans for improving the lives of freed slaves once slavery is abolished.

Slavery is such an atrocious debasement of human nature, that its very extirpation [extermination], if not performed with solicitous care, may sometimes open a source of serious evils.

The unhappy man, who has long been treated as a brute animal, too frequently sinks beneath the common standard of the human species. The galling chains, that bind his body, do also fetter his intellectual faculties, and impair the social affections of his heart. Accustomed to move like a mere machine, by the will of a master, reflection is suspended; he has not the power of choice; and reason and conscience have but little influence over his conduct, because he is chiefly governed by the passion of fear. He is poor and friendless; perhaps worn out by extreme labour, age, and disease.

Under such circumstances, freedom may often prove a misfortune to himself, and prejudical to society.

Attention to emancipated black people, it is therefore to be hoped, will become a branch of our national policy; but, as far as we con-

Excerpted from *An Address to the Public from an Anti-Slavery Society*, by Benjamin Franklin.

tribute to promote this emancipation, so far that attention is evidently a serious duty incumbent on us, and which we mean to discharge to the best of our judgment and abilities.

To instruct, to advise, to qualify those, who have been restored to freedom, for the exercise and enjoyment of civil liberty, to promote in them habits of industry, to furnish them with employments suited to their age, sex, talents, and other circumstances, and to procure their children an education calculated for their future situation in life; these are the great outlines of the annexed plan, which we have adopted, and which we conceive will essentially promote the public good, and the happiness of these our hitherto too much neglected fellow-creatures.

A plan so extensive cannot be carried into execution without considerable pecuniary [financial] resources, beyond the present ordinary funds of the Society. We hope much from the generosity of enlightened and benevolent freemen, and will gratefully receive any donations or subscriptions for this purpose, which may be made to our treasurer, James Starr, or to James Pemberton, chairman of our committee of correspondence.

Signed, by order of the Society,
B. Franklin, *President.*

Philadelphia, 9th of November, 1789.

The Execution of Louis XVI

Hilaire Belloc

Louis XVI married Marie Antoinette in 1770 and became king of France in 1774. Louis was a weak ruler who was much more interested in pursuing kingly pleasures such as feasting, hunting, and hosting lavish parties at splendid palaces. Unfortunately, Louis became ensnared in the French Revolution in 1789, which began when a Parisian mob stormed the prison known as the Bastille on July 14 and seized the munitions stored within. A violent rebellion ensued, and the king attempted to appease the revolutionary leaders by abolishing privileges for the nobility and accepting a more constitutional form of government.

In spite of these concessions, the royal family was forced by revolutionaries to leave their palace at Versailles and move under guard into the royal residence in Paris. In June 1791, the royal family attempted to flee the country but their escape was foiled. The king secretly negotiated the support of Austrian and Prussian forces to help him regain power. When those countries invaded France in 1792, a mob rose up against the monarchy. The king's collusion with Austria was used as a basis for a trial for treason in December. The king was condemned and executed by guillotine on January 21, 1793. Marie Antoinette suffered the same fate on October 16, 1793.

Historian Hilaire Belloc was an expert on the French Revolution. He wrote biographies of several important figures in the revolution, including Robespierre and Marie Antoinette.

Excerpted from *High Lights of the French Revolution* (New York: The Century Co., 1915) by Hilaire Belloc. Copyright © 1915 by The Century Co.

The long trial at the bar of the Parliament was over. The pleas had been heard, and [Louis XVI's old lawyer Chrétien de Lamoignon de] Malesherbes, weighty and with dignity at once of ancient law, of contempt for fate, and of complete self-control, had done all that could be done for the king. The verdict had been given. Louis was found guilty by all of betraying the nation. He had called in the enemy. There remained to be decided by a further vote what his penalty should be.

It was the evening of Wednesday, January 16, 1793. The deputies of the nation were to vote, each publicly and by name, an enormous roll-call of hundreds of men; each was to come up the steps to the tribune, to face the vast audience . . . and to pronounce clearly his decision. Each was free, if he chose, to add to his declaration the motives that had determined it.

The three great chandeliers that hung from the roof of the place were lit, affording a mellow, but insufficient, light in which the faces of the great throng, small dots of white on the black background, were but ill distinguished. Upon the tribune itself a brighter light was turned.

"I Vote for Death"

The sun had long set; the evening meal was over; at eight o'clock the interminable procession began. They came on one by one, arranged in groups by their constituencies. They went up in turn the steps of the tribune from the right, voted in open voice, descended by the left. Among the first was [revolutionary leader Maximilien] Robespierre, because he was of those that sat for the capital. He made a speech (too long) to explain what he was about to do. He protested that if the penalty of death was odious to him, and if he had combated it consistently as a general principle of law, yet did he now support it for this exceptional case. "I remain compassionate for the oppressed. I know nothing of that humanity which is forever sacrificing whole peoples and protecting tyrants. . . . I vote for death."

One after another the deputies for Paris, the extreme men, the men of the Mountain, mounted those few steps, faced the great silent body of their colleagues, while those who had just voted before them were quietly seeking their places again, and those who were about to vote stood lined up before the steps upon the farther side, and one after the other gave his voice for death. Each after so declaring loudly his responsibility, his verdict, and his name, confirmed the whole by the signing of a roll.

The voice of [Minister of Justice Georges Jacques] Danton was heard, the harsh, but deep and strong, voice that was already the first in the country. He had sat all that day by the bedside of his wife, who was to die. He had but just come back from the frontiers and from the army. His huge body was broken with fatigue; his soul was heavy with grief; his powerful brain was aching from a lack of sleep. "I am no politician," he shouted; "I vote for death."

So all night long the dreadful litany proceeded. Men left the hall to take an hour or two of sleep, a snatch of food; yet the hall seemed always full despite the coming and going of single figures, and through the long, cold darkness of that misty weather history heard voice after voice, weak, strong, ashamed, defiant, pitiful, muffled, outspoken, bass, treble, old, and young, repeating at regular intervals: "Death absolute"; "Death with respite"; "Banishment"; "Imprisonment." And history saw, after each such speech or cry (for many spoke as well before they declared the doom), an isolated man, high upon the tribune, beneath the candles, bending over the register and signing to what he had determined and proclaimed.

The dull dawn of winter broke through a leaden sky. No eastern window received it. The tall, gaunt casements of the southern wall overlooking the Tuileries Gardens grew gradually into lighter oblongs of gray. The candles paled and were extinguished. Hardly a third of the list was done. All that short January day (Thursday, the seventeenth of January) the dreadful thing proceeded until darkness fell again, until once more the chandeliers were lit. Once more it was night, and they were still voting, still declaring.

Advocates of the King

At last, when more than twenty-four hours had passed, the business was over. No one was left to come forward to the tribune; and this great sleepless mass, within which some few had noted one by one the voices as they fell, and had already calculated the issue, waited for the counting of the votes and for the recounting. Not only by word of mouth, nor only by the signing of the register, had the precision of so awful an event been secured, but one by one the votes had been written down, folded, and sealed. The clerks of the Parliament opened each packet and arranged the sentences in rows, according to their tenor: for death absolute, for imprisonment, for delay. So one hour went past, and then another; but in the third, when it was perhaps ten o'clock, this silent process was interrupted, and the many that had fallen asleep, or were nodding half asleep after such a vigil, looked up surprised to hear that two letters had reached the assembly, one from some agent of the Bourbon [ruling dynasty] king in Spain to demand a respite; the other from the advocates of the king, who demanded to be heard once more before the chair should announce the result of the voting.

All was interrupted; an immediate and passionate, though short, debate began. The intervention of the King of Spain the Convention would not consider; upon the proposal that the king's advocates should be heard once more a debate was allowed. Many members joined it, though in brief periods. Robespierre, among others, spoke intensely. He demanded that sentence should be read out and given before there could be any consideration of appeal. That opinion (not through him) prevailed, and the opening and arranging of the votes continued. A ceaseless little crackling of tearing papers, the whispered comments of men in groups, now and then some cry from the public in the galleries, broke the silence.

Sentenced to Hang

It was not far from midnight when a further movement among the clerks at the table, a comparison of sums, and heads bent together, scrutinizing the additions, prefaced the last scene of this act. The paper, with the figures written on it, was handed up to the chairman. That chairman was [Pierre Victurnien] Vergniaud. . . . He rose in his place above them, holding that paper before him, and read out in the grave and even voice which had often moved their debates:

"It is with profound sadness that I declare the penalty incurred by Louis Capet [Louis XVI] to be, by the vote of the majority of this assembly, that of death."

Of seven hundred and twenty-one men who had voted, three hundred and ninety-seven had demanded the scaffold, a majority of seventy-three.

It was in complete silence that this memorable sentence fell. That silence was continued for some moments unbroken. The advocates of the king were now permitted to enter, for sentence had been formally delivered, and old Malesherbes, short, strong in figure for all his years, and now so far oblivious of his dignity and name as to be weeping, put forward his last plea. Sentence of death could not be given, by all the traditions of their law, unless two thirds of the bench (for the French will have no single judges) concurred. And again, the prisoner had not had all those guaranties which a prisoner should have. And again, since it was as the head of the whole nation that he had acted, and since it was by the whole nation that he was conceived to be judged, then let the whole nation speak. He demanded an appeal to the French people.

For a third time Robespierre spoke. He spoke with more emotion than his peculiar academic style commonly permitted. Though he was in no way representative as yet of public feeling, though he was still a lesser man among those hundreds, for the third time his opinion coincided with that which was to prevail. He implored the assembly not to reopen the whole issue of civil war by putting this grave matter upon which they had fixedly decided to a general vote of millions. Not for the first time did this unalterable man betray for a moment his own unalterable creed. Later he was himself to perish in punishment divine of such deviations from the conscience of equality and of citizenship. . . .

The appeal of Louis was rejected, and the Convention rose after a continued session of thirty-six hours. . . .

That Sunday [January 20], Louis, in the prison of the Temple, in the great square tower where he and his wife and his children and his sister had now for many months been held captive, suffered his passion.

Final Requests

It is singular, instructive, a lesson in history, to note what the man's temper was during this prodigious time. The curious may examine (displayed under glass in the archives for all to see) the note which he wrote out with his own hand in his prison. It proves in its handwriting and in its composition, in its very erasures, a momentous calm. If courage in the presence of death be a chief index to character, admire so complete a courage present in a man whose lack of judgment, torpor, grave lethargies, whose imbecilities even, had helped to bring him where he was. Louis, but for his death, might pass to history among the negligible figures of her roll; but see how he died!

The note, written finely in even lines, asks for a delay of three days "to permit me to appear before the presence of God." It asks further for the right to have his own confessor and for the guarantying of that confessor (the Abbé Edgeworth) from all anxiety. He asks to see his family, and he recommends to the good-will of the nation all those who were attached to his person.

Here and there he changes a word, scratching out the original expression deliberately, rewriting the substituted expression in a hand as firm as the rest. . . .

Final Visit with Family

The night came early upon that Sunday, for the unbroken, drizzling sky still stretched above Paris, and there was no sunset. Moreover, the insufficient windows of the medieval tower, sunk in their thick walls, were partly boarded to prevent communication with friends outside. After some hours had passed—rather more than two hours in the light of the candles—it was somewhat after eight o'clock and the time for the supreme ordeal, for his family were to be admitted.

For some weeks now he had been separated from them. They had been in the rooms above. His demand for three days had been rejected. He was to die upon the morrow, but he was to be permitted to see his own before he died, and to discuss with his confessor what he nobly called "the great business" of our passage from this life.

There gave upon the stair facing the narrow stone staircase of the Temple a great oaken door, studded with many huge old nails. It opened, and the queen [Marie Antoinette] came in. God! what must we not imagine her to have seemed in that moment, this woman who had so despised him, and yet had been faithful to him, and had principally ruined him; and who had, in these last months, so marvelously changed and grown in soul. The queen came in falteringly. She held by the hand her rickety little son; her somewhat dull little daughter, the elder of the children, followed. The king's sister, the Princess Elizabeth, of a different and more simple bearing, and of a soul longer tried and longer purified, came in more erect, the last of the four.

The king sat down and put his wife upon his left, his sister upon his right. He took the boy, the last heir of the Capetian monarchy, and stood him between his knees, and told him in a clear manner and in a low and even tone the duties of a Christian in the difficult matter of revenge, that it must be foregone. He lifted up the boy's little right hand to give to this direction the sanctity of an oath.

It seems that few words were spoken during that terrible time. The queen clung to him somewhat. He mastered himself well. Altogether these three and the two children were assembled for nearly two hours. A little before ten he himself determined this agony must end.

Marie Antoinette, as was her custom under stress, broke out into passionate protestation. Then she checked herself and admitted doom. But she implored him that they should see him again, and he said to her, perhaps unwisely, that he would see her before he left for his passing. He would see her in the morning. She would have it earlier still. He said it should be earlier by half an hour. She made him promise solemnly enough, and he promised her. Ten o'clock had struck, and the chimes were sounding over Paris and from the great clock of the Temple before she unloosed her hands.

He stood, the women passed out with weak knees (it is said that the girl was half fainting), the oaken door shut behind them, and the iron door outside it clanged to. He heard their soft steps, slow and creaking, mounting the winding stone stairs without, then they were lost, and he was in silence. He prayed a moment and then lay down to sleep. He slept deeply till five in the morning. The men bringing in the vessels for a mass awoke him. He rose and prayed.

The Final Walk

In the full darkness, before it was yet six o'clock, the queen heard a step approaching up the stairs. It could not be the king. She watched from above her candle. It was a messenger come for books of devotion which the king required at his mass and communion. Then she heard the chimes of seven, and the day was breaking; upon her window the falling mist had made a blur, and it was very cold. She waited on until eight o'clock. There was no sound. Her agony was unrelieved. Yet another hour, and she heard steps and the coming and going of many men upon the stone stairs below. No one came up. The sounds sank away. The great door that gave into the courtyard was heard creaking upon its hinges, there was the pawing of horses upon the stones, and the cries of command to the escort, a certain confused noise from the crowd outside the walls. The tower was empty. She had not seen the king.

The king had passed through the prison door. He had gone on foot, with the priest by his side, across the little court to the high wall which surrounded the tower. The guards followed him.

Just before he came to the barrier he turned back to look at the prison. He made a slight gesture as of constraint, and firmly turned again toward the gate.

"We Are There"

Outside this the guards were drawn up, and a roomy carriage of the sort that was then hired in the streets by the wealthy stood at the entrance. Two policemen armed with muskets were awaiting him at the carriage door. As Louis appeared, one of these men got in and took his seat with his back to the horses. Then the king entered, sitting in his proper place upon the right, facing him, and motioned to the priest, Edgeworth, to sit beside him. When they were both thus seated, the second policeman took his place opposite, and he and his colleague set their guns before them. The door was shut, the cab started at a foot's pace.

As they came out on the broad streets . . . , they could see upon each side of the way, three or four ranks deep, the soldiery and militia which guarded those few miles through the town. There was no crowd behind them, or at least but few spectators, and a curious observer might have noted how few and rare were the uniforms, how many of the thousands alined were clothed in workman's dress or in the mere remnants of military coats. Even the windows of the uneven houses they passed (the boulevards were then but half built) gaped empty, and no one stood at the doors.

Before the carriage marched a great multitude of men, all enregimented in some sort of troop, and the greater part of them drummers. These last drummed incessantly, so that this long and very slow procession was confused and deafened with a loud and ceaseless sound. Paris heard that sound rolling up afar from the eastward, crashing past its houses, lost again toward the west.

It was close upon eleven o'clock when the carriage came before the unfinished columns of the Madeleine and turned into the rue Royale.

Louis was reading from a book the Psalms which his confessor had pointed out to him when he noticed that the carriage had stopped. He looked up, turned to the priest, and said in a low voice:

"Unless I am mistaken, we are there." The priest did not answer.

"You Shall Not Bind Me"

They had come to that wide open space which is now called the Place de la Concorde, and as he looked quietly through the windows, the doomed man perceived a great throng of people densely packed about a sort of square of cannon which surrounded the scaffold and guillotine. That fatal woodwork and the machine it bore stood near the entrance of the rue Royale and a little to the east. One of the executioners (who stood at the foot of the scaffold) took the handle of the carriage door to open it. Louis stopped him and, putting one hand on the priest's knee before he got out, said:

"Sirs, I recommend you this gentleman here. See to it that after my death no insult shall be offered him."

They said nothing in reply, but when the king would have continued, one of them cried:

"Oh, yes, yes. We will see to it. Leave it to us."

The king opened the door, and came out into the freshness of that damp air. Above, the sky was still quite gray and low, but the misty drizzle had ceased. They made as though to take off his coat and his collar. He moved them aside, and himself disembarrassed his neck. Then one came forward with a cord and took his hands.

"What are you at?" he cried.

"We must bind you," said the man.

"Bind me!" answered the king. "I will never allow it! Fulfil your orders, but you *shall* not bind me!"

There was a struggle in which he turned to the priest as though for counsel or for aid, but they bound his hands behind him.

A Loud Moaning

The few steps up to the scaffold were very steep. The Abbé Edgeworth supported him so bound, and thought for a moment, as he felt the weight upon his arm, that the prisoner was losing courage. But even as he turned to glance furtively at the king, in that crisis Louis had strengthened himself, and stood upright upon the broad stage. With a few rapid and determined steps he took his way toward the guillotine, standing to the right of the instrument. Some yards in front of him and below a score of drummers were at the ready with sticks lifted, balanced as drummers balance them between the knuckles of the hand. He cried out, standing erect with his stout figure and heavy, impassive face, "I die innocent of all the—" at which moment there came a sudden cry of command, and the drums beat furiously. To that sound he died; and those who were present relate that immediately afterward there arose from the great mob about, which had hitherto held its breath, a sort of loud moaning, not in anger or in hatred, but in astonishment of the spectacle and of things to come.

The French
Reign of Terror

J.F. Bosher

On September 22, 1792, the ruling body known as the National Convention established a constitutional republic in France. After sending the king to the guillotine in 1793, a radical faction known as the Jacobins took control of the government. When the Jacobins attempted to purge the government of all opposition, a period known as the Reign of Terror ensued.

By July 1793, Jacobin leader Maximilien Robespierre headed the National Convention. Robespierre believed that ruthlessness was justified in the name of revolution, and so established several repressive committees to seek out those who might be a threat to the power of the Jacobins. In the following months, tens of thousands of innocent people were beheaded by the guillotine before Robespierre and his allies were overthrown on July 27, 1794. Like so many before him, Robespierre died by the guillotine.

In this excerpt, J.F. Bosher, professor of history at York University in Ontario, Canada, exposes the methods of the French Reign of Terror. Bosher has taught at Cornell University, London University, and the University of British Columbia. He has written several books about French and Canadian history.

The regime that ruled France by terror from early June 1793 until late July 1794 was not a simple one. It was different from what went before and after, and it aroused emotions of enthusiasm or horror so strong that even two centuries later they are still likely to move the reader to take sides. . . .

The regime as a whole is not easy to judge. On the one hand, it gave a vigorous leadership that preserved the republic against the assaults of its enemies within and without; on the other, these successes were won by the terrorizing of millions of people, the arrests of hundreds of thousands, the massacre of 100,000 or more in the genocidal pacification of the Vendée [region of western France], and the execution of 15,000 or 16,000 after the mock trials of revolutionary tribunals. Again, on one hand, the Terror treated nobles, priests, and the rich with a rigor satisfying to many a reader's sense of social justice. On the other, no more than one-third of the victims were nobles, clergy, or rich commoners. Just over one-third were property-owning peasants or lower middle-class townsmen, and just under one-third came from the urban working class. The Jacobin dictatorship was not the rule of one particular social class, however "classes" may be defined. Careful scholars in every corner of the subject resort to political rather than social explanations.

The Jacobin Dictatorship

The [organization known as the] Mountain, men from the Jacobin Club, ruled the Convention in alliance with the militants of the Paris sections. This was a dictatorship because the Mountain was a minority in the Convention—267 men, according to one scholarly list—and the section militants were a minority in Paris, a tiny minority in France. Neither of these minority groups was representative of a particular social class. Their principal opponents were, after all, of similar social origin. In the convention about half the 749 deputies were lawyers (406), and the other half were also from middle-class occupations: businessmen (67); clergymen, including 9 Protestants (55); civil servants (51); medical men (46); farmers, but not peasants (38); soldiers and sailors (36); writers (30); academics (11), artisans (6); and clerks (3). A disproportionately large fraction of these, some 40 percent, came from large towns. On the whole, the older men from smaller communities less exposed to national politics tended to support the Girondins, though the Girondin leaders were themselves among the youngest. The youngest men with the most political experience, usually in their late thirties or early forties, including most of the 191 from the Legislative Assembly, tended to support the Mountain. This large contingent from the Legislative Assembly is hard to identify with the rump left sitting after the purge of 10 August 1792, always thought to have been Girondin in sympathies. . . .

During the fourteen months of the Jacobin dictatorship the Mountain ruled the Convention and the nation through two committees.

The first of them, the Committee of General Security (Comité de sûreté générale), had been set up as early as 2 October 1792 on the model of the Surveillance Committee in the Legislative Assembly and, before that, of the Research or Information Committee created by the Constituent Assembly on 28 July 1789. The purpose of all these committees was to deal with treason, subversion, foreign agents, counterfeiters, and all other conspirators against the State. Like any institution in a dictatorship, the Committee of General Security was soon packed with men of the ruling group. In fact, it had been reorganized on 21 January 1793 as a group of twelve Jacobins. . . .

They were assisted everywhere in France by local imitations of themselves which sprang up spontaneously here and there, notably in some of the Paris sections, but were legally set up by a decree of 23 March 1793. These were Surveillance Committees, often called Revolutionary Committees, perhaps 20,000 of them in all, which volunteered to spy on their neighbors in order to denounce royalists, traitors, Girondins, aristocrats, . . . wealthy men, hoarders, and other counterrevolutionaries. The political purposes of these committees were clear from the first.

Trials and Massacres

Surveillance and denunciation were one thing; arrests, trials, and sentences were another. Police and criminal courts had already been reorganized under municipal and departmental authorities. Early in March 1793 the Mountain proposed a Revolutionary Tribunal in Paris that might expedite the trial of suspects and secure rapid convictions, as [author] Robert Lindet put it, "by all possible means." This tribunal, [Minister of Justice Georges Jacques] Danton argued, "is to replace the supreme tribunal of the people's vengeance." There would have been no massacres in September 1792, he thought, if there had been a Revolutionary Tribunal then: "[L]et us use terror so that the people will not need to! . . ." The Revolutionary Tribunal was created immediately on 10 March with five elected judges, twelve jurors, and a public prosecutor. The prosecutor, an efficient civil servant with legal training named Antoine-Quentin Fouquier-Tinville, was entitled to try anyone on his own initiative—even suspects arrested out in the provinces—except members of the Convention, executive ministers, and army generals, whom he could arrest only on orders from the Convention, usually from one of the two main committees. The property of anyone sentenced to death was to escheat to the republic.

The first trial began on 6 April, but the tribunal was hampered by a general reluctance to give up employment in order to serve as judges and jurors. In its first six months it sentenced only 70 people to death. By the end of its first year, however, it had guillotined more than 500, and by the end of July 1794, when the dictatorship was overthrown, the score was nearly 2,700. Only at [the cities of] Nantes and Lyons were there more victims of revolutionary "justice." In the course of 1793 and 1794 the tribunal supplanted the ordinary criminal courts, but its political complexion discouraged the barristers [lawyers] from pleading before it. The profession of barrister was abolished by the Convention on 24 October 1793 in favor of a system in which anyone could act as counselor in cases before the tribunal. Defendants were exploited by unscrupulous individuals who played upon their fears.

Farces and Nightmares

The trials were at once farces and nightmares. Fouquier-Tinville, who presided over them, acted on orders from the Convention's committees, and the judges fell into step with him. Late in the evening, after the day's work, he used to visit the committees to discuss cases with them and receive his orders. The jurymen, drawn mainly from the Paris sections and the Jacobin Club, did nothing to distinguish guilt from innocence, and could not have done so even if they had wished to. Charges were hopelessly vague, and the tribunal had neither the time nor the inclination to seek the truth in particular cases, especially after the Law of Suspects voted on 17 September 1793 to prevent delays. At least two jurors passed the time sketching the prisoners, and others made ribald jokes about them and their almost certain death. For example, Clément Charles François de L'Averdy (1724–93), the controller general of finances from 1763 to 1768, now seventy years old, was tried for the crime of throwing wheat, the people's food, into a pond on a property he had not visited for years. The remarks he made in his own defense were pointed, intelligent, and utterly convincing, but he was judged guilty and executed on 23 November 1793.

Rather than face such a nightmare, many prisoners took their own lives, as Étienne Clavière did with a knife on 8 December 1793, Jacques Roux with a knife on 10 February 1794, and Condorcet probably with poison. Three Girondins . . . shot themselves in the fields near Saint-Émilion to escape the execution their friend [Martin-Michel-Charles] Guadet and his family suffered there, but [one of them], not quite dead, was dragged off to the guillotine. Others showed transcendent courage. Charlotte Corday, the handsome twenty-five-year-old Norman girl charged with [journalist Jean-Paul] Marat's murder, answered all questions firmly and went to her death, after a two-hour ride in a tumbril through the raving crowds, with perfect self-possession. She, at least, was charged with a recognizable crime and was guilty of it.

Tribunals of Repression

The repressive Committee of General Security and the Revolutionary Tribunal were parts of a dictatorship crowned with the principal committee of the Convention, the Committee of Public Safety (Comité de salut public). Founded on 6 April 1793, this group soon took charge of the country in the manner of an emergency wartime cabinet. Eight of the twelve men in it at its height, including a former nobleman, Hérault de Séchelles, and an arthritic cripple, Georges Couthon, had been trained in the law (Barére, Billaud-Varenne, Lindet, Prieur de la Marne, Robespierre, and Saint-Just); two were engineers and army officers (Carnot and Prieur de la Côte-d'Or); one had been an actor and playwright (Collot d'Herbois), and another a Protestant minister (Jeanbon Saint-André). All were capable and energetic, but three of them did outstanding service: Barére, prodigiously active in matters of policing, war, munitions, and the navy; Lazare Carnot, a great strategist and war leader; and Robespierre, who presided over the committee and the nation with a clear and unwavering determination, turning his hand to all sorts of tasks. They were too busy, like most cabinets, to keep minutes and were in any case supposed to be working in secret. Consequently, there is some uncertainty about how they divided their many tasks among them, and the thousands of orders they penned and signed do not show specialized functions for most of them. Their headquarters was a green room in the Tuileries Palace, where they spent many hours each day around a table, but several of them went off on special missions to armies or to provinces troubled by uprising.

Eighty-two representatives on mission (*représentants en mission*), only a few of whom ever served on the Committee of Public Safety, were sent out on 9 March 1793 to raise 300,000 men for the armies on the foreign frontiers. Even more than their predecessors of August and September 1792, they served as agents of the dictatorship in Paris. A series of decrees in the weeks following their departure removed legal impediments to tyranny by terror: death for émigré and nonjuring priests as soon as caught (18 March); death for rebels against recruiting and other war measures (19 March); the Surveillance Committees in villages and town sections to check passports and the identities of foreigners and other strangers (21 March); death for émigrés who returned to France (28 March). They were assisted in many departments by committees set up by local Jacobin clubs to organize recruiting, forced loans, and dictatorial violence. In about half the departments they were soon also assisted by "revolutionary armies," civil contingents of the populace organized to carry out revolutionary and dictatorial purposes. Robespierre proposed these as early as May, and by the end of the year about forty of them were roaming about the countryside, seizing food from peasants and hoarders and valuables from all and sundry, arresting rebels and other suspects, and trying to destroy the parish life of the church in the brief dechristianizing campaigns of the winter 1793–94. In all, perhaps 30,000 men joined the revolutionary armies. None played a bigger part in terrorizing the nation than the representatives on mission. A decree of 29 December sent 58 more members of the Convention out on missions, with unlimited authority, each to serve the dictatorship in two departments.

The most active and violent were those in provinces that rose in revolt against the Jacobin dictatorship. After 7 June 1793 a Federalist government at Lyons would take no further orders from Paris and prepared to defend the city with 10,000 volunteers under the Comte de Précy, a former member of the Garde royale. General François-Christophe Kellermann besieged Lyons from 8 August 1793 on, and when he had starved it into submission on 9 October, Collot and Fouché organized a savage repression. Their Tribunal of Seven executed about 20 people a day in November. From 4 to 7 December, some 360 men, women, and children were murdered by grapeshot from cannons near the ditches they were to be buried in, and by April 1794 almost 2,000 people had been killed. Meanwhile, other representatives were on missions at neighboring towns, Georges Couthon and Étienne-Christophe Maignet at Clermont-Ferrand, and Claude Javogues in the Loire Department, where he executed 15 people on 11 December, 21 ten days later, and 208 on 5 December. "Javogues" most constant preoccupation," [author] Colin Lucas tells us, "was with repression.". . .

Denouncing One Another

The Jacobin dictatorship, like all dictatorships, defended itself by executing its political enemies on various pretexts. Vague accusations of counterrevolution, intrigue, and corruption sufficed to get rid of the Girondins, thirty-one of whom were executed on 31 October 1793, and of many others at various times. By a natural turn of events, however, the rulers soon began to denounce one another. In April 1794, for example, Robespierre, Saint-Just, and Couthon had organized a police surveillance bureau to work for the Committee of Public Safety, and this aroused the mistrust and hostility of the Committee of General Security. Soon all the members of this committee except Philippe Lebas and Jacques-Louis David were hostile to the Committee of Public Safety. Disagreements and jealousies among the Jacobins and sections led to political struggles, and these led to the guillotine. . . .

Death to the Leaders

When the Jacobin leaders executed [those loyal to their cause], they were sawing off the branch on which they themselves were perched. The militants of the Paris sections had put them into power in the uprising of 31 May–2 June 1793 and had supported their dictatorship ever since. The moderate majority in the Convention and moderate opinion across the country in various guises—Girondins, *fédérés, muscadins,* and counterrevolutionaries—had been intimidated by repression organized by Jacobins and Paris sections. Stunned and confused by the execution of the [members of the political extremist group the] Hébertists, the Paris sections lost the will to turn out the mobs that had terrorized Paris on behalf of the Jacobin dictatorship. This change was not immediately visible. But on 27 July 1794, when the Jacobin leaders were challenged in the Convention, no Paris mob appeared in their defense.

The occasion was provided by one of those bitter quarrels within the ranks of the Jacobin leaders that confused their supporters and subordinates. A plan to betray Robespierre revealed weaknesses in the ruling committees to the Convention and moved the moderate majority to turn against its dictatorial leaders. The political struggle that followed in Paris was sharp and decisive. On the same day and the next, eighty-three of the Jacobin leaders, including Robespierre himself, were guillotined in the terrifying process they had themselves devised. The remaining leaders . . . expected to carry on as before but soon found themselves swept aside in a reaction against the dictatorship of the past months. A new government came into being, the so-called Thermidorian regime named for the month of this sudden reversal, and by the end of the year it had dismantled the institutions of the Terror and even closed down the Jacobin Club.

Child Laborers in the Industrial Revolution

Paul Mantoux

Before the Industrial Revolution of the late 1700s, most goods were manufactured by small groups of artisans. With the invention of the steam engine and advances in large machinery design, the factory system became the main method of production. The system allowed faster and more standardized production, but these benefits came at a high price for the small children who labored fourteen hours a day in factories where dangerous machinery and unhealthy working conditions were prevalent.

The following excerpt explains how children were exploited by factory owners during the early stages of the English Industrial Revolution in the late 1700s.

Paul Mantoux is one of many contemporary French social critics—including Voltaire—who wrote about England and the English.

The feeling of repulsion which [working in a factory] aroused is easily understood, as to a man used to working at home or in a small workshop, factory discipline was intolerable. Even though at home he had to work long hours to make up for the lowness of his wage, yet he could begin and stop at will, and without regular hours. He could divide up the work as he chose, come and go, rest for a moment, and even if he chose be idle for days together. Even if he worked in the master-manufacturer's house, his freedom though less

Excerpted from *The Industrial Revolution in the Eighteenth Century* (New York: Macmillan, 1928) by Paul Mantoux.

complete was still fairly great. He did not feel that there was an impassable gulf between himself and his employer, and their relations still retained something of a personal character. He was not bound by hard and fast regulations, as relentless and as devoid of sympathy as the machinery itself. He saw little difference between going to a factory and entering [an army] barracks or a prison. This is why the first generation of manufacturers often found real difficulty in obtaining labour. They would have found it still more difficult had there not been a [transient] population available, which the changes in rural conditions were driving from agriculture into industry and from the country to the towns. Other workers were attracted from the poorer parts of the Kingdom, from the bogs of Ireland and from the mountains of Scotland or Wales. Thus the origin of factory labour is to be found partly in a class of men forcibly uprooted from their employment, and partly among populations to whom industry offered better opportunities than did their former employment.

Hiring Small Children

In the textile trades the manufacturers found another way out of the difficulty, by resorting largely to woman and child labour. Spinning was quickly learned and needed little strength, while for certain processes the small size of the children and their delicacy of touch made them the best aids to the machines. They were preferred, too, for other and more conclusive reasons. Their weakness made them docile, and they were more easily reduced to a state of passive obedience than grown men. They were also very cheap. Sometimes they were given a trifling wage which varied between a third and a sixth of an adult wage; and sometimes their only payment was food and lodging. Lastly they were bound to the factory by indentures [contracts] of apprenticeship for at least seven years, and usually until they were twenty-one. It was obviously to the spinners' interest to employ as many as possible and thus to reduce the number of workmen. The first Lancashire factories were full of children. [Founder of the British Conservative Party] Sir Robert Peel had over a thousand in his workshops at once.

Sent Like Cattle to a Factory

The majority of these wretched children were paupers, supplied (one might almost say sold) by the parishes [county division associated with a church] where they belonged. Especially during the first period of machine industry, when factories were built outside and often far from the towns, manufacturers would have found it impossible to recruit the labour they needed from the immediate neighbourhood. And the parishes on their side were only too anxious to get rid of their paupers. Regular bargains, beneficial to both parties if not to the children, who were dealt with as mere merchandise, were entered into between the spinners on the one hand and the Poor Law [welfare] authorities on the other. Lots of fifty, eighty or a hundred children were supplied and sent like cattle to the factory, where they remained imprisoned for many years. Certain parishes drove even better bargains and stipulated that the buyer should take [mentally impaired] in the proportion of one to every twenty children sent. At the beginning these 'parish apprentices' were the only children employed in the factories. The workmen, very justifiably, refused to send their own. But unfortunately this resistance did not last long, as they were soon driven by [poverty] to a step which at first had so much horrified them.

The only extenuating circumstance in the painful events which we have now to recount as shortly as we can, was that forced child labour was no new evil. In the domestic system of manufacture children were exploited as a matter of course. Among the Birmingham ironmongers apprenticeship began at seven years of age. Among the weavers of the north and the south-west children worked at five or even four years old, as soon in fact as they were considered capable of attention and obedience. Far from regarding this with indignation, men at that time thought it an admirable system. [Economist and author Andrew] Yarranton recommended the establishment of 'industrial schools' such as he had seen in Germany. There, two hundred little girls under a matron's rod sat spinning without a moment's relaxation and in complete silence, and were beaten if they did not spin quickly or well enough: 'In these parts I speak of, a man that has most children lives best; whereas here he that has most is poorest. There the children enrich the father, but here beggar him.' When [author Daniel] Defoe visited Halifax he was lost in admiration at the sight of four-year-old children earning their living like grown-up people. . . .

Cruel Servitude

It might be said that in the earlier forms of industry the child was at any rate an apprentice in the true sense, for he learned a trade instead of merely being a part of the plant, as he was in the factory. But real apprenticeship could only begin when the child was old enough to benefit by it, and therefore for several years the child could only be a workman's drudge, paid either nothing or next to nothing. It might also be said that the conditions under which the child lived were less unfavourable to its physical development; but with regard to hygiene we know only too well the condition of the domestic workshop. Was it kindly treated and not overworked? Under the sting of necessity parents were often the most exacting, if not the harshest of taskmasters.

But, even with these reservations, we must acknowledge that the fate of these parish apprentices in the early spinning mills was particularly miserable. Completely at the mercy of their employers, kept in isolated buildings, far from anyone who might take pity on their sufferings, they endured a cruel servitude. Their working day was limited only by their complete exhaustion, and lasted fourteen, sixteen and even eighteen hours. The foreman, whose wages were dependent on the amount of work done in each workshop, did not permit them to relax their efforts for a minute. In most factories forty minutes were allowed for the chief or the only meal of the day, and of these about twenty were taken up in cleaning the machines. In some factories work went on ceaselessly day and night, so that the machines might never stop. In such cases the children were divided up into shifts, and 'the beds never got cold'. Accidents were very common, especially towards the end of the overlong day, when the exhausted children almost fell asleep at their work. The tale never ended of fingers cut off and limbs crushed in the wheels.

Discipline was savage, if the word discipline can be applied to such indescribable brutality, and sometimes such refined cruelty as was exercised at will on defenceless creatures. The well-known catalogue of the sufferings of the factory apprentice, [former child laborer] Robert Blincoe, makes one sick with horror. At Lowdham (near Nottingham), whither he was sent in 1799 with a batch of about eighty other boys and girls, they were only whipped. It is true that the whip was in use from morning till night, not only as a punishment for the slightest fault but also to stimulate industry and to keep them awake when they were dropping with weariness. But at the factory at Litton matters were very different. There the employer, one Ellice Needham, hit the children with his fists and with a riding whip, he kicked them, and one of his little attentions was to pinch their ears until his nails met through the flesh. The foremen were even worse and one of them, Robert Woodward, used to devise the most ingenious tortures. It was he who was responsible for such inventions as hanging Blincoe up by his wrists over a machine at work so that he was obliged to keep his knees bent up, making him work almost naked in winter with heavy weights on his shoulders, and filing down his teeth. The wretched child had been so knocked about that his scalp was one sore all over. By way of curing him his hair was torn out by means of a cap of pitch [tar]. If the victims of these horrors tried to escape their feet were put in irons. Many tried to commit suicide, and one girl, who took advantage of a moment when the supervision relaxed and threw herself into the river, thus regained her freedom: she was sent away, as her employer was 'afraid the example might be contagious'.

Unhealthy Environment

Of course, not all factories witnessed such scenes, but they were less rare than their incredible horror would lead one to suppose and were repeated until a system of strict control was set up. Even if they had not been ill-treated, excessive labour, lack of sleep and the nature of the work forced on children during the critical period of their growth, would have been quite enough to ruin their health and deform their bodies. The food, too, was often bad and insufficient. They had black bread, oatmeal porridge and rancid bacon. At Litton Mill the apprentices used to struggle with the pigs fattening in the yard in order to get some of the food in their troughs. The factories were usually unhealthy, as their builders cared as little for health as they did for beauty. The ceilings were low in order to economize as much space as possible, the windows were narrow and almost always closed. In the cotton mills fluff filled the air and gave rise to serious lung diseases. In flax-spinning mills, where wet spinning was usual, the air was saturated with moisture and the workers' clothes were dripping wet. Overcrowding in unventilated rooms, where the atmosphere was further vitiated by candle smoke at night, favoured the spreading of a contagious disorder resembling prison fever. The first cases of this 'factory fever' broke out near Manchester in 1784. It very soon spread to nearly all the industrial districts and there were many deaths. Lastly, the promiscuity of both workshops and dormitories gave scope for immorality, and this was unfortunately encouraged by the bad behaviour of some of the employers and foremen, who took advantage of it to satisfy their low instincts. Thus to a puritan conscience the factory, with its mixture of depravity and suffering, of barbarity and vice, offered a perfect picture of hell.

Among those who lived through the cruel period of apprenticeship, many bore its brand for life in the shape of crooked backs, and limbs deformed by rickets or mutilated by accidents with machinery. With 'flaccid features, a stunted growth, very often tumid bellies', they were already marked down as the victims of all the infections to which, during their later life, they were but too frequently exposed. Their moral and intellectual condition was no better. They left the factory ignorant and corrupt. During their miserable period of servitude not only did they receive no teaching of any kind, but in spite of the formal clauses of their indenture of apprenticeship they did not even acquire enough technical knowledge to enable them to earn their living. They had learned nothing beyond the mechanical routine to which they had been bound during so many long hard years, and they were thus condemned to remain mere slaves tied to the factory as of old the serf to the soil.

No Law to Restrain Them

It must not be assumed that the status of all workers under the factory system was like that of the apprentices in the spinning mills. But, even though adults were not treated with quite the same revolting cruelty, their life in the factory was hard enough. They, too, suffered from too many working hours, from overcrowded and unhealthy workshops, and from tyrannical foremen and overseers. With them the despotic employer, instead of physical violence, resorted to fraud; one of the most frequent abuses of which the workmen had to complain was that, in order to lengthen the working day of which every minute meant money to the employer, they were literally robbed of their rest hours. During the dinner hour the speed of the factory clock appeared miraculously to accelerate, so that work was resumed five or ten minutes before the hour had actually struck. Sometimes the means used to the same end were even simpler and less hypocritical: the meal times and closing times were at the discretion of the employer, and the workers were forbidden to carry watches.

Here we come to the real cause of the evils attributed to machine industry, namely the absolute and uncontrolled power of the capitalist. In this, the heroic age of great undertakings, it was acknowledged, admitted and even proclaimed with brutal candour. It was the employer's own business, he did as he chose and did not consider that any other justification of his conduct was necessary. He owed his employees wages, and once those were paid the men had no further claim on him: put shortly, this was the attitude of the employer as to his rights and his duties. A cotton spinner, on being asked whether he did anything to help sick apprentices, answered: 'When we engage a child, it is with the approbation of the parents, and it is an engagement to give a certain quantity of money for a certain quantity of labour. If the labour is not performed, the child is supported by the parents.—Then there is no security afforded to the child, that in sickness the master will support it?—It is an act of bounty in the master.' Pure bounty, indeed, on which it was wiser not to count. The same man, when questioned as to why he had decided to stop his machinery at night, explained that he did it in order to allow water to accumulate in a tank, as the stream of the neighbouring river was insufficient: 'Then if the stream had been more ample, you would have continued your night work?—As long as the trade had been sufficiently lucrative.—Then there is nothing now to restrain you from working day and night, but want of water or want of trade?—I know of no law to restrain me for so doing: I never heard of any.' This was unanswerable, so long as the law remained unchanged.

English Convicts Populate Australia

Russel Ward

The following excerpt details the founding of Australia in the late eighteenth century by British felons who were shipped to that continent because English jails were full.

The first European to travel to Australia was Dutch navigator Abel Tasman in 1642. Few Europeans returned to the country until 1770 when English captain James Cook charted part of the coastline and claimed possession of eastern Australia for Britain on his first voyage around the world. As Great Britain began colonizing this vast continent, it was in the process of losing the American colonies during the Revolutionary War.

Great Britain had been emptying its jails and sending felons to the American colonies for more than 150 years. After the war began, Britain could no longer use America as a dumping ground for criminals and determined that Australia was the best place to send its criminals.

Russel Ward was born in Australia in 1914 and was professor emeritus of history and deputy chancellor at the University of New England.

When it [the Revolutionary War] ended in 1783 Britain had won Canada from the French but lost her own settlements in North America. The thirteen colonies on the Atlantic seaboard from New England to Georgia had federated to form a new nation, the United States of America. The Peace of Versailles [that ended the war] left British statesmen with one major problem—how to preserve what was left of the Empire, principally India, and one minor one—what to do with her surplus criminals now that the North American colonies would no longer take them. . . .

The least talented person in the government was probably Thomas Townshend, Viscount Sydney, Secretary of State. To him fell the less important but more pressing task of finding a place suitable for the reception of Britain's felons.

Steal or Starve

The matter was urgent because, as it seemed to contemporaries, crime and criminals had been multiplying at an alarming rate. Throughout the eighteenth century the 'agricultural revolution' transformed the face of the English countryside. More and more enclosure acts were passed through parliament by and for the landed gentry and their friends; for large 'capitalist' farms, run on scientific lines, produced much more food for sale, and profit for their owners, than the traditional kind of land-use. As the change proceeded thousands of small tenant farmers, poor labourers and their families with ancient traditional rights to some forms of land-use, found themselves expropriated [deprived of property]. Most of them moved to the growing industrial towns . . . but much was lost even by those who found work in the new factories driven by water or steam power. They left, perforce, a settled life in a village community made secure by friendship and traditionally sanctioned relationships involving mutual obligations with squire and parson. They became, often, 'hands' in an impersonal factory, living among strangers in jerry-built terrace houses, working for inhumanly long hours at low wages and bereft of all sense of 'belonging' or personal worth: and these were the lucky ones. Those who could not find work had often to steal or starve.

Citizens with property worth stealing naturally worried mightily about the increasing criminality of those to whom they referred as 'the lower orders': but their ideas for stemming the flood of larceny, mayhem and murder were limited. The British governing classes . . . thought only of terrifying potential malefactors by hanging more and more of the few who were caught. . . . By the end of the eighteenth century hanging crimes included picking pockets of goods worth more than one shilling, shop-lifting of goods worth more than five shillings, and cutting down trees in an avenue or garden.

Alas, for the property-holders: neither the preachings of the clergy nor fear of the scaffold deterred many poor people from following the paths of wickedness in which they had been trained by desperate or demoralised parents. This was partly because police forces were so inefficient that wrong-doers had an excellent chance of escaping scot free, and partly because the very severity of the laws defeated their purpose. When the penalty for stealing goods of or above the value of a shilling was death, juries often found the value to be less—despite the most cogent evidence to the contrary. . . .

Transporting Convicts

Until 1776 most of them had been shipped to the American colonies where their services, for the term of their sentences, were sold to planters and other employers by the contractors who took them off the hands of the British government. . . . The founding fathers of the United States of America [however, thought] it beneath the dignity of the new nation to continue receiving British gaol- [jail] birds. . . . Meanwhile successive Secretaries of State for Home Affairs sought for suitable places of exile. . . .

At last in 1787 the King's speech to parliament announced that a plan had been formed 'for transporting a number of convicts in order to remove the inconvenience which arose from the crowded state of the gaols in different parts of the kingdom'. A new empire and a new receptacle for unwanted criminals was to replace the lost American colonies [in Australia]. . . .

Struggle for Survival

In May of the same year the First Fleet of eleven store-ships and transports set sail for Botany Bay [a small inlet south of present-day Sydney]. Most of its complement of something more than a thousand felons and their gaolers [jailers] disembarked in the virgin bush at Sydney Cove eight months later, on 26 January 1788. It had been—for the period—a slow but more than usually healthy voyage.

The first governor and commander-in-chief was Arthur Phillip, a sensible and, by contemporary standards, unusually humane naval captain. . . . Phillip knew . . . that the Government saw the new settlement as a 'strategic outlier' to imperial interests in Asia as well as a conveniently remote convict depot. This would account for his being almost the only person in the First Fleet who foresaw the time when the miserable little gaol might become a prosperous and civilised country: but the immediate struggle for survival taxed his strength to the limit.

His human cargo had been dumped on the shore where Sydney now stands. About three-quarters of them were convicts—men, women, and children; many were aged or infirm, and nearly all unwilling to work. The remainder were mainly Marine Corps officers and men, sent out as a guard; but from the moment of landing the officers manifested a keen appreciation of their station in life. They refused to compromise what they regarded as their dignity by supervising the work of felons, except in the case of those who had been assigned to them personally as servants. Thus the best-behaved—or most sycophantic—convicts had to be made constables and placed in other positions of some responsibility. Most of the colonists were criminals from the slums of London and other great cities. There was hardly a gardener or farmer among them. Seeds refused to sprout in the alien soil, and for the first two years the infant colony was threatened with famine. . . . Phillip placed his private stock of food in the communal store and decreed the same scale of rations for bond and free. The 'starving time' had passed by the time he sailed for England in December 1792, and the day when the colony would be self-supporting seemed not quite as far off as before. There was one convict in the First Fleet who had been bred to farming, James Ruse. Phillip gave him every encouragement and in April 1791 title to the first forty acres of land ever granted by the British Crown on the Australian continent. By that time Ruse had succeeded in producing enough to keep himself and his family.

Tough Life for Women

Only about one convict in every four in the First Fleet was female. This gross imbalance between the sexes generally increased throughout the whole period of transportation. When the last 'exile' landed in Western Australia in 1868, about 162,000 had been transported of whom about 25,000, or one in every six or seven were women. The scarcity of women in the early days disfigured Australian life for long afterwards, creating a much cruder, male-dominated, 'frontier' society than developed in most other colonies where Europeans settled in the nineteenth century. Surprisingly the reasonable men in the British Government, who drafted Phillip's commissions, recognised the danger and sought to provide against it. Phillip was to order the commanders of any ship visiting islands in the south seas 'to take on board any of the women who may be disposed to accompany them to Sydney', providing that no deception or compulsion was employed. Possibly because he feared that the Polynesian women would in fact be brutally kidnapped if the scheme were put into effect, the man of the enlightenment ignored the proposal. No women were present when the officers and marines hoisted the Union Jack and 'christened' Sydney Town about noon on 26 January 1788. . . . When the female convicts landed on a Sunday eleven days later, most un-sabbath-like scenes ensued. As darkness fell, men and women, convicts and marines, joined in an orgy of rum and fornication. A tropical storm poured down on the revellers, seemingly lashing them on to fulfil the biblical command to Noah and his sons to be fruitful, to multiply, and replenish the earth.

Contemporary observers, whether male or female, agreed that the women convicts were even more profligate, vicious and irredeemable than the men, but recent research shows that all have been tarred with the sins of a minority. At least one woman convict in every five was a prostitute at the time of her arrest. In the early years of the system most others were forced into prostitution on the transport ships, where they lived promiscuously with the sailors or took a protector from among them. Those whose 'innocence' survived till their arrival at Port Jackson or Hobart Town were almost always forced into prostitution in the new country, if only because prisoners had to find their own board and lodging. Only the luckier or more attractive women were able to cohabit with only one man, at least for a time. As late as 1811, as soon as female convicts disembarked, officers, non-commissioned officers, privates and free settlers took it in turns to have women assigned to them

> *not only as servants but as avowed objects of intercourse, which is without even the plea of the slightest previous attachment as an excuse, rendering the whole colony little less than an extensive brothel.*

Up till about the same date women were sometimes flogged for real or imagined misbehaviour, but rarely or never later on. . . . Hardened old harridans and at least relatively innocent new arrivals, all alike were put to work weaving rough cloth for 'Government'. Yet the life of a Factory woman was not one of unrelieved hard labour and boredom. Because of the scarcity of white women, and because the authorities believed that embracing holy matrimony improved the character of both spouses, a sort of marriage bureau was conducted at Parramatta every Monday morning. The best behaved women were paraded by the Matron. Dressed in whatever finery they could muster, they conversed with free but unmarried men in search of a helpmeet. Any couple who fancied each other were then given a special licence and married. . . .

Despite the profligacy and drunkenness forced on them by a crude and massively male-dominated society, the majority of women convicts did improve vastly in morals, if not necessarily in manners. The most cogent proof of this is that they bore and brought up the first two generations of native-born, white Australians, people whom even the sternest moralists proclaimed to be ethically superior in every way to their parents and, more often than not, to the generality of free immigrants.

Killing the Natives

Phillip's instructions also enjoined him to 'open an intercourse with the natives, and to conciliate their affections, enjoining all our subjects to live in amity and kindness with them'. No one could have tried harder to carry out this order. On 15 May 1788 in his first despatch to his master, Lord Sydney, Phillip wrote 'it was my determination from my first landing that nothing less than the most absolute necessity should ever make me fire upon them.' Two years later he was still better than his word. On 7 September 1790 at Manly Cove . . . the unarmed Governor of New South Wales walked along the beach holding out both hands in a gesture of peace towards an armed Aborigine. For answer the black man hurled his spear so forcefully that the barbed point transfixed Phillip's right shoulder. The butt-end of the three metre-long spear kept striking the ground as this gentleman of the age of enlightenment returned painfully to his boat. No serious efforts were made to punish the offender.

The captain-general could not, however, control the passions of his white subjects as he could his own. From the very first day of contact many convicts and marines stole from the Aborigines their fishing and hunting tackle, their women and sometimes their lives, just as the British government . . . had already stolen their land. The first-comers fought back as well as they could. In the first three years up to December 1790 they had killed or wounded seventeen Whites. When Phillip's gamekeeper, M'Entire, was killed in that month, the Governor's stock of calm reason came to an end. He despatched two punitive expeditions with orders to bring back in bags the severed heads of six Aborigines from what was thought to be the offending tribe. Both expeditions failed even to make contact with the Aboriginal enemy, but from that time onwards no one set in authority over white Australians made such efforts as Phillip had done to see that they lived 'in amity and kindness' with black ones, and few indeed tried so hard to understand them.

The abyss of incomprehension which separated the two races was graphically illustrated in May 1791. Phillip decided to make an example of a convict caught in the act of stealing fishing tackle from Dar-in-ga, the wife of Colbee. The man was severely flogged in the presence of many Aborigines who had been made to understand the reason for his punishment, but 'there was not one of them that did not testify strong abhorrence of the punishment, and equal sympathy with the sufferer'. Aborigines never could understand people who, in cold blood, deliberately inflicted pain on a fellow human being. Unlike nearly all other people on the earth they never engaged in any form of cold-blooded torture. . . . Their humane and conciliatory temper, like their social organisation, and the inferiority of their weapons, remained a fatal weakness in their efforts to resist the implacable and bloodthirsty European invaders. The temper of North American Indians, for instance, was very different and their resistance to White conquest correspondingly more sustained and somewhat more successful.

General Debauchery

Thus with relatively slight pressure toward closing their ranks against the black natives, white Australian pioneers had ample scope for falling out with each other. The historian may doubt whether there was any more quarrelsome society in the world than that of early New South Wales, though even at this period quarrels were usually fought out in law courts, drawing rooms, and grog shops with words and fists rather than with more lethal weapons. . . .

The general debauchery was both sustained and aggravated by the oceanic tide of Bengal rum which was for many years the principal commodity imported. It was an age of prodigious drinking in which London gin-shops advertised that customers could get drunk for a penny and dead drunk for twopence, but the specially selected colonists at Sydney and Hobart Town outdrank all others. The New South Wales Corps, recruited for the peculiar service of keeping order at 'Botany Bay', replaced the Marine detachment on Phillip's departure in 1792. It proved a thorn in the flesh of successive governors from 1795 till its departure in 1810, earning in popular usage the sobriquet of the 'Rum Corps'. During its existence, and for most of the following decade, coinage was in such chronically short supply that rum, often used as a generic term for spirits, became the commonest medium of incentive payments to convicts and the commonest article of barter, so common that some historians have held that it functioned as the *de facto* currency of the colony during this period. The traditional words of 'The Convicts' Rum Song' give a romanticised, or heroic, picture of the place rum occupied in the community and hint at the reasons for its importance.

> *Cut yer name across me backbone,*
> *Stretch me skin across a drum,*
> *Iron me up to Pinchgut Island*
> *From today till Kingdom-come!*
> *I will eat yer Norfolk dumpling*
> *Like a juicy Spanish plum,*
> *Even dance the Newgate Hornpipe*
> *If ye'll only gimme RUM!*

'Pinchgut Island', originally little more than a barren rock in Sydney Harbour, served as a place of solitary confinement, and occasionally of execution, for particularly refractory convicts in the early days. Later officially renamed Fort Denison, the older term has persisted in popular usage. A 'Norfolk dumpling' symbolised prison conditions at Norfolk Island, after 1825 the most appalling of all penal settlements for twice-convicted felons. The 'Newgate hornpipe' meant, of course, the 'dance' of death on the gallows. Nevertheless legend has exaggerated the quantity, though not the quality, of brutality inflicted on the 'government men' under the convict system. Probably fewer than 15 per cent of all those transported ever saw the inside of such penal hells as Norfolk Island, and probably fewer than half were ever flogged at all. Soldiers in the army, equally subject to the lash, very often committed crimes in Australia because they were convinced that they would be better off as convicts.

CHRONOLOGY

1701
Frederick I, father of Frederick the Great, becomes king of Prussia.

1702
England and France enter into the War of the Spanish Succession.

1703
Russian czar Peter the Great orders construction of a new city to be called St. Petersburg.

1713
St. Petersburg replaces Moscow as the capital of Russia.

1715
Louis XIV, the Sun King of France, dies.

1725
Peter the Great dies.

1728
Sailing under the Russian flag, Danish explorer Vitus Bering discovers the strait between Alaska and Siberia later named the Bering Strait.

1740
Frederick the Great becomes king of Prussia.

1754
Lieutenant Colonel George Washington warns the French that they are to leave Fort Duquesne or be forcibly removed; the French and their Indian allies easily defeat Washington's forces.

1756
The Seven Years' War begins in Europe as Prussia and Great Britain battle Austria, Russia, France, and others. In America the British battle the French in Canada and the western frontier in the French and Indian War.

1759

The French lose Quebec, Canada, to the British.

1762

Catherine the Great becomes empress of Russia after overthrowing her husband, Peter III.

1763

Prussia wins the Seven Years' War in Europe; the British defeat the French in North America, thus gaining control of the entire North American continent from Canada to Florida and west to the Mississippi River.

1764

Britain passes the Sugar Act, which taxes sugar and imported goods in the American colonies; this evokes protests that eventually provoke the American Revolution.

1765

Britain repeals the Sugar Act and instead invokes the Stamp Act, taxing all documents and inflaming American protest against English rule.

1767

The British Parliament passes the Townshend Acts, which impose a tax on lead, paper, tea, paint, and glass; Samuel Wallis, a British sea captain, is the first European to travel to Tahiti.

1768

Englishman James Cook sails to Tahiti, New Zealand, and Australia.

1770

On March 5, British soldiers kill five American protesters in Boston; the event is known as the Boston Massacre.

1773

On December 16, the Boston Tea Party takes place when several dozen colonists disguised as Native Americans dump 342 chests of tea into Boston Harbor to protest the British tea tax.

1774

In response to the Boston Tea Party, British politicians pass the Intolerable Acts, which close Boston Harbor to all commerce until the tea is paid for; this act unites the colonists against the British and leads to the Revolutionary War.

1775

On April 19, a column of British soldiers on a mission to collect arms in Lexington, Massachusetts, are attacked by the patriot militia in the first battle of the Revolutionary War.

1776

On July 4, the Declaration of Independence is signed in Philadelphia, claiming American independence from British rule; George Washington's Continental Army crosses the Delaware River on Christmas Eve and scores a stunning victory against German Hessian mercenaries in Trenton, New Jersey, on Christmas morning.

1777

On October 4, the British capture Philadelphia, home of the Continental Congress.

1778

The French join the revolutionary cause and supply desperately needed money and troops to aid American independence.

1781

In the final battle of the Revolutionary War on October 19, British general Charles Cornwallis surrenders 8,000 troops to the 17,000-man patriot force in Yorktown; this victory leads to a negotiated peace with the British in 1783.

1783

On September 3, the Treaty of Paris, negotiated by John Jay and Benjamin Franklin, is ratified, securing British recognition of American independence.

1787

The Constitutional Convention meets in Philadelphia to draft the U.S. Constitution.

1789

A riot by hungry peasants at the Bastille prison in Paris touches off the French Revolution.

1790

The Constitution is fully ratified by all thirteen states.

1792

Austrian and Prussian allies invade France in an unsuccessful attempt to help French king Louis XVI regain his throne.

1793

Convicted of treason for his part in the Austrian invasion, Louis XVI is executed by guillotine on January 21.

1793–1794

Approximately thirty-five thousand people are executed on trumped-up charges of treason during the French Reign of Terror.

1794

Maximilien Robespierre, leader of the Reign of Terror, is himself executed by guillotine on July 28.

1799

Napoléon names himself emperor of France and the French Revolution ends.

Mortimer J. Adler, ed., *Great Books of the Western World*. Vol. 35, *Montesquieu and Rousseau*. Chicago: Encyclopædia Britannica, 1992.

Maurice Ashley, *The Age of Absolutism 1648–1775*. Springfield, MA: G. & C. Merriam, 1974.

Alan Axelrod and Charles Phillips, *What Every American Should Know About American History*. Holbrook, MA: Bob Adams, 1992.

Hilaire Belloc, *High Lights of the French Revolution*. New York: Century, 1915.

Mary Sumner Benson, *Women in Eighteenth-Century America*. Port Washington, NY: Kennikat, 1966.

Andrew S. Berky and James P. Shenton, eds., *The Historians' History of the United States*. Vol. 1. New York: G.P. Putnam's Sons, 1966.

Sally Smith Booth, *The Women of '76*. New York: Hastings House, 1973.

J.F. Bosher, *The French Revolution*. New York: W.W. Norton, 1988.

Richard Cobb, gen. ed., and Colin Jones, ed., *Voices of the French Revolution*. Topsfield, MA: Salem House, 1988.

Alfred Cobban, ed., *The Eighteenth Century: Europe in the Age of Enlightenment*. New York: McGraw-Hill, 1969.

David Colbert, *Eyewitness to America*. New York: Pantheon, 1997.

Diané Collinson, *Fifty Major Philosophers: A Reference Guide*. London: Routledge, 1988.

David Cordingly, *Under the Black Flag*. San Diego: Harcourt Brace, 1995.

Jean de Crèvecoeur, *Crèvecoeur's Eighteenth-Century Travels in Pennsylvania and New York.* Trans. and ed. Percy G. Adams. Louisville: University of Kentucky Press, 1961.

Vincent Cronin, *Catherine, Empress of All the Russias.* New York: William Morrow, 1978.

Thomas E. Crow, *Painters and Public Life in Eighteenth-Century Paris.* New Haven, CT: Yale University Press, 1985.

Will and Ariel Durant, *The Age of Louis XIV.* Vol. 8 of *The Story of Civilization.* New York: Simon and Schuster, 1963.

Will and Ariel Durant, *The Age of Voltaire.* Vol. 9 of *The Story of Civilization.* New York: Simon and Schuster, 1965.

Charles W. Eliot, ed., works of Thomas Jefferson in *The Harvard Classics: American Historical Documents 1000–1904.* New York: P.F. Collier, 1910.

Olaudah Equiano, in *The Mammoth Book of Eye-Witness History.* Ed. Jon E. Lewis. New York: Carroll Graf, 1998.

Brian M. Fagan, *Clash of Cultures.* New York: W.H. Freeman, 1984.

Benjamin Franklin, *Poor Richard's Almanack.* Mount Vernon, VA: Peter Pauper Press, n.d.

Peter Gay, *Age of Enlightenment.* New York: Time-Life Books, 1966.

Lorenzo Johnston Greene, *The Negro in Colonial New England.* New York: Atheneum, 1968.

George R. Havens, *The Age of Ideas.* New York: Free Press, 1965.

Christopher Hibbert, *The Days of the French Revolution.* New York: William Morrow, 1980.

David Horowitz, *The First Frontier: The Indian Wars and America's Origins 1607–1776.* New York: Simon and Schuster, 1978.

William Mann, *Music in Time.* New York: Harry N. Abrams, 1982.

Paul Mantoux, *The Industrial Revolution in the Eighteenth Century.* 1910. Reprinted. New York: Macmillan, 1961.

D.W. Meinig, *The Shaping of America*. Vol. 1, *Atlantic America 1492–1800*. New Haven, CT: Yale University Press, 1986.

Yehudi Menuhin and Curtis Wheeler Davis, *The Music of Man*. New York: Methuen, 1979.

Nancy Mitford, *The Sun King*. New York: Harper & Row, 1966.

Samuel Eliot Morison, *The Oxford History of the American People*. New York: Oxford University Press, 1965.

Thomas L. Purvis, ed., *Colonial America to 1763*. New York: Facts On File, 1999.

Parke Rouse Jr., *The Great Wagon Road*. New York: McGraw-Hill, 1973.

Louis de Rouvroy, Duke of Saint-Simon, *Memoirs of Louis XIV and His Court and of His Regency*. Vol. 2. New York: P.F. Collier & Son, 1910.

George Rudé, *Europe in the Eighteenth Century*. New York: Praeger, 1973.

Isidor Schneider, ed., *The Enlightenment*. New York: George Braziller, 1965.

Henri Sée, *Economic and Social Conditions in France During the Eighteenth Century*. New York: Cooper Square, 1968.

Henry Thomas and Dana Lee Thomas, *Living Adventures in Science*. Garden City, NY: Hanover House, 1954.

Russel Ward, *Australia Since the Coming of Man*. New York: St. Martin's, 1987.

George Washington, *George Washington Writings*. New York: Literary Classics, 1997.

Russell F. Weigley, *The Age of Battles*. Bloomington: Indiana University Press, 1991.

Stephanie Grauman Wolf, *As Various as Their Lands: The Everyday Lives of Eighteenth-Century Americans*. New York: Harper-Collins, 1993.

William Wood and Ralph Henry Gabriel, *The Winning of Freedom*. Toronto: Glasgow, Brook, 1972.

Donald R. Wright, *African Americans in the Colonial Era.* Arlington Heights, IL: Harlan Davidson, 1990.

Gilette Ziegler, *At the Court of Versailles: Eye-Witness Reports from the Reign of Louis XIV.* New York: E.P. Dutton, 1966.

Howard Zinn, *A People's History of the United States 1492–Present.* New York: HarperPerennial, 1995.

INDEX

aborigines, 266–67
absolutism, 15
  see also monarchies
Academy of Painting and
  Sculpture, 122
Adams, John, 195
Adams, Samuel, 190, 195
Africa, 91, 94
African Americans. *See*
  slaves/slavery
Age of Enlightenment. *See*
  Enlightenment
Albany Conference, 161–62
Aleuts, 137–38
America
  attacks/riots against the rich
    in, 191–93
  British convicts shipped to,
    264
  conditions for success in,
    233–34
  European claims to, 149–50
  immigrant settlement, 35–36
  Polish immigrant's
    impressions of, 234–38
  population, 21–22
  Russian discovery of, 133,
    135–36
  union of colonies, plan for,
    150–51, 163
  see also American
    Revolution; French and
    Indian War; Native
    American Indians; United
    States
American Revolution, 187
  British surrender, 28–29
  causes, 25–28
  declaring, 28

major battles of, 26
persuading lower classes to
  join cause of, 195–97
ploys of Founding Fathers for,
  188–89
Stamp Act riots, 193–94, 225
upper class shaping opinions
  of lower classes for, 189–91
see also Boston Massacre;
  Declaration of Independence
Amherst, Jeffrey, 155
anti-Federalists, 29
architecture, 19–20
aristocracy. *See* monarchies
Arouet, François Marie, 113
  see also Voltaire
art, 19–20
  see also Paris Art Salon
Articles of Confederation,
  226–27
Ashley, Maurice, 47
Assiento (treaty agreement of
  1713), 91
Attucks, Crispus, 195, 203
Augusta, Sophie Fredericke.
  See Catherine the Great
Australia
  British convicts sent to,
    264–66
  British vs. aborigines in,
    266–67
  prison at, 268
  use of rum in, 268
Austria
  monarchy in, 42–44
  and Seven Years' War, 19,
    145–46, 147
  and War of Spanish
    Succession, 18, 47–48, 49